Wings over Hellas

Ancient Greece from the Air

Wings over Hellas

Ancient Greece from the Air

RAYMOND V. SCHODER, S. J.

with 140 colour photographs by the author
138 line drawings and 1 map

NEW YORK
OXFORD UNIVERSITY PRESS · 1974

Publication of this book at so reasonable a
price was made possible by a generous grant
from the John and Helen Condon Trust.
R.V.S.

Plans drawn by Sarah Lillywhite
Map drawn by John Woodcock

Library of Congress Catalog Card No.
74–78754

Printed in the Netherlands

Dedicated to the Officers and Pilots of the Hellenic Air Force
whose friendly and effective cooperation
made this book possible

Contents

CONTENTS

CONTENTS

CONTENTS

Introduction

Readers of this book participate in a high privilege – seeing Greece as the ancient gods did on their way down from Olympus!

Seen from the air, an archaeological site immediately takes on new meaning. It is understood as a unit, not piecemeal in sequence as is necessary on the ground. The inter-relationships of its buildings in size, position and arrangement become more clear. Its geographical context of hills, rivers and sea is fully visible, often clarifying the site's natural advantages and making obvious why it was originally chosen for a city or sanctuary.

The aim of this book is to present all important excavated sites of ancient Greece, both mainland and islands and from Minoan to Roman times, from this advantageous point of view as a new aid to archaeology and to historical studies as well as to visitors to the sites. This airphoto approach should bring a new perspective towards understanding ancient Greece.

Only ancient sites are included, though many medieval centres are also meaningful from the air and I have photographed them also. Further, it is the archaeology, not the geography, of Greece that is here emphasized.

Though I already knew Greece well from many extensive study-trips throughout the country, I learned much from the aerial perspective, and I have found that others also enjoy and appreciate these photos. It is this wider enthusiasm, including that of many of the best scholars of Greek archaeology, which has induced me to make my air photos available to all lovers of ancient Greece, both amateur and professional. I hope that the book will be of real use, as well as of widespread interest.

This project was possible only because of the generous and friendly cooperation of the Hellenic Air Force, and I wish to record my sincere and warm appreciation for their essential help. Once the concept and value of the undertaking was established with the Air Force

Chief of Staff several years ago, my efforts were most helpfully promoted and carried to completion. I am pleased to dedicate the book to these good friends and skilled collaborators.

It may be of interest to know some details of the adventures and procedures involved in taking these photographs. I took them all with a small hand-held camera using 35mm film – as opposed to professional or special airphoto equipment. Most of the views are taken at an oblique angle, not directly down as in air-mapping technique. This allows much better results for my purpose, which is not a ground-plan but a meaningful perspective of a whole site from on high.

Since I knew the archaeological significance of the sites, as well as the requisite photographic techniques, I could manoeuvre the plane – by directives to the pilot – to that angle, distance, and height which best bring out the meaning of the structures and their geographical context and most effectively highlight the more important items. This was not always easy, and it involved planning the suitable time of day in order to have the lighting from the proper angle. Since we had to do many sites on any given day's flight, I arranged the sequence of places as far as possible on considerations of preferable lighting, but this was not always possible on the optimum level without involving many more flights than were available to me. So some compromises were necessary, with not all conditions ideal. Weather could have been better over some sites – even in June it was often cloudy or erratic.

Apart from a few photos taken from commercial planes, the work involved thirteen days of flying with the Air Force, five to seven hours at a time. One flight was in August of 1962, the rest in August 1967 and June 1968. Despite the famous good climate of Greece I was, in fact, many times hampered by excessive cloudiness or haze, and had to cancel or postpone planned flights at least a dozen times. Some days it was clear enough but too windy for this risky low-level flying; twice we had to give up after getting aloft, and wait for better conditions.

The photos were mostly taken through the open door of a rather aged DC 3 ('Dakota') plane. We removed the door and left it on the ground. I was tied to the inside floor by a six-foot strap, adjusted to allow me to stand or kneel at the door's edge just inside the air-stream without likelihood of falling out. This was from the photographic viewpoint excellent as there was nothing in the way but air – no glass or wing or narrow opening. Generally we flew at about 1000 feet, but sometimes lower where safe, and occasionally higher where necessitated by mountains or boisterous air currents.

Since we were flying past the site at fairly close range at over 100 miles per hour, little time was available for composing the view-point to best effect. I had to anticipate as much as possible what would be best and be ready to press the shutter release at the appropriate instant. I used 1/500th of a second to stop motion blur. To insure getting a variety of views, both over-all and close-up details, I had four lenses at the ready on the floor beside me: standard, wide-angle, long-range, and telephoto, and often had to change lenses furiously as we went by a site or circled for a second or third 'run'. Since each lens has its own different principles of use and of setting, and differing arrangements for adjustments, this procedure was fairly complicated in view of the minimum time available. I also had to be constantly checking on exposure rating with a light-meter, since angles and heights and the presence or absence of vegetation around a ruin affect that important setting considerably.

Finding the sites from the air was often difficult. All Greece is mountainous, and most mountains look alike from above – as do most villages, with their uniform red-tile roofs. I would plan in advance a day's itinerary and discuss it with the pilot (often it was a different pilot each day), indicating on a map for him and on another for me the sites to be located. I sometimes also made up individual small guide-plans, sketching the relation of a desired site to better-known places or landmarks and specifying the direction of approach which I needed. Even so, it often took considerable searching to spot a specific site hiding in the numberless hills and valleys and often sharing in colour the tone of the local stone and earth. I would pass on to the pilot the necessary directives for angle of approach and lateral distance. This was sometimes by hand signals down the length of the cabin to the co-pilot (while the captain kept his eye on adjacent mountains!), or by courier through word or note in English or Greek; later by intertele-phone, though that meant holding the mechanism in my hand along with the camera and light-meter, and it was not always effectively audible over the roaring engines and air-stream, and sometimes not even operative.

We would circle a site, once found, to determine the best approach and distance, then make one or more passes for photographing. The swirling about which this entailed some-times led to dizziness and air sickness on my part; and the exposure to air blast and at times to rarified atmosphere (particularly for Mt Olympus) induced temporary ill effects on ears and bloodstream. Mid-day lunch had to be brought along to be nibbled between sites. The physical strain was often very considerable – from the uncomfortable position for long hours on hard floor or bench, from extended kneeling, from muscular tension in holding steady, and from reduced air pressure and oxygen when high over mountains.

The hardships were worth it, however, for the memorable experiences and for the resulting photos. I hope that the latter will be of interest to many, and will help make better understood the unique quality of ancient Greek cities and shrines in their marvellous natural context and unified relationships.

The sites are arranged alphabetically accord-ing to Modern Greek spelling in phonetic equivalents. This was required by the pub-lisher's need for a basis of uniform sequence of plates since the book is appearing in several languages. There is no universally agreed sys-tem of transliterating these names into English, and the nomenclature here adopted is a com-promise among the variant forms in use today in Greece on maps and road signs. The resultant spelling is sometimes strange and arguable, but it does serve a necessary practical purpose and will be helpful to travellers faced with modern bilingual place names.

Each photograph is accompanied by a matching sketch map with key structures numbered for identification by the appended list. General data on a site's history and cultural interest are provided to make its archaeological significance more meaningful. These accompanying commentaries supply brief data on the major monuments visible, highlighting details and aspects of special importance or interest. No attempt is made to give a detailed description, since that is readily available in the sources cited in the appended Bibliography.

Professional archaeologists will discover nothing new in these commentaries. Others, however, should find them useful background towards understanding the photos, and as a brief synthesis of the topography of Greece. A great deal of information is compressed, or implied, in these short accounts – which strive to be accurate and up-to-date summaries of the most significant information, and a guide and stimulus to further reading. It must be remembered that there is a good deal of disagreement and controversy among experts on some buildings' dates, purposes and details; my notes reflect the position I take on such matters.

In the irksome question of the spelling of proper names, the norm here followed is sensible and familiar usage rather than pedantic consistency and precise equivalence to the ancient sounds. The excuse is English tradition, which has handled this problem very freely.

Because of the expense involved in producing colour plates the number of photos given of each site had to be very limited. It was often difficult to select the best one for inclusion and the decision was based on what would be most instructive and interesting at each site. Over-all views were usually given precedence, but detailed close-ups are also included when of special usefulness.

Unfortunately, all my efforts to perfect the coverage in the book during the beautifully clear weather of October and November 1972 came to nothing. Although the Air Force was ready and eager to complete the project, and Drs Platon and Orlandos had given cordial permission for new air views of their important recently expanded excavations at Zakros and Messene, I was prevented from taking the desired new photos and from adding Lykosoura and Kerkyra City as planned. I trust that my readers will understand, and share my regret.

The text of the book was written in the autumn and winter of 1972 at the American School of Classical Studies in Athens. Its admirably complete library of books and periodicals in many languages was a great asset in my extensive research and in preparing the Bibliography. I would like to thank the staff of the School for their friendly assistance and support, especially the Director, Dr James McCredie, and the librarians. Eugene Vanderpool was often of great assistance on complicated problems of topography and interpretation, always generous with his remarkable fund of archaeological information.

I am most appreciative of the cooperation and enthusiastic support for my project by Thames and Hudson since it was first proposed to them several years ago.

The objective of this book is to provide a new experience and perspective on all important excavated sites of ancient Greece. It does not seek to discover hidden ruins not visible from the ground. My aim is to report what can be seen from the air, with all the special interest and the often illuminating insights which that involves. If the book also provides pleasure and excitement, and a challenge to visit Greece or to see it again in a new dimension, all the more satisfaction to both user and author!

RAYMOND V. SCHODER, S.J.
Loyola University, Chicago

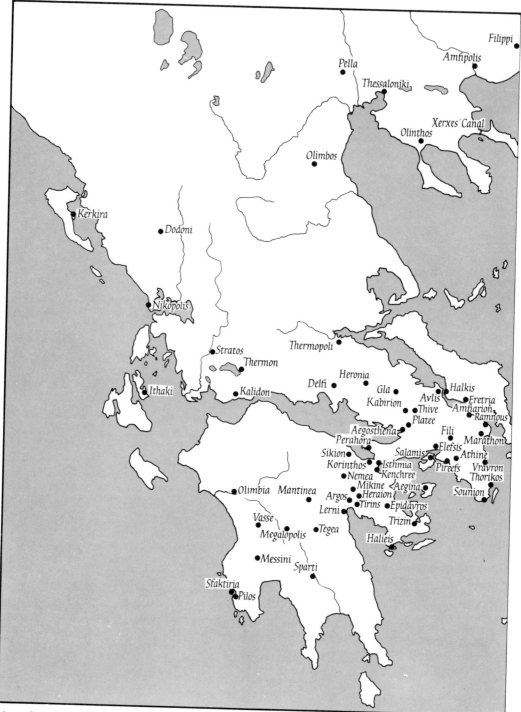

Map of sites mentioned in the text

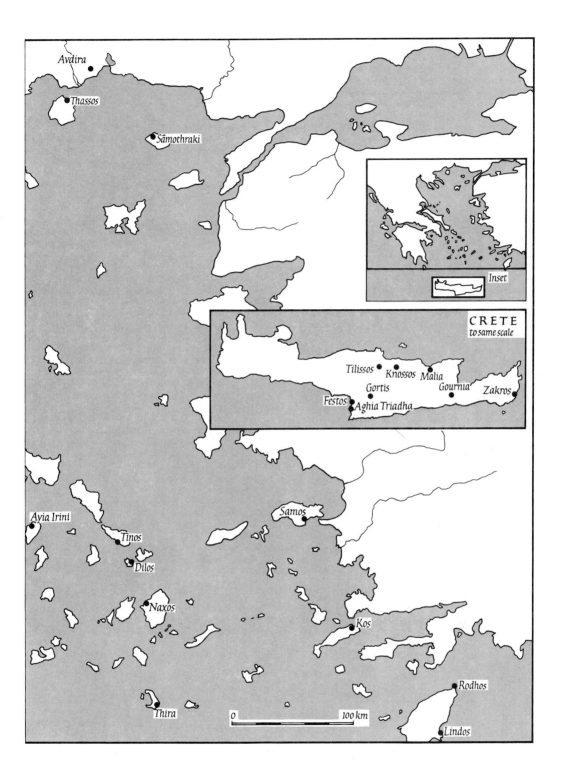

Avdira

Thassos

Sámothraki

Inset

CRETE
to same scale

Tilissos
Knossos
Malia
Gortis
Gournia
Zakros
Festos
Aghia Triadha

Ayia Irini

Samos

Tinos

Dilos

Naxos

Kos

Rodhos

Thira

Lindos

0   100 km

Aegina/Aegina : The Aphaia Temple

Aegina is located about 12 miles out in the middle of the Saronic Gulf, directly south of Salamis and Eleusis. This pleasant triangular island played an important role in Greek history and served as capital of Greece from 1826 to 1828 after the achievement of freedom from the Turks. There is evidence of Neolithic settlement as early as the late fourth millennium BC, and of later Minoan and Mycenaean occupation. Repopulated by Dorians from Epidauros in the tenth century BC, Aegina became a formidable commercial power in Archaic times due to its outstanding naval skills. It was a centre of art, notably pottery and bronzes, and seems to have been the first Greek state to adopt coinage – its famous 'turtles' becoming the monetary standard of Doric Greece. It fought valiantly at Salamis and Plataea, but was harshly conquered and put down by jealous Athens in 457–455 BC. After Athens' defeat in 404 BC, Sparta restored Aegina's exiled citizens, but its days of power and glory never revived. Only meagre remains of its Archaic and Classical city survive near the port. Its chief antiquity is the fine Doric temple to Aphaia near the northeast corner of the island.

Aphaia, a local goddess not worshipped elsewhere, had a shrine on a hill-top overlooking the sea from at least the seventh century BC. This was reconstructed in the sixth century and again at the beginning of the fifth, around 490 BC, at the end of the Archaic period. An inscription identifies the cult, and Pindar wrote a hymn in Aphaia's honour. The setting of the temple among a verdant pine forest, fragrant and delightfully green, with the sea below and a great vista to the Argolid, Salamis, and Athens, is one of the most charming in Greece. Excavations since 1900 by Furtwängler and others have recovered important pedimental sculpture (now mostly in Munich), as well as clearing the temple's considerable remains.

This temple is the finest example of late Archaic architecture, and it introduced some refinements of proportion and inclination of columns and inter-relation of blocks that later temples such as the Parthenon adopted. Though small in dimension, the temple dominates its context. It is built on a terrace-platform with a larger terrace below. Made of local limestone covered with a marble stucco, it has an unusual plan of 6 × 12 columns. Inside the cella is a two-storeyed colonnade to support the roof – perhaps the pioneer instance of this technique. At the back was the cult statue of Aphaia, made of ivory. The sculptures of the west pediment, executed between 500 and 490 BC, are notably more typical of the Archaic period than those of the east pediment (perhaps a replacement *c.* 480 BC of earlier work destroyed in the interval),

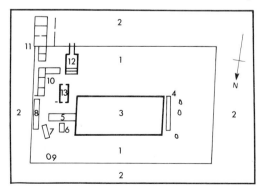

1 Temple-platform terrace
2 Outer terrace
3 Aphaia temple
4 Trench showing circular structure
5 Ramp
6 Site of Archaic altar
7 Sixth-century altar
8 Classical altar
9 Votive column
10 Archaic priests' houses
11 Classical priests' quarters
12 Classical Propylon
13 Sixth-century Propylon

which are freer and better unified and include the great kneeling Hercules, one of the earliest statues of the incipient Classical style. The Propylon, off the southeast corner of the temple, gives an uncommon approach from the side. Beyond lie rooms which probably served as living and administrative quarters for the priests.

Aegosthena/Aigosthena

At the easternmost tip of the Gulf of Corinth, on the southern slopes of Mt Citheron, the fort of Aigosthena protected the approaches to Megara and indirectly also Athens farther to the east. It is an excellent example of Greek military architecture of the late fourth or early third century BC, and its southeast tower is the finest extant proof of the great care and skill employed in the best Greek fortifications, with neatly regular rows of dressed limestone blocks. This tower rises over 30 ft above the high general wall, with interior flooring at various levels and small openings for light and observation. Other towers at intervals of 160 ft provide defensive points all along the double sweep of wall – a loop around an acropolis rock on the east and a curtain wall running westward to the sea. There is no evidence of a sea wall, and none of a southern wall to parallel the extant north wall to the coast, though its existence is supposed as an obvious completion of the defence system. The acropolis circuit is some 600 ft across, and the north wall is three times that length from the acropolis edge to the sea. The masonry is mostly refined polygonal but in places there are regular blocks about 3 ft long and $1\frac{1}{2}$ ft high and thick. Though built for defensive purposes, these walls are still a work of art.

There was a shrine at Aigosthena to Melampus, a legendary prophet and promoter of the Dionysiac cult, who was said to understand the language of birds and beasts. The Spartan army retreated there after defeat at Leuctra in 371 BC. A bust of Hadrian, and an inscription referring to him as 'founder' of the city, indicate an imperial visit in the second century AD.

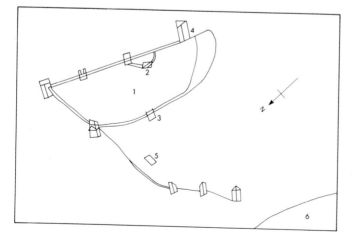

1 Acropolis
2 Byzantine church
3 Gate
4 Southeast tower
5 Byzantine basilica
6 Gulf of Corinth

Aghia Triadha/Haghia Triadha

Two miles west of the great Minoan palace of Phaistos is an unusual complex of buildings named Haghia Triadha after a nearby double-naved Venetian church. An ancient paved road joins it with Phaistos. Lacking some structural features of Minoan palaces, but much more elaborate and ornate than any known house of the period, these ruins probably belong to a royal villa of the king of Phaistos in a pleasant setting nearer the sea. It is possible, however, that some king used these buildings as his regular palace, perhaps while the great one at Phaistos was being rebuilt. The main construction was in the later sixteenth century BC (Late Minoan I), though after the earthquake which proved disastrous to all palaces in Crete *c.* 1450 BC there was considerable rebuilding and continued use beyond the Minoan and Mycenaean periods into Geometric times. Earlier habitation in the Early Minoan and even Neolithic periods is also evidenced. Italian excavations from the beginning of the present century have recovered not only complex and impressive architecture but many notable art treasures: pottery, steatite vases, frescoes, and a remarkable painted sacrophagus showing a funeral ritual at a king's or noble's tomb.

The western portion of the L-shaped site is the royal villa or palace. Living and reception rooms, in the middle and western sections, were elegantly paved and brightly decorated with frescoes. The southwest wing served mainly as storerooms, the southeast wing perhaps the servants' quarters. Between them was an open court with altars and a shrine nearby. In the heart of the royal residence was a treasure room in which 19 copper ingots in the shape of ox hides, each weighing 64 pounds, were found: obviously a form of currency. The archives nearby contained signet seals and cupboards for records. Stairs led northward to a lower level and a paved ramp running westward towards the sea.

The northern complex includes several houses, some of the same period as the villa, but many of them dating from the Late Minoan III rebuilding in the fourteenth and thirteenth centuries BC. An open oblong court resembles the agora or market centre of later cities. On its east side is a remarkable series of eight rooms, probably shops and storerooms, with a long colonnade across their western front, its pillars alternately square and round as indicated by their extant bases. This is unique in Minoan

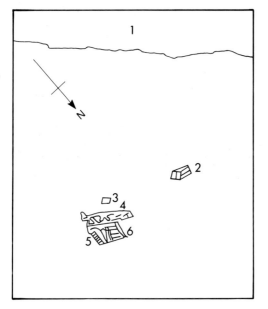

1 Sea
2 Haghia Triadha church (double nave)
3 Haghios Georgios chapel
4 Royal villa
5 Storerooms/shops, with portico
6 Houses

For colour plate see overleaf.

architecture. (At Phaistos and Mallia a wall intervenes between rooms and portico in similar structures there.) It is late in date and may indicate Mycenaean innovations: the somewhat similar stoa-like structure at Gla is comparable. Another Mycenaean feature is the later large rectangular room built over the remains of the royal villa at its centre, apparently a megaron.

A short distance to the northeast of the house and market area are Minoan cemeteries and tholos tombs.

1 (see p. 19)
2 (see p. 19)
3 Haghios Georgios chapel
4 Royal villa
5 Storerooms/shops, with
   portico
6 Houses
7 Agora
8 Stairs
9 Ramp to sea
10 Megaron
11 Living rooms
12 Archives
13 Storerooms
14 Treasury (ingots)
15 Main court, with altars
16 Shrine
17 House (servants'?)

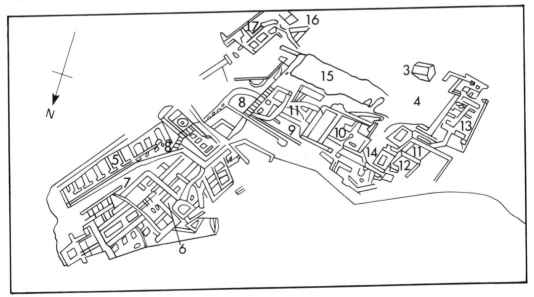

Amfiarion/**Amphiareion**

Amphiaraos was king of Argos, endowed with a gift of prophecy. He took part in the expedition of the Seven against Thebes. Afterwards he was swallowed up by the earth near Thebes, but a cult developed near Oropos on the borders of Boeotia and Attica opposite Eretria, at a sacred spring where his spirit was believed to continue prophetic and healing activity. The shrine and ritual here had many similarities to that of the Asclepieion at Epidauros. Herodotus records that even the Persian general Mardonius consulted this oracle before the battle of Plataea.

Those who sought the deified hero's guidance and healing aid had to sacrifice a ram on the altar in front of his temple, then, wrapped in the ram's skin, sleep in the stoa and hope for a revelation in a dream. They had to abstain from wine for three days and from all food for one day. Those who were answered were expected to throw gold or silver coins into the Sacred Spring, which was near the front of the temple, downhill from the altar towards the stream flowing through the ravine. Many shells have been found nearby from which the sick drank the healing water of the spring.

The temple is unusual in design: no columns on the outside, but two rows of five each within the cella, which has a porch across its northern front with six pillars and a small porch with two columns at the back, leading from the *adyton* to the priests' quarters at the rear. The

base for the cult statue is still in place at the back of the cella, and a table for offerings in the centre. The temple is Doric, built in the fourth century BC.

West of the altar, on a low terrace, is a row of statue bases, of Hellenistic and Roman times; over 30 can be counted. A stone bench runs in front of them.

The Stoa of Incubation is located northeast of this terrace. Built around 387 BC, it is a long rectangular structure with 41 Doric columns along the front and 17 Ionic columns inside, dividing the space into two naves down the stoa's length. Along the back wall ran a bench on which worshippers slept to await a salutary dream. Fifty-three of the marble feet which supported this bench have been recovered. The smaller rooms at each end of the building may have been reserved for women. The building north of the stoa is of uncertain purpose; it was converted in Roman times into a mineral bath.

The small theatre above the stoa was probably used for religious pageants connected with the cult and for musical competitions in the special festivities at the shrine every four years after their initiation in 332 BC. The stage building is of stone, a Hellenistic feature. Five marble thrones of honour carry scroll ornamentation.

Across the stream are remains of what were probably hostels for pilgrims. Among these ruins is a well-preserved ancient water-clock

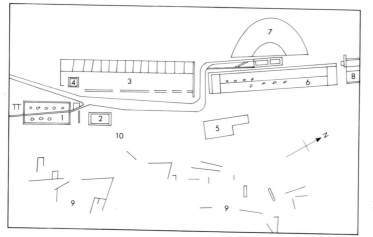

1 Temple
2 Altar
3 Terrace of statues
4 Water reservoir
5 Museum
6 Stoa of Incubation
7 Theatre
8 Greek building/Roman baths
9 Hostels, houses etc.
10 Site of Sacred Spring (hidden in the photo by trees)

(*klepsydra*), indicating time by its float.

Excavations were carried out by Leonardos between 1884 and 1930, and Petrakos, 1958–60.

The natural beauty of the site and its approaches is outstanding. This was an asset to the shrine's recuperative role in ancient times.

Amfipolis/**Amphipolis**

When Xerxes passed here in 480 BC on his way to attack central Greece, the town later called Amphipolis was known as Ennea Hodoi (Nine Roads) and belonged to the Edonians, a people of Thrace. Other powers coveted its possession because of its admirable situation on a hill protected on the north, west and south sides by a great loop of the large river Strymon some three miles inland from the sea, where it controlled the approach from the northern Aegean to the Strymon plain and the western access to the rich gold and silver mines and fine timber of Mt Pangaios. Both Miletus and Athens tried to establish colonies there, Athens finally suc-

ceeding in 437 BC. When in 424 BC it surrendered without a struggle to the Spartan expedition under Brasidas, Athens, in dismay, sent a force to recover it under the generalship of Thucydides – who for his failure to retake the city (though he did occupy its harbour town, Eion) was exiled and turned to writing his celebrated *History of the Peloponnesian War*. In a subsequent unsuccessful attempt in 421 BC to re-establish control the Athenian demagogue, Kleon, was killed, as also was Brasidas. Philip of Macedon captured the city in 358, and the Romans, after their victory at Pydna in 168 BC, made Amphipolis the capital of Macedonia

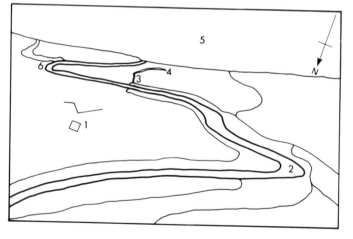

1 Ancient city site, Christian basilicas
2 River Strymon
3 Lion monument
4 Modern road to Thessalonike
5 Sea (Strymonic Gulf)
6 Site of Eion (ancient harbour)

Prima, one of the northern republics under their rule. It was a major stop along the Via Egnatia from the Adriatic to Byzantium.

Very little is visible today except the splendid setting. Excavations by Pelekides in the 1920s, and more recently by Lazarides, have revealed parts of the extensive defence wall on the north, east and south edges of the high plateau; it had polygonal facings and towers at key places. The agora, centre of the ancient city, is probably located where the Christian basilicas have been uncovered on the high northern level of the plateau. An ancient bridge crossed the Strymon to the west, and to the east have been found a shrine of Klio and tombs of various periods.

Across the modern bridge over the Strymon, along the road to Thessalonike, stands an imposing ancient monument: a colossal lion reconstructed from its fragments by Oscar Broneer in 1936–37. It squats upright on its haunches with a majestic but not very fearsome mien. There is reason to believe that it was a memorial to Laomedon, a sailor from Mytilene who lived some years at Amphipolis and became one of the close companions of Alexander, an official of his fleet in India, and later Governor of Syria. It is quite similar to the Theban lion at Chaeronea, but was probably put up somewhat later, towards the end of the fourth century. Some scholars suggest that this Laomedon was also the person for whom the splendid 'Alexander Sarcophagus' from Sidon (now in the Istanbul Museum) was made. Among its sculptured reliefs is depicted a lion hunt – perhaps the famous one in which Laomedon participated with Alexander.

Argos/**Argos**: The City

Inhabited by the Pelasgoi in pre-Greek times, Argos was the chosen centre of the early Greek Danaoi, and after the Mycenaean age was the most powerful city in the northern Peloponnesus. For centuries it vied with Sparta, on its own and in alliance with Athens, Corinth, and the Achaean League in turn, but never gained control in the south. Its early king Adrastus led the Seven against Thebes, and in the seventh century its energetic and imaginative despot Pheidon promoted the wide use of coinage and a new standard of weights and measures. In Archaic and Classical art it had a vigorous school of its own which produced the famous Hageladas and Polyclitus and some fine painted pottery. The Romans favoured Argos and rebuilt some of the city both before and after the devastating attack of the Goths in AD 395. Dutch and French excavations from 1902 to 1930 and since 1952 have uncovered many tombs from all periods and some of the civic structures in the agora area, on the slopes and summit of Larissa hill, and on the lower hill, Aspis, and the ridge (Deiras) connecting the two hills. Ancient fortifications once encircled the whole region, including both hill-top citadels.

At the top of Larissa, a high conical peak northwest of the central city, remains of Mycenaean and sixth-century BC polygonal walls and later fortifications have been identified, and foundations of two temples to Athena and to Zeus Larissaios inside the massive Byzantine-Frankish-Venetian fort that crowns the summit.

Along the southeast foot of Larissa are several major structures. The theatre is very tall and capacious, its central portion cut into the rock, with 81 of its rows of seats still in good preservation. It has two horizontal *diazoma* aisles, and could hold nearly 20,000 people, making it one of the largest in Greece. It dates from the end of the fourth or early third century BC, with considerable reworking in Roman times of the stage building and adaptation to naval combat in place of plays.

Below the theatre and a little to the south are extensive Roman baths with a great apsidal hall, a cold pool in the centre, and three hot baths at the east end. To the south is the Roman Odeion, cut into the rock-slope on the site of the late Classical Greek auditorium for the administrative assembly, whose straight rows of rock-cut seats are partly visible above the 14 curved rows of the Odeion. The construction is dated to the first century AD, some hundred years before the baths. To the north, within the ancient city limits, a late Roman house of the fifth century AD has been found; it had interesting mosaics representing the various months, which are displayed in the museum along with fine pottery and sculpture.

None of the eighteen temples mentioned by Pausanias has yet been found. Part of the ancient agora sector has however recently been excavated, along with many tombs in the area. At the edge, near the baths, is a large hypostyle hall, perhaps the Bouleuterion council hall. To the south is a long stoa with wings at each end, and north of that a Nymphaeum with a circular core and 8 Corinthian columns around the water basin. The hypostyle hall and stoa were much reworked in Roman times after the destruction by the Goths.

The rest of ancient Argos lies hidden beneath the modern city.

1 Theatre
2 Roman baths
3 Roman Odeion
4 Hypostyle hall (Bouleuterion?)
5 South Stoa
6 Nymphaeum

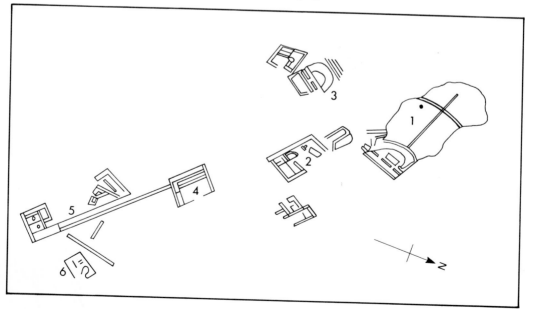

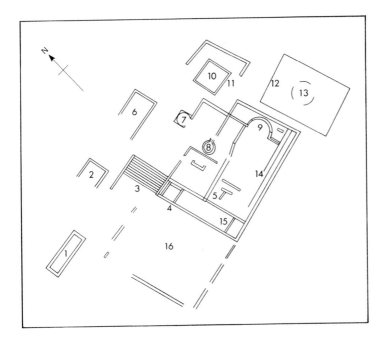

ASPIS

1 Cistern
2 Stoa
3 Steps
4 Altar site
5 Site of Apollo temple?
6 Site of Oracle?
7 Early Christian baptistery
8 Byzantine baptistery
9 Site of Apollo temple?
10 Cistern
11 Site of Athena sanctuary
12 Terrace (of Leto?)
13 Round building (tholos)
14 Byzantine church walls
15 Entry into Apollo sanctuary
16 Courtyard of Byzantine church

Argos/**Argos: Aspis**

Below Larissa to the northeast is a low circular hill known as Aspis because it looks from afar like a great shield lying on the ground. It was to become the original citadel of Argos. There is evidence of prehistoric habitation there at least as early as 2000 BC. Mycenaean tombs have been excavated on its southwest lower slope, and there was a fort on its summit; some sixth-century BC walls are visible still.

Farther north, on the western slope at the edge of Deiras ridge, is the ancient sanctuary of Apollo and Athena, worshipped here under special local names: Apollo of the Ridge (also Pythian) and Sharp-eyed Athena. It was built on four terraces, the central one Apollo's temenos, Athena's to the northeast, and south of that another which may have been reserved for their mother Leto. The structures are badly preserved, and further confusion results from the overlying remains of a fifth-century AD early Christian basilica and a later medieval Byzantine church.

Along the east edge of the lower terrace is a long stretch of ten steps cut into the rock for access to the central terrace of Apollo. At the foot of Apollo's terrace is a great altar, nearly 50 ft long and 15 ft wide judging from its remains. Tripods and statues also stood here. The altar is probably from the late Classical period. A formal entrance to the Apollo temenos seems to have been above the altar to the south. Scholars argue whether the temple was located towards the lower (western) or upper part of the temenos, or even a good way west of the steps and altar where a cistern is now to be found.

Athena's sanctuary lies to the northeast, where a deep cistern can be seen at its centre. The terrace southeast of this has remains of a circular building within its spacious rectangular enclosure. Dated to the sixth century BC, this tholos may have been part of Athena's precinct, but some think it belonged to Leto.

An oblong structure of unbaked brick north of the Apollo temenos may have been the oracle site, the *manteion*, which had an inner colonnade. A stoa stood near to and northwest of the rock steps. There also seems to have been an Asclepieion somewhere in the general sanctuary area, perhaps at the eastern end.

Athine/**Athens: General**

There has been continuous habitation at Athens for nearly 5000 years. Located some three miles in from the sea, the site is desirable primarily because of its acropolis hill, the finest in all Greece. Roughly oval in shape, well over 1000 ft long and 420 ft wide, its summit is 512 ft above sea-level and 300 ft higher than the plain. This gift of Nature called for human use, and traces of Neolithic occupation have been found along the south slope and there is evidence for a town of the Middle Helladic period. In Mycenaean times the Acropolis was fortified and had a palace, the primitive Greek dynasty here being traditionally traced back to Kekrops in the early sixteenth century BC. Around 1300 BC Theseus was said to have united several small communities in a broad surrounding area into a single domain, setting under way Athens' growth to greatness, already praised by Homer. Athens seems to have twice driven off the Dorian intruders who took over much of Greece at the end of the second millennium and it remained vigorous during the Geometric age.

By the eighth century BC it controlled all Attica and had become a major centre of art. In the Archaic period its Proto-attic pottery and later black-figure vases and strong sculptural style were widely admired. In the mid-sixth century Pisistratus promoted cultural leadership, instituting the Great Dionysia festival which later gave birth to Greek drama, establishing an official text of Homer, and raising the Panathenaic festival to national prestige. Constitutional reforms by Draco, Solon, and Cleisthenes brought a basic democracy which stimulated Athens' pride and development. Her leadership against the two Persian invasions established Athens' glory, and literary, artistic, and speculative geniuses

1 Stadium	7 Cave of Pan	12 Agora
2 Olympieion	8 Athena Nike temple	13 Gymnasium court
3 Acropolis	9 Odeion of Herodes	14 Odeion of Agrippa
4 Parthenon	Atticus	15 Tholos
5 Erechtheum	10 Areopagus	16 Hephaisteion
6 Propylaea	11 Ancient houses	17 Site of temple of Ares
		18 Stoa of Attalos
		(reconstructed)
		19 Library of Hadrian
		20 Roman Agora
		21 'Tower of the Winds'

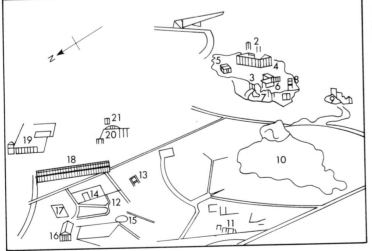

made it an unrivalled cultural dynamo, especially in the fifth century BC under Pericles – who proudly called Athens 'the Greece of Greece' and started the great building programme that made the Acropolis an architectural marvel of still-vibrant fame.

Meanwhile Athens had become a pre-eminent commercial and naval power, but came into disastrous conflict with Sparta in the Peloponnesian War and was humiliatingly defeated. It soon recovered, however, and annihilated the Spartan fleet off Cnidos and re-established leadership of the island states. It fell to Philip of Macedon in the battle of Chaeronea in 338 BC, but Alexander treated Athens with honour. So also did the Romans, who took control of Greece in the second century BC – except for Sulla who pillaged Athens in 86 BC. Hadrian, in contrast, gave it important new buildings. But in a changed world Athens faded steadily. It was sacked by Herulian Goths in AD 267 and seized by Alaric a century later. In the Byzantine Empire it was insignificant. Franks and Venetians ruled it in the Middle Ages, and the Turks for 400 years till 1833. The following year it became the capital of free Greece – which it never achieved in ancient times. It is now threatened anew by its strangling traffic and polluted smog.

The Areopagus hill northwest of the Acropolis has a chasm on its northeast slope where Aeschylus' trilogy *Oresteia* ends with Athena calming the Furies and making them guardians of justice. In Classical times it was the seat of a venerable Council which ruled on criminal homicide and upheld the Constitution. Mycenaean tombs and Greek and Roman houses have been found on its slopes and below.

Athine/Athens: The Acropolis

The chief glories of the Acropolis are the Parthenon and Erechtheum, buildings of extraordinary subtlety and refinement of design. The neighbouring structures were splendid too and the ensemble when intact must have made an impression of unique grandeur. As Plutarch said when they were already 500 years old, these buildings 'were created in a short time for all time. . . . A perpetual newness blooms upon them untouched by the years, as if they held within them some everlasting breath of life and an ageless spirit intermingled in their composition' (*Pericles* 12–13).

The Parthenon was ordered by Pericles to replace an earlier temple on the site ('pre-Parthenon') destroyed by the Persians in 480 BC when still incomplete, itself replacing an Archaic limestone temple from the sixth century (probably the 'Hecatompedon' of ancient mention) demolished shortly after Marathon. Phidias was in over-all charge of planning and decoration, with Iktinos as the architect and Kallikrates as chief contractor. Begun in 447 BC, it was basically finished in nine years and complete with sculpture by 432. It has an unusual pattern of eight columns across the front and 17 down the sides. There is a slight curvature of stylobate and architrave, a small inward inclination of the columns, progressive narrowing of the space between columns, and other ingenious refinements. All is of Pentelic marble, even the roof tiles. Though Doric, it had a continuous Ionic frieze around the outer cella wall, representing the Panathenaic procession. The east pediment's sculpture showed the birth of Athena among the gods; the west her struggle with Poseidon for Attica. Within stood her splendid gold and ivory statue by Phidias, nearly 40 ft high.

The Erechtheum is the finest masterpiece of Ionic style, beautifully delicate and brilliantly designed to incorporate venerable shrines from Mycenaean times of Athena Polias and Erechtheus/Poseidon while accommodating two ground levels (the tall-pillared North Porch is 9 ft deeper than the South Porch with its famous Caryatid maidens substituting for columns and humanizing the whole structure). The frieze around the building under the roof was in white marble figures clamped onto a blue-grey background. Colour enlivened the upper elements: blue, red, and gold décor on the snowy marble capitals and ceiling coffers. Adjacent to the combined temple was the ancient tomb of Kekrops, Athena's sacred olive tree, and Poseidon's 'sea'. Just to the south are the foundations of a sixth-century structure seemingly replacing one of Geometric times. It is probably the 'Old Temple of Athena' referred to in ancient sources, but also possibly an administrative building from the days of Pisistratus. Near here was the old Mycenaean palace and stairs down the north cliff, with other stairs farther west.

The formal entrance to the Acropolis was on the west, through a noble Doric portal, the Propylaea. The columns along the ramp at the centre are Ionic, to allow for needed height without being massive. The north wing was used as a display gallery for paintings (Pinakotheke). To the southwest, on the hill's edge from which Theseus' father Aegeus plunged to his death, stands that tiny Ionic gem the Athena Nike temple, completed in 424 BC. It has four slim columns at each end but none down the sides. Its frieze dramatized Athenian battles with Persia. At the opposite edge a Hellenistic victory tower, 29 ft high, later honoured the Roman admiral Agrippa.

At the foot of the south slope Herodes Atticus built a large Odeion, now restored for summer use. Next to it lies a long stoa, its back arches largely intact. Above this are two sanctuaries to Asclepius, each with temple, altar, incubation hall, and sacred spring. The western one dates to 420 BC, the other a century later.

The great theatre of Dionysos was rebuilt c. 330 BC in stone, replacing the wooden seats and stage of Sophocles' day. Stage and orchestra were remodelled in Roman times to suit Nero. Behind is a stoa open to the south and the sixth- and fifth-century temples of Dionysos. To the east is Pericles' Odeion, a square roofed music hall with 81 interior pillars.

Athine/Athens: The Agora

Because of its ruinous state and the overlay of later buildings on those of an earlier period, the Agora is a notoriously complicated archaeological site. American excavations and detailed studies since 1932 have greatly clarified the area, but problems remain and the northern sector is not yet fully uncovered.

This region north of the Acropolis was inhabited from late Mycenaean times through the Geometric and Archaic periods, as tombs and wells from the eleventh to seventh centuries show. The original Agora seems to have been at the west end of the Acropolis but from at least the early fifth century BC Athens' civic centre developed in this lower terrain, where there were already at least some private houses along the west side. Growing need of ready access to Eleusis and Piraeus, whose roads entered Athens here, gave impetus to the location of new public buildings in this area. There was no over-all plan, and Athens' Agora was remarkably casual and open until Hellenistic and Roman times. It was devastated in the Herulian raid of AD 267 and after the sixth century AD was abandoned.

Its most striking monument today is the Stoa of Attalos along the east side, rebuilt in 1953–56 and serving as both a museum and an example of this type of public building. Given to Athens by an admiring king of Pergamum around 145 BC, it is 382 ft long and 66 ft deep. There were 21 square rooms at the back on each of its two floors, serving as shops. The outer colonnade facing the Agora had 45 Doric columns on the lower level, with double Ionic ones above. Inside, 22 columns supported the long ceiling – those of the upper storey having special Pergamene capitals. A tall pillar with a chariot above it stood at the centre in front in honour of Attalos, and in front of that was the speakers' platform, the Bema. Several other stoas, earlier and later in date, lined the Agora's edges. Near the southeast corner the Roman T. Flavius Pantainos built a library around AD 100. Opposite it, where the Byzantine church now stands, was a Nymphaeum fountain-house of semicircular design, east of which was a small temple and to the south the ancient mint for Athens' famous coins.

The large oblong area between the Middle and later South Stoas was in Roman times incorporated into a huge gymnasium built after the Herulians destroyed most of the Agora's buildings. At the west end of this sector was the Heliaia, a square walled enclosure for the city's major law court, with room for 1500 jurors! It dates from the mid-fifth century BC and survived till the third century AD. Adjacent was a fountain-house and a water-clock. Just north of the Middle Stoa's west end were Roman-era

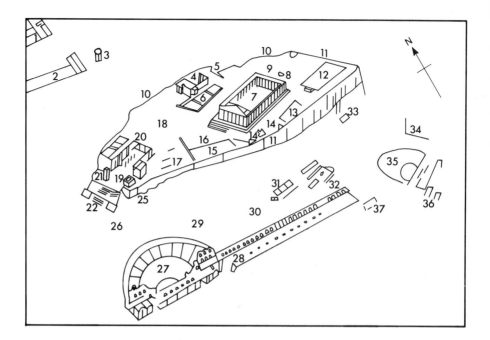

THE ACROPOLIS

1 Library of Hadrian
2 Roman Agora
3 'Tower of the Winds'
4 Erechtheum
5 Mycenaean stairway
6 Old Athena temple?
7 Parthenon
8 Temple of Rome and
  Augustus
9 Site of Zeus Polieus temenos
10 Themistocles' wall
11 Kimon's wall
12 Acropolis museum
13 Phidias' workshop?
14 Trenches of pre-Parthenon
   retaining walls
15 Chalkotheke
16 Athena Ergane temenos
17 Artemis Brauronia temenos
18 Site of Athena Promachos
19 Athena Nike temple
20 Propylaea
21 'Tower of Agrippa'
22 Beulé Gate, third century
   AD
23 Grotto of Erinyes/
   Eumenides
24 Areopagus
25 Site of Aigeion
26 Site of Aphrodite Pandemos
27 Odeion of Herodes Atticus

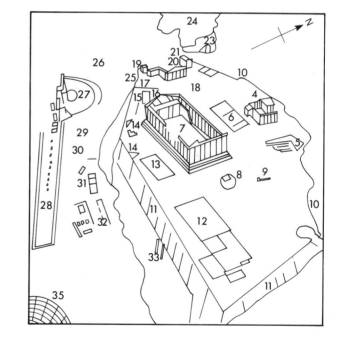

28 Stoa of Eumenes (or
   Roman?)
29 Site of Aphrodite temenos
30 Site of Themis temenos
31 Older Asclepieion
32 Later Asclepieion

33 Thrasyllos monument and
   Corinthian columns
34 Odeion of Pericles
35 Theatre of Dionysus
36 Temples of Dionysus
37 Nikias monument

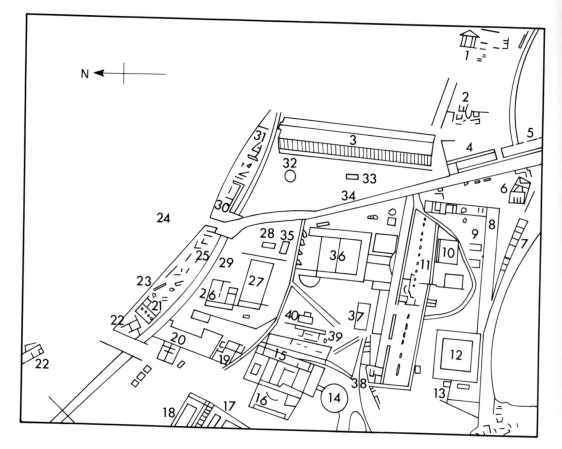

The Agora

1 Roman Agora
2 New excavations along street to Roman Agora
3 Stoa of Attalos
4 Library of Pantainos
5 Southeast Stoa
6 Byzantine church of Holy Apostles (eleventh century)
7 Old South Stoa (I)
8 Late South Stoa (II)
9 South square
10 Roman gymnasium's court
11 Middle Stoa
12 Heliaia
13 Southwest fountain-house
14 Tholos
15 Metroön
16 Bouleuterion
17 Garden of the Hephaisteion
18 Hephaisteion
19 Temple of Apollo Patroös
20 Stoa of Zeus Eleutherios
21 Royal Stoa
22 Stoas along Panathenaic Way to Dipylon
23 Site of Stoa of Herms?
24 Site of Stoa Poikile?
25 Unidentified later ruins
26 Roman building
27 Temple of Ares
28 Altar of Ares
29 Site of the Altar of the Twelve Gods
30 Augustan colonnade
31 Hadrianic basilica
32 Fountain
33 Bema (speakers' platform)
34 Panathenaic Way to Acropolis
35 Harmodios and Aristogeiton base?
36 Odeion of Agrippa (later a gymnasium)
37 Southwest temple
38 Civic offices
39 Eponymous Heroes base
40 Altar of Zeus Agoraios?

civic administrative offices; east of them a small temple of uncertain dedication, and to its north the presumed location of the Altar of Zeus Agoraios, perhaps moved here from the Pnyx hill assembly place. Nearby is a long narrow platform for statues of the Eponymous Heroes, reputed founders of the various political 'tribes' of Athens. The platform's walls also served as posting place for public notices; a stone fence surrounded the enclosure. Adjacent was the Metroön, a sanctuary to the Mother of the Gods which was also the repository for State archives. Some think it covered the Bouleuterion council hall of the time of Cleisthenes, one of the earliest structures in the Agora area, itself replacing an older one from the days of Solon. The later Bouleuterion from the end of the fifth century BC was behind it to the west, its auditorium making an arc.

The circular Tholos was built c. 470 BC as government headquarters where a group of Prytaneis officials was on duty day and night.

It had its own kitchen for their meals. North of the Metroön was a temple to Apollo Patroös, patron of Athens and all Ionians. Opposite was the Temple of Ares, moved here in the days of Augustus, and north of that the Altar of the Twelve Gods of Olympus, with a stone enclosure wall, here since the sixth century BC.

The Stoa of Zeus Eleutherios, where Socrates often talked, had projecting wings, as did the smaller adjacent Royal Stoa, headquarters of the Archon-King in charge of religious ceremonies and trials for impiety or murder. The Odeion, a huge roofed concert hall, built by Augustus' minister Agrippa, was rebuilt two centuries later, and c. AD 400 was replaced by a vast gymnasium. On a low hill west of the Agora there still stands the Temple of Hephaistos, begun before the Parthenon, notable as the best preserved of Greek temples anywhere. It was long confused with the Theseion, the shrine of Athen's founder, which is still undiscovered, but probably lies southeast of the Agora.

Athine/Athens: The Roman Agora and the Olympieion

Apart from a small business sector where the Panathenaic Way entered the Agora at its northwest corner, the main commercial district of ancient Athens was east of the Stoa of Attalos in what is known as the Roman Agora, or market, because it was extensively developed at that later period, though presumably Athenians considered it merely the eastern part of

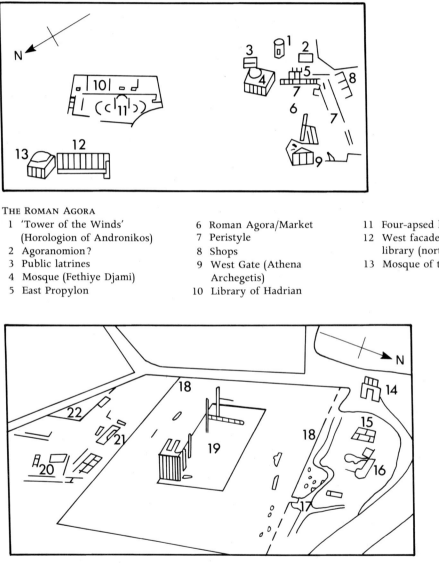

THE ROMAN AGORA

1. 'Tower of the Winds' (Horologion of Andronikos)
2. Agoranomion?
3. Public latrines
4. Mosque (Fethiye Djami)
5. East Propylon
6. Roman Agora/Market
7. Peristyle
8. Shops
9. West Gate (Athena Archegetis)
10. Library of Hadrian
11. Four-apsed later hall
12. West facade of Hadrian's library (northern half)
13. Mosque of the Bazaar

OLYMPIEION

14. Arch of Hadrian
15. Greek house
16. Roman baths
17. Propylon to Olympieion
18. Temenos wall of Olympieion
19. Olympieion
20. Sanctuary of Kronos and Rhea
21. Temple of Apollo Delphinios
22. Temple of Hera and Panhellenic Zeus

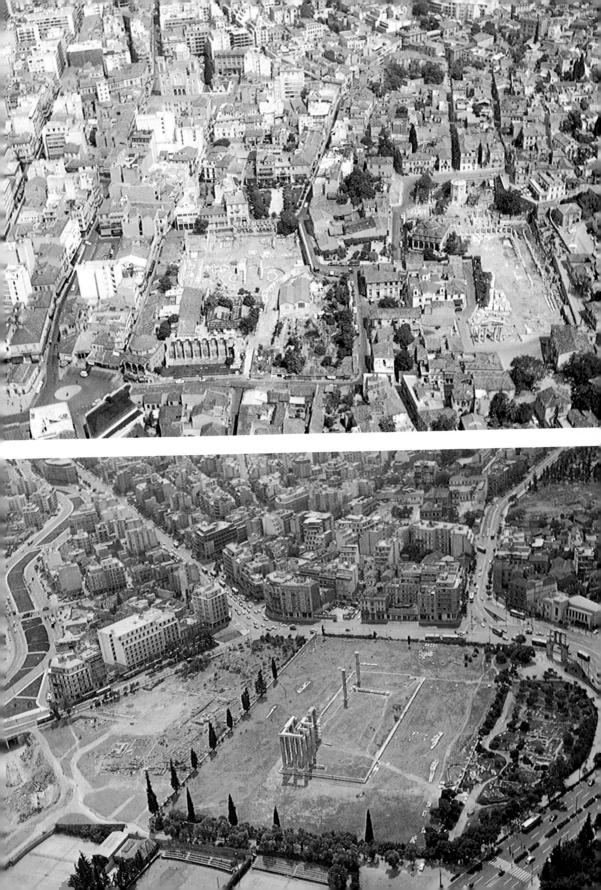

their single Agora. It was entered through a formal gateway dedicated to Athena Archegetis ('Leader') erected by the munificence of Julius Caesar and Augustus in the late first century BC, as its inscription records. Four Doric columns supported an architrave and pediment above which were three statues, one of them of Lucius Caesar, adopted 'son' of Augustus. The central portal was for vehicles, a smaller one at each side for pedestrians. Behind was a paved vestibule and other columns leading into the market square – which was framed by colonnades at a later date, probably a gift from Hadrian. Behind these were shops at the south and east ends. The East Gate was a pillared propylon with a square inner court. East of it was the Agoranomion, offices for the market supervisors; and, opposite, public latrines.

Of great interest is the 'Tower of the Winds' farther east. This was constructed in the first century BC by the astronomer Andronikos of Kyrrhos, probably a Syrian, to be both a weather-vane and a city clock. Time was indicated by sundials on the exterior and by an ingenious device inside which told the hour by the level of its water. Each of the eight outer faces of the tower is oriented to one of the cardinal directions and bears the name and symbol of the appropriate wind. Zephyros (West) is a handsome youth in floating garment scattering flowers; Boreas (North) is bearded, grim, in heavy clothes; Notos (South), who brings rain, is emptying an urn; the others are similarly thematic. The roof is an eight-segment pyramid of marble slabs held in place by a round keystone at the summit.

North of the market is another walled rectangle of similar size: the library of Hadrian. The only entrance is on the west, a simple projecting porch at the top of six steps, with seven unfluted marble columns standing out from the wall at each side of the door but anchored to the wall at their top by the architrave; the northern section of these survives. Within was a large courtyard garden, with the reading rooms around and at the back, the main bookshelves being in special rooms along the east side. This admirably assured a quiet retreat from the noisy city outside. Pausanias admired 100 splendid marble columns inside the court. Much later a square hall with four projecting apses was built at the centre, where a pool had long been. This was replaced in the sixth century AD by a Byzantine church, some of whose interior columns still stand.

A third of a mile southeast of the Acropolis is the temenos of Zeus Olympios on a site which was inhabited from prehistoric times. Nearby is the Kallirrhoe Spring, the most abundant in Athens, and the bed of the Ilissos river (now mostly underground). Deucalion was said to have built a temple here to Zeus after the great flood, which ended in a chasm nearby. Remains of a primitive temple have been traced under the later structure, which was begun c. 515 BC by the sons of Pisistratus, but was abandoned when scarcely above ground. In 174 BC work was resumed for ten years by order of the Syrian king Antiochus Epiphanes under the Roman architect Cossutius, who changed to Pentelic marble and to the Corinthian order. Still unfinished, it was completed by Hadrian 650 years after its start. It was the largest temple in Greece, 354 ft long, 135 ft wide, with a double row of 20 columns down the sides and three rows of eight across the front and back, and a height of 90 ft. It contained a gold and ivory statue of the god. To the south are several other temples recently uncovered; to the north beyond the Propylon and through the peribolos wall are Roman baths and Greek houses dating from the fourth century BC. Farther on the Arch of Hadrian divides the old Athens of Theseus from the new one of Hadrian, a fact that its inscription neatly points out.

Athine/Athens: The Stadium and the Kerameikos

The gleaming marble Stadium at the foot of Ardettos hill (on whose summit the ancient Heliasts took their annual oath) is an accurate reconstruction undertaken for the revival of the Olympic Games here in 1896 at the great expense of George Averoff of Alexandria. As Herodes Atticus had similarly done in 144 AD, he had the seats and supporting walls restored

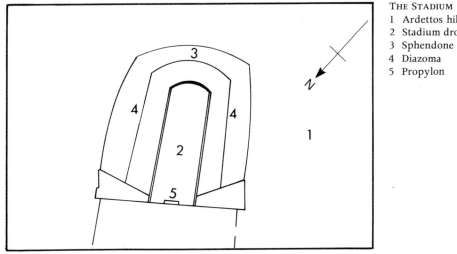

THE STADIUM
1 Ardettos hill
2 Stadium dromos
3 Sphendone
4 Diazoma
5 Propylon

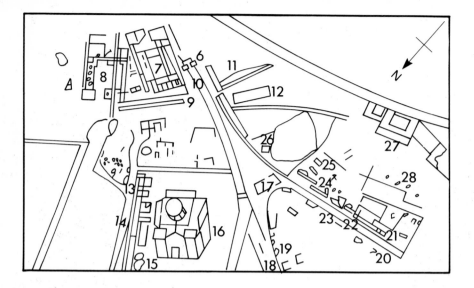

THE KERAMEIKOS

in Pentelic marble. The original structure put up by Lycurgus in 331 BC for the athletic contests of the Panathenaic festival had provided stone foundations for temporary wooden seats. The track (*dromos*) was an Attic stade in length, a little over 600 ft (the modern one is 670 ft). A row of pillars ran down the centre, some of them in the form of double herms. A single course ended at the closed south end (the semicircular *sphendone*); for a double length the runner had to stop and reverse direction, not continue in a loop as in modern practice. The seats for 60,000 or more spectators are in 47 rows, with a *diazoma* aisle dividing them behind the 24th. Seats of honour were in the bottom row of the arc's end. There are five vertical aisles in the curved end and 12 in each side. A Doric stoa provided shelter along the top of the *sphendone*; the Propylon at the north end was

in the Corinthian style. Mosaic-paved rooms for contestants were located under the east wing at the north end. Its mathematically harmonious proportions make the Stadium a work of beauty, enhanced by the clean glint of the marble.

Northwest of the Agora along the Panathenaic Way is the Deme of Kerameikos, the ancient pottery and tile production centre. The inner, industrial, section was included in Themistocles' wall in the early fifth century BC; the outer Kerameikos was primarily the chief cemetery of ancient Athens. Greek and German excavations since 1863 have clarified the important gates and other monuments and recovered valuable examples of ancient pottery.

Here the Sacred Way to Eleusis passed through the city walls by the small Sacred Gate, which also admitted the canalized course of the

Eridanos stream, partly covered over at this point by a vaulted roof. Since Themistocles' time it had two towers inside the wall.

Fifty yards to the northeast was the main entrance to the city from the Academy, Kolonos, Thria, and Piraeus (via the *Hamaxitos* route) leading into the Agora by the Dromos, later becoming the Panathenaic Way. An earlier gate at this busy spot was replaced by Lycurgus around 330 BC and came to be known as the Dipylon ('Double Gate'). Its outer towers were set back a little inside the circuit wall and had a wide pier between them. A similar inner gate on the city side lay behind the intervening paved court with its lateral ramparts.

Between the Dipylon and Sacred Gate was the Pompeion, a storehouse for the special floats and equipment for the Panathenaic and Eleusinian processions. It contained a statue of

Sophocles and painted portraits of comic poets. The Classical Age structure was destroyed in Sulla's siege in 86 BC, and Hadrian accordingly had a new Pompeion built.

Northeast of the gates and wall was a necropolis area in use since sub-Mycenaean times in the twelfth century BC and throughout the Geometric era. Fine vases found here from the eighth century BC established the 'Dipylon' style. Farther west are burials of later periods and this section has been more fully explored. Some tombs remain *in situ*, others are now in various museums. Notable examples still here or in replica are those of Eukoline holding a bird among her family (with a dog at her feet), the famous Hegeso stele of gentle sadness, the memorial of 13 Spartan officers who helped liberate Athens from the Thirty Tyrants, Dionysios' noble bull, a Molossian hound guarding the tomb of Lysimachos, the knight Dexileos' relief, Pamphile seated before her mother Demetria, and a monument to the Tritopatores (ancestors). In this area Pericles delivered his famous funeral oration praising Athens and her dead.

Avdira/**Abdera**

On the Thracian/Macedonian coast northeast of Thasos in a swampy environment, Abdera claimed to have been founded by Hercules in honour of Abderos who had been killed nearby by the famous horses of Diomedes. Historical evidence indicates that the site was colonized from Asia Minor, primarily Klazomenai, in the middle of the seventh century BC and later expanded by an influx of Greeks fleeing Persian domination of their native Teos, near Klazomenai to the west of Smyrna. After the Persian Wars Abdera joined the Delian Confederacy. Though its population was not noted for its intellectual ability, it eventually became the centre of famous and influential schools of philosophy and science. Protagoras was born there about 480 BC, later becoming the pioneer Sophist. Leucippus' original philosophical system made Abdera prominent, as did the brilliant atomic theory of Democritus, a native of Abdera in the fifth century BC – a theory explaining physical reality which was respectfully demolished by Aristotle but has had profound and lasting influence through some of its basic intuitions. Alexander the Great's advisor, Anaxarchos, also came from Abdera. The city survived Roman occupation of the area but slowly disappeared, probably depopulated on account of its bad climate. Excavations in 1950–56 and 1966–67 by Lazarides have uncovered part of the ancient city and produced important vases and terracottas. The silver coins are especially fine.

The setting of the town on a low hill, jutting out into the sea with a good bay and reasonably fertile fields around, helped Abdera prosper. On a slope away from the sea a considerable length of the walls and a poorly preserved theatre remain. The photo shows details of finds in the western part of the city – a mixture of Classical, Hellenistic, and Roman structures.

In the Roman period the West Gate through the city walls was surrounded by houses, public buildings, and tombs; originally constructed in the fifth century BC, the gate was rebuilt by the Romans. Houses to the east of the gate belong to all periods of Abdera's history. Both Greek and Roman civic buildings are probably lying under the soil and awaiting future excavation.

Avlis/**Aulis**

When Helen of Sparta ran off to Troy with its wandering prince Paris, her aggrieved husband Menelaos and his brother Agamemnon, king of mighty Mycenae, called on other Greek princes to assemble at Aulis with fleet and soldiers for a concerted attack on Troy. It was here, then, just south of the narrows between Euboea and the mainland at Chalcis, that in Marlowe's dramatic phrase Helen's beauty 'launched a thousand ships and burnt the topless towers of Ilium'. Here too, according to Homer and Euripides, Agamemnon was forced to sacrifice his daughter Iphigeneia in order to obtain favourable winds from the gods to sail to Troy. Thereafter the town was eternally famous, but never of much size or historic importance.

The hilly promontory of clover-leaf configuration has a bay on either side. The one to the north is small but relatively deep and well protected; the southern is more open and shallow. Scholars argue as to which served as the mustering place for the Greek fleet, since neither is fully adequate. Presumably both did, with those who came first getting the more desirable anchorage.

A Mycenaean necropolis has been partly located along the north edge of the smaller bay.

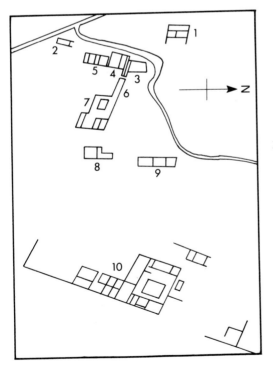

1 Roman houses
2 Roman baths (?)
3 West Gate
4 Roman tombs
5 Roman houses
6 Street
7 Houses: Greek and Roman, *c.* fourth century
   BC to *c.* third century AD
8 Houses
9 Hellenistic houses, third to second centuries BC
10 Roman houses

1 Promontory
2 South bay

3 North bay
4 Temple of Artemis, etc.

5 Modern cement factory
6 Mycenaean necropolis

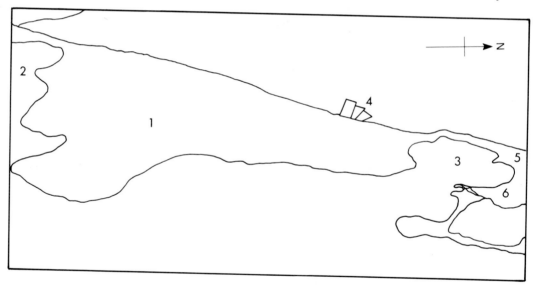

In 1941 a temple was discovered which is identified by an inscription as sacred to Artemis. It was excavated between 1956 and 1961 by Threpsiades along with some surrounding houses and a kind of pilgrims' hotel. He also found workshops of potters and vase-painters and a sacred spring near the front of the temple. Further excavation will no doubt one day reveal more of the ancient town.

The temple of Artemis is rather unusual in design: a long nave with eight columns inside, a sacred *adyton* at the rear with statue-bases and altars traceable, and across the front an extra large porch (*prostoön*) with four columns across its length. This seems to be a Hellenistic rebuilding of an earlier and simpler two-columned porch. The nave itself dates to the fifth century BC. In Roman times the temple was partially reconstructed and altered, and a thermal bath establishment was added nearby.

Pausanias saw two marble statues in the temple, one holding torches, the other representing Artemis shooting with bow and arrow. There were also remains inside of the great plane tree mentioned in the *Iliad* in connection with the sacrifice of Iphigeneia. On the hill he was shown 'the bronze threshold of Agamemnon's tent'. He remarks on the palm trees growing at the site and mentions the local potters.

Delfi/Delphi : The Setting and the Oracle

Greece, with all its splendid and varied scenery, has no more spectacular context for an ancient site than Delphi. It arouses universal awe and long remembrance. The sanctuary is perched high up on the north slope of the Pleistos torrent gorge, with the foothills of Parnassus towering another thousand feet above it. The orange and tan Phaidriades ('Shining Rocks') reflect Apollo's radiance and evoke by their grandeur a mood of reverence and a sense of man's insignificance before Nature and the divine. No wonder, then, that here grew up the greatest oracular centre in Greece, its fame spreading afar to Italy, Asia Minor, and Egypt. Gifts, memorials, and monuments in honour of Apollo crowded his temenos, vying with one another for space and visibility. Many of the later ones were indeed meant to glorify the donor (individual or city-state) rather than to express piety, but in any case they were there because of the oracle's unique fame and international audience.

In pre-Greek times there was here a cult of Ge (Mother Earth) and her serpent-son Python next to the sacred Omphalos, reputed navel of the Earth and centre of the world. Around 1000 BC Apollo replaced the more primitive cult, though vestiges of it remained near his temple. He probably came from Dorian Crete, as the earlier Mycenaean settlement here did not evict the prehistoric goddess. He was said to have slain the dragon in heroic combat and was ever afterwards honoured as Pythian Apollo. Homer calls the site Pytho. The name Delphi, in common use from the seventh century BC onwards, is probably connected with Apollo's attributes. Dionysus too was honoured here in a secondary role and ruled the sanctuary in winter months when Apollo was away. Poseidon also had his small temenos.

Though Dodona was a more ancient oracle among the Greeks, from the seventh century BC Delphi was pre-eminent. Even Rome consulted it, much later, on how to save herself from Hannibal after the disaster at Cannae. King Croesus of Lydia sent queries and rich gifts, and Amasis of Egypt honoured Delphi though he had Zeus Ammon nearer at hand.

As monuments and shrines multiplied, an official sanctuary area was delimited in the sixth century BC by a wall. It became so crowded with memorials that Pliny counted over 3000 statues there even after it had been looted of many by Sulla, Nero, and the Phocians. The nearby city Krisa and its port-town Kirrha (near modern Itea) exploited pilgrims to the shrine until they were destroyed by Athens, Sicyon, and other Greek states in the First Sacred War *c.* 590 BC. An Amphyctionic League was established of many cities to manage and protect the sanctuary, but Delphi's autonomy was often suppressed by seizure of control by Phocians (who in 356 BC robbed much of its wealth and art), Macedonians, Aetolians, and Romans. Attacks by Xerxes' troops in 480 and Brennus' Gauls in 279 BC were frustrated by thunderous rockslides from the Phaidriades. After the fourth century AD Delphi was abandoned and fell into decay. French excavations since 1892 have restored it to the world's admiration.

The Delphic Oracle long had unrivalled reverence throughout Greece and abroad. It rarely foretold future outcome or obscure events. Rather it offered guidance, supposedly based on Apollo's superhuman wisdom, on important decisions of individuals and city-states: whether to marry, undertake a certain business risk, enter legal litigation, start a colony or a war, etc. In cases of clear alternatives, the choice was mostly indicated by lot. If a verbal response was needed, the Pythia had to

1 Phaidriades cliffs (W: Nauplia/Rhodini; E: Hyampeia/Phleboukos)
2 Castalian Gorge
3 Stadium
4 Theatre
5 Temple of Apollo
6 Sacred Way
7 Sanctuary wall
8 Treasury of the Athenians
9 Hellenistic Stoa
10 Museum
11 Gymnasium area
12 Marmaria: sanctuary of Athena Pronaia
13 North slope of the Pleistos Gorge

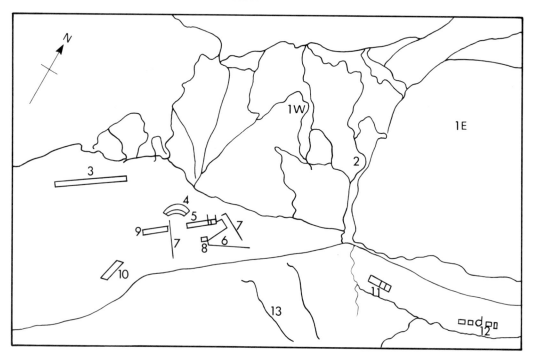

transmit Apollo's advice received in mystic communion on her golden tripod in the temple's *adyton*. The response, in wretched verse, needed interpretation. A ritual of purification and sacrifice preceeded the oracular pronouncement.

Delfi/Delphi: The Apollo Sanctuary

The heart of Delphi was the great Apollo temple on an upper terrace at the end of the Sacred Way. The extant ruins are from its fourth-century phase, completed c. 329 BC after nearly 40 years of rebuilding. Though with late Classical refinements, it followed the plan of the famous Archaic temple built between 536 and 505 BC from contributions of many cities. The Alcmaeonid family of Athens supervised the work and paid for a marble pronaos and the pedimental sculpture by Antenor. This temple collapsed in an earthquake in 373 BC. Its own antecedent, apparently built in wood with bronze-clad walls, had burned down in 548 BC after standing for a century or more. Both the Alcmaeonid and the fourth-century structures are mostly of Corinthian limestone, Doric in style, with archaic proportions of 15 columns down the sides and six across the front and back. They stood on a laboriously levelled artificial terrace; a retaining wall (*ischegaon*) was added at the north end before the final rebuilding. The pronaos porch, with maxims such as 'Know Thyself' and 'Nothing in Excess', held a statue of Homer. In the cella was an altar to Poseidon, statues of Zeus and the Fates, and the throne of Pindar. Nothing remains of the sacred *adyton* where the Pythia spoke; it was probably at the back, in a secret area, and contained the Omphalos and the 'tomb of Dionysos'. At the east front was a ramp and beyond that the great Altar of the Chians in bluish and white marble with double step-back.

At the northwest corner was a large niche with bronze statues by Lysippos showing Alexander in a lion hunt being rescued by Krateros. Nearby stood the wonderful surviving bronze charioteer in a four-horse chariot: a memorial given by Polyzalos of Gela in Sicily about 475 BC. Higher up was the theatre, with its splendid view over all the sanctuary. Built in the fourth century, it was restored in 159 BC by Eumenes II and later by the Romans. Northeast of the temple towers a pillar which once held a statue of Prusias, king of Bithynia.

Near it stood a colossal bronze Apollo Sitalkas ('Protector of Food'), described in ancient sources but since totally lost. Aemilius Paullus' memorial of his victory at Pydna was also a column; near it the Messenians' Nike celebrated their triumph with Athens over the Spartans at Sphacteria. To the north in a rectangular exedra were once displayed statues of Thessalian nobles (some now in the museum) put up by Daochos of Pharsala about the time that Alexander invaded Asia. At the northern end of the temenos was the club-house (Lesche) of the Cnidians, whose elaborate paintings by Polygnotus are described in great detail by Pausanias. To the southeast was a stoa, the gift of Attalos of Pergamum. East of the Altar of the Chians intertwined bronze serpents holding aloft a golden cauldron – part of them surviving in Istanbul – formed a striking memorial to the Persian defeat at Plataea. Behind this the Rhodians dedicated a gilded chariot of the Sun; grooves for the horses' hooves hint that they may have been the magnificent four now on the balcony of San Marco in Venice. At the east corner of the fine polygonal wall below the temple terrace is the Athenian stoa, with seven wide-spaced Ionic columns, housing spoils from Salamis and cables from Xerxes' bridge across the Hellespont. South of this was the sanctuary and spring of Ge (Earth), sacred here long before Apollo, and the prophetic Sibyl's rock. An Archaic Naxian sphinx guarded the site from a 33 ft high column.

Over 20 cities' treasuries throughout the sanctuary displayed their special art and trophies of victory over other Greeks for international publicity. Corinth's is the oldest, c. 640 BC. Fine Archaic frieze sculpture survives from those of Sicyon and Siphnos, while the walls of Athens' preserved text and musical notation of hymns to Apollo. Farther east Argos built two arcs with statues of its kings and of the Epigonoi, and a model Trojan Horse. Near the entrance Athens commemorated the victory at Marathon, and Sparta its victory over Athens.

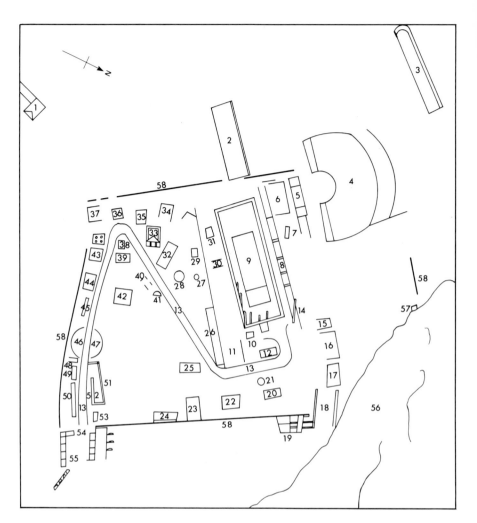

THE APOLLO SANCTUARY

1 Museum
2 Hellenistic stoa
3 Stadium
4 Theatre
5 Stage building
6 Krateros and Alexander group
7 Charioteer base
8 Ischegaon retaining wall
9 Temple of Apollo
10 Aemilius Paullus monument
11 Site of Messenians' Nike?
12 Altar of the Chians
13 Sacred Way
14 Prusias column
15 Exedra with statues
16 Daochos monument
17 Neoptolemos heroön
18 Stoa of Attalos I
19 Roman ruins
20 Rhodian chariot base
21 Plataea Serpent column base

22 Treasury (unidentified)
23 Prytaneion
24 Cyrene treasury?
25 Corinthian treasury
26 Stoa of the Athenians
27 Naxian Sphinx column
28 Sibyl's Rock
29 Shrine of Ge
30 Steps down to well (Cassotis basin?)
31 Pythia's house?
32 Bouleuterion
33 Athenian treasury
34 Etruscan treasury?
35 Potidaean treasury
36 Boeotian treasury
37 Theban treasury
38 Megarian treasury?
39 Syracusan treasury
40 Cnidian treasury
41 Exedra
42 Aeolian treasury (Clazomenae?)

43 Siphnian treasury
44 Sicyonian treasury
45 Tarentine ex-voto
46 Epigonoi monument
47 Kings of Argos monument
48 Trojan Horse base
49 Argives' Seven against Thebes
50 Athenians' Marathon monument
51 Lysander and Spartans group?
52 Arcadian heroes with Apollo
53 Corcyran Bull
54 Main entrance to sanctuary
55 Roman agora outside entrance
56 Phleboukos cliff over Castalian Gorge
57 Lesche of Cnidians
58 Temenos wall (sixth and fourth centuries BC)

Delfi/Delphi: The Stadium, Gymnasium and Marmaria

The stadium at Delphi is the best preserved anywhere in Greece. It is cut into the hillside at an elevation of 2100 ft on a level considerably above that of the sanctuary, which lies to the southeast. Its length of six *plethra* (about 580 ft) constituted a Pythic stade, somewhat shorter than the distance at Olympia. The starting and terminal lines at each end are in marble, with grooves for the runner's feet to help getting off to a sure start, and there are 18 lanes marked out by cuttings for upright posts. The track and the raised mound along the south side supporting six tiers of seats date from the fifth century BC, but the whole structure was re-worked in Roman times and Herodes Atticus paid for new stone seats along the north, where there are 12 tiers, mostly well preserved. Vertical stairs at frequent intervals divided all seating areas into rectangular sections. Total capacity was about 7000 – considerably less than the 40,000 at Olympia. Special backed seats

of honour for officials are visible. The entrance was at the southeast end towards the sanctuary. An elaborate triple Roman arch near the entrance was also erected at Herodes Atticus' expense.

The Pythian Games were originally held every eight years, but after reorganization in 582 BC they occurred in the late summer of every fourth year, though in Roman times they reverted to eight-year intervals. They were primarily musical contests, as was suitable in Apollo's honour – competitions with the lyre, flute, hymns, and choral song. Included was a special choral pageant presenting Apollo's victory over Python. Literary and rhetorical displays were also prominent, and later tragedies and comedies were added. The athletic events were held in the stadium (the others probably in the theatre). They never matched Olympia's in prestige, but rated among the four chief such festivals. Pindar wrote victory

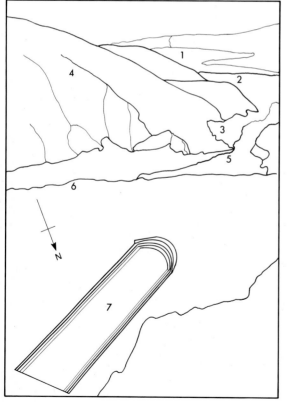

THE STADIUM
1 Gulf of Corinth
2 Itea (ancient Kirrha to the east)
3 Sacred Plain
4 Mt Kirphys
5 Pleistos Gorge
6 Modern town of Delphi
7 Stadium

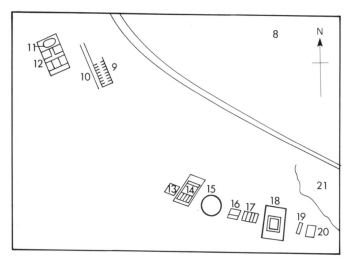

THE GYMNASIUM AND
MARMARIA

 8 Phleboukos base
 9 Xystos running track
10 Paradromos open track
11 Cold water pool
12 Palaestra court
13 Priests' house?
14 New temple of Athena
    Pronaia
15 Tholos
16 Massilian treasury
17 Dorian treasury
18 Old temple of Athena
    Pronaia
19 Altar
20 Gate to sanctuary
21 Terrace of heroa (Phylakos
    Pyrrhos)

odes for winners here also; his *First Pythian Ode* is probably the most splendid choral composition ever created. Horse races were held in a special Hippodrome in the plain far below, near Krisa. That fertile Sacred Plain was supposed to support the sanctuary's expenses but was often illegally exploited by neighbouring Phocians and Amphissa. At its southern edge near modern Itea was the harbour on the Gulf used by many pilgrims to the oracle.

In the other direction, nearly a mile southeast of the sanctuary, is the gymnasium area. The palaestra section included a peristyle court, north of which was a large circular pool; hot baths were added in Roman times. On a higher level to the east were two practice running tracks, each the length of a Pythian stade. The lower one was open to the sky, and known as the *paradromos*. The upper, *xystos*, was roofed over like a long stoa.

Farther around the curving terrace is the marmaria ('marble') sector, primarily the special sanctuary of Athena Pronaia ('Guardian of the Temple'). There are Mycenaean remains here evidencing an ancient cult. An Archaic Doric temple here of the seventh century was destroyed by a rock-slide during the Persian intrusion in 480 BC. It was soon replaced but the fifth-century temple was also damaged by another fall of boulders at the time of the Gauls' attack in 373 BC, and a new one was then built farther west. Between them is a treasury in Doric style and an elegant Aeolic one erected by distant Massilia (Marseilles). More notable is the fine Tholos, a circular structure of marble built in the early fourth century BC by Theodoros of Phocaea, who wrote a book about its design principles. Its ring of 20 Doric columns enclosed a cylindrical cella with a Corinthian inner colonnade.

Dilos/Delos: General and the Northern Sector

Though the smallest of the Cyclades, of which it is the centre point, Delos is the most famous and archaeologically the most important. As mythical birthplace of Apollo and Artemis, it developed into the chief religious sanctuary of Greece, though it was overshadowed by Delphi on the oracular level. Prehistoric remains on Mt Kynthos' summit imply inhabitation before 2000 BC. The Mycenaean settlement was situated by the harbour and had considerable wealth and power. Ionian colonists in the tenth century BC brought the cult of Leto, while the later Dorians revered Artemis – as Geometric Age remains under the Artemision indicate. From the seventh century BC onwards, the worship of Apollo gained predominance; yet in later centuries his birthplace welcomed the cult of other gods: Hera, Zeus, Athena, Poseidon, Aphrodite, the Kabeiroi of Samothrace, and Egyptian divinities. In Archaic times a confederation of island states under the leadership of Naxos administered and supported the growing sanctuary, but soon Athens took over and considered Delos its own special domain, like Eleusis. The Athenians purified Apollo's island by the removal of graves in the days of Pisistratus and again in 425 BC. No one was

allowed to be born or to die there, in honour of the god. After the Persian Wars, Delos was the centre of the Athenian-led Confederacy, though the common treasury was transferred to Athens in 454 BC and used to finance the great new buildings on the Acropolis.

Athens revived the old Apollonian festivals in 426 BC and instituted the Delian Games, held every fourth year in February for competitions in music and athletics as well as sacred ceremonies; a special state ship, reputedly Theseus', sailed from Marathon to inaugurate the festival. A simpler celebration, the Apollonia, was held every May.

Delos was mostly under Athenian control, but had short periods of independence tempered by political intervention of the Macedonians, Ptolemies, and Romans. It was made a free port by Rome in the second century BC, and took over from Rhodes as the chief international exchange centre for Aegean commerce and prospered richly. It also was the main slave market of Greece. Foreign merchants from Rome, Alexandria, Berytos (Beirut), Tyre and Corinth had major offices in Delos. Its wealth led to danger. Mithridates' forces looted and razed Delos in 88 BC, slaying or enslaving

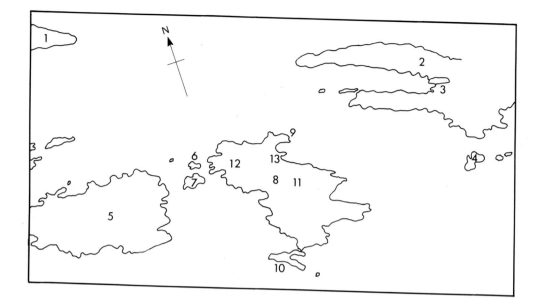

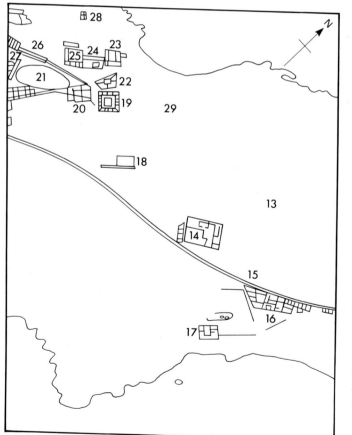

1 Tenos
2 Mykonos island
3 Mykonos town
4 Prasonisi
5 Rhenea
6 Little Rhevmatiari
7 Rhevmatiari islet (Hekate)
8 Delos
9 Patiniotis Point
10 Kherronisio
11 Mt Kynthos
12 Sanctuary of Apollo
13 Northeast sector
14 Gymnasium
15 Site of stadium
16 Houses in the stadium area
17 Synagogue
18 Archegesion
19 Granite palaestra
20 Lake palaestra
21 Sacred Lake
22 House by the lake
23 House of the Comedians
24 House of Diadoumenos
25 Poseidoniasts of Berytos
26 Terrace of the Naxian
   Lions
27 Agora of the Italians
28 House on the hill
29 Site of the Hippodrome

its citizens. Rome rebuilt it, but it was again sacked in 69 BC by pirates and never recovered its pre-eminence. Rome even tried to sell the island but found no buyers. Venetians and Turks used its ruins as a marble supply for buildings elsewhere. French excavations since 1873 have uncovered, and clarified in numerous publications, the complex tangle of ruins and revealed the Delians' way of life.

Near the bay of Gourna on the northeast side of the island, protected by Patiniotis Point from the ceaseless Cycladic winds, lay a sports compound and a residential section. The stadium location is easily identified; along its west side ran a *xystos* (a stoa-like covered running track) while to the east were houses and, farther off, a first century BC synagogue with a porch along its east side overlooking the sea. The gymnasium, rebuilt in the Athenian period, had a large square interior courtyard with 13 Ionic columns along each side and rectangular exedrae benches. The Archegesion to the west, dating from the sixth century BC at least, was the cult centre of the legendary founder of Delos, Anios. West of it lay the Hippodrome for the Delian Games, two sports palaestras near the Sacred Lake, and a fine house of trapezoidal plan around a peristyle court.

Dilos/Delos: The Sanctuaries and the Theatre Area

From at least Mycenaean times the cult centre on Delos was located near the Sacred Harbour of the Classical era. Artemis was worshipped here in the Geometric Age and later the Apollo sanctuary was established nearby, eventually overshadowing all others. The Ionic temple of Artemis built *c.* 175 BC on a granite platform encloses remains of an Archaic sanctuary which is itself built over a long narrow shrine of Proto-Geometric or Mycenaean origin. An adjacent building of Athenian style was probably the Keraton with the altar of horns used in the primitive ritual of the Crane-Dance established by Theseus after slaying the Minotaur in Crete. The whole complex was set apart by an L-shaped Ionic stoa to the north and east. Five treasuries to the east formed an arc facing the Apollo temples – of which there were three,

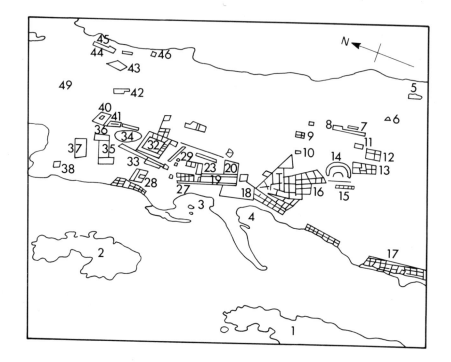

side by side, all unusually oriented to the west to face the primitive cult site. The northernmost is the sixth-century poros temple, probably decreed by Pisistratus. It had columns only across the west front. A huge archaic statue of Apollo by Naxian artists dominated its small cella. The southernmost 'Great Temple of Apollo' was twice as large, the only peripteral temple in Delos: 6 × 13 Doric columns. Started by the Delian Confederacy c. 478 BC, it was not completed until the end of the fourth century BC. Between the two is the Athenian temple erected by special workmen between 425 and 417 BC in Pentelic marble also brought from Athens. Its brilliant architect adapted its design to that of both its neighbours: side walls were substituted for pillars, as with the poros temple, but there were six Doric columns across the front and back. Inside the west front colonnade were four thin rectangular pillars between the antae, as in the Nike temple on the Athenian Acropolis, and windows on each side of the central west door, making a light-filled porch. A semicircular platform in the cella supported seven statues. The akroteria decoration of the roof was the most elegant anywhere, with groups of figures including Dawn and the North Wind Boreas.

Just south of the three Apollo temples is the curious Naxian house, an oblong structure from the seventh or early sixth century BC, replacing a much earlier one facing a primitive shrine that is the oldest in the area. It had a door in the north side as well as at the east and west ends, and inside a row of eight extremely slender pillars supporting the roof. The pronaos had two columns between the antae. An east porch was added later, with four columns across it. Outside to the north towered a colossal Apollo statue 30 ft high, an archaic Naxian marvel of the seventh century BC, of which gigantic fragments survive.

South of the Apollo temples ran the Avenue of Processions from the Agora of the Competeliasts along the South Stoa edge, to the east of which lay the large Agora of the Delians. A long building east of the temples, known from its decoration as the 'Sanctuary of the Bulls', seems to have been the Neorion, housing a trireme, probably dedicated by Antigonos Gonatas to commemorate a victory over the Ptolemies. He also built the long stoa north of the sanctuary, near which is the ancient Minoe fountain and the semicircular Theke or tomb of Arge and Opis, Hyperborean maidens who attended Leto and Apollo. West of the stoa

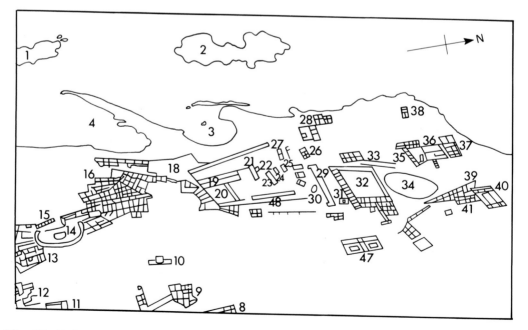

near the sea a large hypostyle hall with 44 Doric and Ionic pillars served as a merchants' exchange.

The large agora of the Italians resident on Delos begins the northern sector. Beyond is the Sacred Lake, now dry, west of which runs the Terrace of the Naxian Lions, gaunt archaic beasts in a long row guarding the area. There are several fine houses west of the lake, and the meeting place of the shipping merchants from Beirut dedicated to Poseidon/Baal.

Other great houses are near the theatre, many with fine mosaics. A large cistern collected rainwater. A complex of rooms south of the theatre seems to have been a hotel. On the slopes above are sanctuaries of foreign gods, and on Mt Kynthos' summit are shrines of Zeus and Athena.

Dodoni/**Dodona**

Deep in the mountains of Epirus, on the borders of Thesprotia, was the most ancient oracle in Greece, probably going back to the pre-Greek inhabitants ('Pelasgians'). Homer describes Dodona as a land of bitter winters where special prophet-priests called 'Selloi' interpret the mind of Pelasgian Zeus, sleeping on the ground and never washing their feet in order to preserve their sensitivity to chthonic inspirations through the earth. Achilles prayed to this god, and Odysseus consulted his will as revealed in the sacred lofty oak at Dodona.

From other ancient sources it appears that Zeus was here called Naios, and that Dione, a sky-goddess and mother of Aphrodite, was later associated with him in the cult. Legend said that a pigeon, flying from Thebes in Egypt and lighting in an oak at Dodona, ordered in

1 Acropolis wall with towers
2 Theatre
3 Stadium
4 Stage foundations
5 Hypostyle hall/Bouleuterion
6 Temple (to unidentified deity)
7 Votive offerings
8 Temple of Aphrodite
9 Sanctuary of Zeus
10 Votive bases
11 Later temple of Dione
12 Older temple of Dione
13 Christian basilica
14 Temple of Hercules

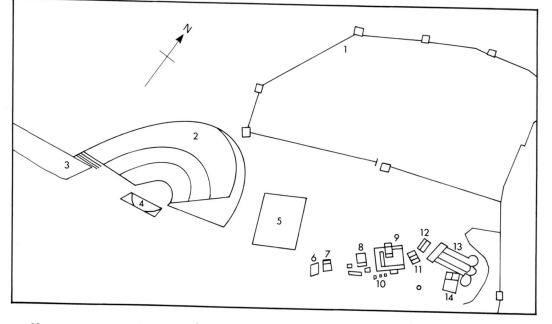

an intelligible voice the founding of an oracle there. Zeus' mind was thought to be revealed to the Selloi by the rustling of oak leaves, by the cooing and flight-patterns of the sacred doves, by the babbling waters of a spring, by the casting of dice, and by the gong-like sound of a bronze vessel struck by a whip held by a doll and blown by the wind. The Selloi are sometimes called Helloi, and are perhaps associated with the early name for Greece: Hellas. Clients presented their petitions and questions to the oracle on leaden tablets, many of which have been found.

By the fifth century BC Delphi had taken over as the chief oracle site, but Dodona was much consulted in later Greek times and was still known in the Roman era. A Christian bishopric was active there in the fifth and sixth centuries AD. The town (on the hill north of the sanctuary) and adjacent sacred buildings were destroyed by the Aetolians in 219 BC in their war against the Achaean League, but were promptly rebuilt in the reign of Philip V in the late third and early second centuries BC. It was again devastated in the seventh century AD,

probably by invading Goths. Its ruins were first identified and excavated by Carapanos in 1873.

Dodona's theatre is one of the largest in all Greece, accommodating 18,000 spectators. Its cavea of seats has a double *diazoma* (horizontal aisle) with 15 rows in the bottom section, 16 in the middle, and 21 in the upper part. There was probably an early hillside theatre, replaced by Pyrrhus in the early third century with the extant stone structure – later repaired by Philip V after the Aetolian destruction in 219 BC. Restored to a usable condition in 1960–63, ancient dramas are now presented there.

Next to the theatre Philip V built a stadium with 20 rows of seats. On the other side, a hypostyle hall with two inner rows of columns was the assembly place for the governing Koinon. The Zeus sanctuary enclosed the Sacred Oak and had a temple with an Ionic porch and a facing Propylon with six Ionic columns across the front and two down the sides, as rebuilt after 219 BC. Nearby are temples dedicated to Dione, Aphrodite, and to Hercules. The Christian basilica dates to the reign of Justinian, around AD 550.

Elefsis/**Eleusis**

Eleusis, some 14 miles northwest of Athens, was inhabited from prehistoric times. Here in Greek legend Demeter came (*eleusis* means 'arrival') in search of her daughter Kore (Persephone) who had been carried off to Hades to be Pluto's queen. Demeter gave Triptolemus, Eleusis' prince, the knowledge of wheat and sent him far and wide to teach men agriculture. From Mycenaean times a sacred ritual each spring and autumn commemorated the carrying off of Kore to Hades after the summer harvest and her return when the autumn rains bring nature to life again. These Eleusinian Mysteries were a high point of ancient religion, giving initiated devotees a hope of survival after death and a happier lot beyond the grave than other men. Their secret has been kept inviolate, but probably consisted in a sacred mime or pageant representing the death and rebirth of nature as the myth dramatized it, with awesome

1 Houses
2 Postern gate (Pylis)
3 Prytaneion?
4 Great Propylaea
5 Stoa
6 Temple of Artemis and Poseidon
7 Kallichoros Well
8 Roman triumphal arch
9 Roman baths
10 Roman portico
11 Inner Propylaea
12 Plutonium
13 Church of Panayia
14 Roman megaron
15 Temple of Kore?
16 Altar
17 Sacred Way
18 Terrace cut in rock
19 Telesterion
20 Early Telesterion of Pisistratus
21 Stoa of Philon
22 Roman enclosure wall
23 Pericles' wall
24 Lycurgus' wall
25 Bouleuterion
26 Portico
27 Sacred House
28 Museum

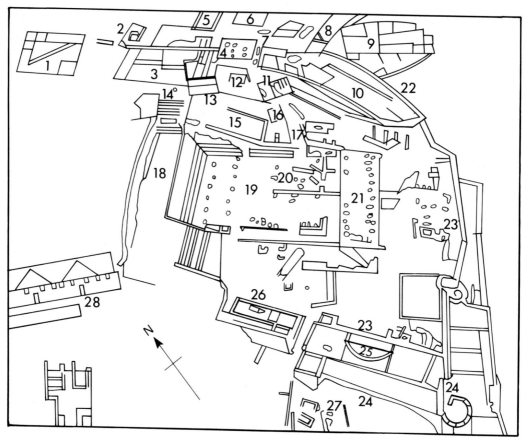

ceremonies in the dark Telesterion hall climax-
ing in a thrilling burst of light through an
opening in the roof. A special Sacred Way led
from Athens along which the ritual processions
marched.

Eleusis long rivalled Athens in early days but
was firmly taken over in the seventh century
BC. Buildings at the Sanctuary of the Great
Goddesses have a complex stratigraphy owing
to changes and additions from Mycenaean to
Roman times. Greek excavations since 1882,
especially in the 1930s and more recently, have
helped to clarify the maze of ruins.

Since entrance to the uninitiated was for-
bidden under penalty of death, a massive
fortified wall surrounded the sanctuary. Part
of this structure dates to Pericles' regime in the
fifth century BC, and part was built a century
later when Lycurgus guided Athens. The

northeast sector is Roman. Outside these
ramparts to the southwest the Sacred House
incorporates an Archaic temple on the site of
the sanctuary's ritual centre in the Geometric
period. The earliest centre seems to have been
a Mycenaean 'palace' (*anaktoron*) of the goddesses which was included in the Archaic (Pisis-
tratean), Classical, and Roman versions of the
great Telesterion hall which is the sanctuary's
chief monument. This remarkable structure,
170×175 ft, had in its full development 42
interior pillars and was one of the largest
roofed-over spaces in the Greek world. Around
all its inner walls ran a bank of eight rows of
steps, cut into the rock on the west and north,
to hold some 3000 initiates standing. Along its
southeast side a fine porch in white marble,
the Stoa of Philon, was added in the later
fourth century to the rebuilt Telesterion

designed for Pericles by Iktinos, architect of the Parthenon. Northeast of the great hall was, in all probability, a special temple to Kore, and beyond that one to Pluto at the traditional spot where he carried off Persephone and where she reappeared each autumn to initiate new life.

The Classical Bouleuterion was at the southwest corner of the enclosure, and the Prytaneion probably at the northwest. Cicero's friend, the proconsul Appius Claudius Pulcher, constructed a formal entrance to the sanctuary (the Inner Propylaea) around 54 BC. In the midsecond century AD Antoninus Pius added the much more elaborate Great Propylaea in Pentelic marble and on the pattern of the entry gate of the Acropolis at Athens. It had a splendid paved forecourt, before which stood a Roman temple to Artemis Propylaea and Poseidon, with an altar for each divinity outside. The Kallichoros Well, mentioned like so many other details of the Eleusinian cult in the *Homeric Hymn to Demeter*, lies east of the Propylaea.

The city walls ran around the acropolis hill west of the sanctuary. Mycenaean graves have been explored at the northeast foot of the hill, some supposedly belonging to the Seven against Thebes.

Epidavros/**Epidauros: The Sanctuary**

Reputedly a son of Apollo and Koronis, Asclepius learned the healing arts from the centaur Chiron (who taught Achilles music and warfare) and was later deified. His cult was introduced from Trikka in Thessaly to many Greek cities from the sixth century BC onwards: notably Cos, Corinth, Athens, Pergamum, and Epidauros – which in the fourth century BC became his greatest centre. The sanctuary here is in a charmingly wooded setting among low hills and wide valleys some five miles inland from the sea and the small town of Epidauros. Most of the buildings date from a great expansion of the sacred precinct in the fourth century BC when the shrine's fame had spread throughout Greece and abroad. Every four years an athletic and cultural festival was held there shortly after that at Isthmia.

The temple of Asclepius is surprisingly small: 77 × 38 ft. It is Doric, with six columns across the front and back, and eleven down the sides. It was designed by the local architect Theodoros in the early fourth century BC, apparently on somewhat earlier foundations. Timotheos supervised the sculpture, the most notable item of which is a large gold and ivory statue of Asclepius on a throne, with staff, serpent, and dog, made by Thrasymedes of Paros in imitation of Phidias' colossal Zeus at Olympia. He also made the wood and ivory doors with their golden nails. The floor was of black and white marble in a pattern. The statue rested in a pit in the floor, into which worshippers presumably descended as part of the ritual. There was an access ramp outside on the east and to the south a great altar. Extant building records show that it took four years and eight months to build the temple, at a cost of 24 talents (equivalent to some 140,000 day's wages). It is of limestone imported from Corinth, with decorative marble brought from Attica. A fine of up to 50% could be imposed for late completion of some of the contracts.

North of the temple was the Abaton, a long hall in two sections, the western of which had a level beneath the ground floor common to both. There were benches along the walls and an interior colonnade. Here the sick lay in hope of a miraculous cure or medical attention, posting memorial tablets on the wall if healed. Apparently this 'dormitory' function was earlier provided by a square building southeast of the temple which goes back to the sixth century BC; originally an altar of Apollo, it was later used as a house for his priests.

The Tholos behind the temple was considered by many ancients to be the most beautiful building anywhere. Designed by Polykleitos and built between 360 and 320 BC at a cost twice that of the temple, it was bigger and more ornate than the earlier round building at Delphi – 72 ft across the lowest of its three circular steps, 48 ft across the cella core. The outer ring of 26 Doric limestone columns enclosed a walkway outside the circular cella, within which was a circle of 14 Corinthian

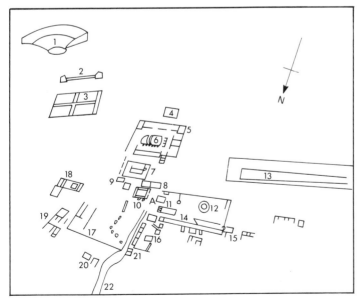

1 Theatre
2 Museum
3 Katagogion (hotel)
4 Greek baths
5 Gymnasium
6 Odeion
7 Palaestra/Stoa of Kotys
8 Temple of Artemis
9 Temple of Themis
10 Priests' house/older Abaton?
11 Temple of Asclepius (A : altar)
12 Tholos
13 Stadium
14 Abaton
15 Fountain-house
16 Roman library and baths
17 North hall
18 Sanctuary of the Egyptian gods
19 Roman baths
20 Roman houses
21 Temple of Aphrodite
22 Path to the Propylaea and the town

columns in marble, their capitals the finest known. The floor was a spiral pattern of alternate black and white diamond-shaped marble plates. The ceiling was richly decorated with meander, acanthus, wave moldings and rosettes. The low conical roof was gilded, and the exterior metopes were, for the first time, decorated not with sculptured figures but with brightly coloured rosettes. Below the floor was a triple circular wall with narrow entries and blocked off passages forcing three changes of direction to reach the core: some kind of mysterious labyrinth for the cult and perhaps for the sacred snakes.

There are other small temples, to Artemis, Aphrodite, and Themis; a stadium, palaestra and gymnasium, into whose centre an Odeion was built in Roman times; baths, both Greek and Roman, a large hostel with four colonnaded courtyards and 160 rooms, and a Roman library.

Epidavros/**Epidauros: The Theatre**

Pausanias, who had seen all major glories of Greek architecture intact, was moved by the theatre at Epidauros to special admiration for its unrivalled harmonious symmetry and beauty. Vast numbers of others before and since have shared his awe. Fortunately this finest of all ancient theatres is also the best preserved. Its beautiful setting all alone on the wooded slopes of Mt Kynortion, looking out across a placid valley to distant rolling hills, reinforces the tranquillizing effect of its subtly related proportions of design. A man's spirit is reassured and calmed by this radiant manifestation of order, intelligent control of space, and delight in a balanced structure that breathes beauty. This theatre contributed to the healing role of Asclepius' sanctuary by its own artistry of form and by endowing with suitable dignity a holy place dedicated to Dionysos and to the dramatic interpretation of the meaning of life. It is a triumph of intelligible art.

The uniquely satisfying effect of the theatre, as well as its perfection of acoustics, is clearly due to a purposeful design. Its architect Polykleitos was also responsible for the splendid tholos there, as Pausanias points out. Both structures show unusual attention to harmonious proportion, internal integration, and the mystique of circular forms. The orchestra area is a complete circle – practically alone among Greek theatres, and the cavea is a segment of a sphere, as the air view clearly reveals. The triple ring of gutter, *diazoma* (horizontal aisle), and upper walkway are of the same width – 4 Doric ells. The whole theatre was constructed on this basic measure, the Pheidonian ell: $1\frac{1}{2}$ Doric ft (49 cm./19.3 inches), as was the Parthenon. The stone ring surrounding the orchestra, for instance, is one ell; the lower cavea radius (from orchestra centre to *diazoma*) is 80 ells, the upper cavea radius 40, the proscenium (stage front) 45 ells across and 7 high, etc. The divisions of the cavea are especially neat: 12 wedges of seats in the lower segment, each becoming two above the *diazoma* – except at the outer edges where one is omitted at each end to provide direct access to the *diazoma* and also to balance the lower sector's pattern of one wedge beyond the diameter-line across the orchestra centre and parallel to the stage. The number and location of the 13 aisles seem determined by the properties of an imaginary pentagon inscribed in the orchestra circle, which arranges them at 18° intervals and puts an aisle at each of the cavea's three axes (diameter-line and right angle to that), and at equal distances between them in the most aesthetically pleasing arrangement in the history of theatre design.

The whole tone of the structure is set by the basic orchestra circle, so pleasing to the eye from every angle of the theatre and the key to its built-in harmonies. The stone at its centre focuses attention and served as guide to movements of the chorus (it was not an altar, as often stated).

Further, the mystical mathematics of the Golden Section and of the Grand Tetractys is consciously worked into the theatre's pattern – the 21 upper rows of seats being in .618 ratio to the lower 34 as these 34 are to the total of 55, this number 55 being also the sum of the first ten digits in counting, with 21 the sum of the first 6 and 34 the sum of the remaining 4. (For

1 Upper walkway
2 Upper cavea
3 Diazoma
4 Prohedriae (seats of honour)

5 Lower cavea
6 Gutter
7 Orchestra
8 Stage buildings

9 Support wall
10 Parodos entry portals

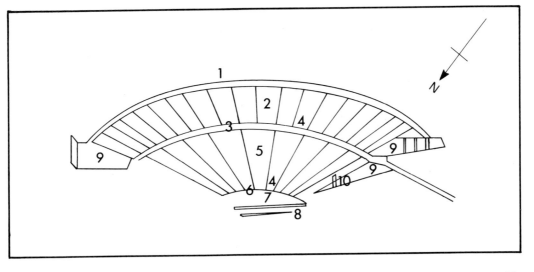

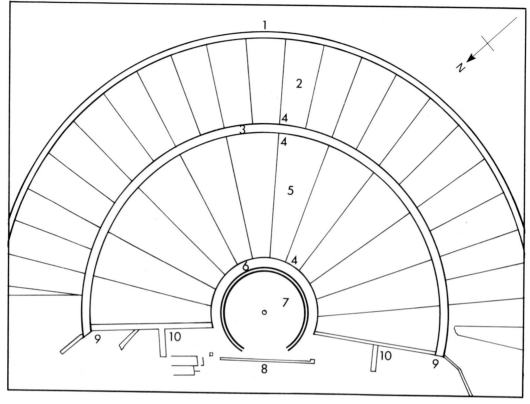

EPIDAUROS: THE THEATRE
1 Upper walkway
2 Upper cavea
3 Diazoma
4 Prohedriae (seats of honour)
5 Lower cavea
6 Gutter
7 Orchestra
8 Stage buildings
9 Support wall
10 Parodos entry portals

details and clarification of all these design factors see my article on this theatre as a work of art, cited in the Bibliography).

Above the theatre, farther up Mt Kynortion, is a small hill-top sanctuary of Apollo Maleatas, much older than the cult of Asclepius, with an altar from at least the seventh century BC amid evidence of a Mycenaean cult, a fourth-century temple, and a later stoa. This sacred area remained in use through Roman times.

Eretria/**Eretria**

Because it had aided the Greek cities in Ionia, especially Miletus, in their revolt against Persian domination, Eretria was devastated by Darius in 490 BC on his army's march to Marathon and humiliation. The city recovered somewhat, however, and fought back with Athens and her allies at both Salamis and Plataea ten years later. It became part of the Second Athenian Confederacy in 377 BC, but fell under Theban control a few years later, then Athenian again, Macedonian in 349, and from the early second century BC was under Roman control. Its greatest prosperity and power had been long before in the eighth and seventh centuries BC, when it vied with Chalcis and sent many colonies abroad. The vases it produced in the late Geometric and Archaic periods are outstandingly fine.

Remains of the city are extensive and scattered, many lying under the modern town near

the sea. The cleared area in the photo here is a mile inland at the foot of the acropolis hill. Early American excavations in the 1890s were supplemented by those of Kourouniotis and Petrakos nearer the sea. The Swiss, under Karl Schefold, are now uncovering many houses and expanding the site considerably.

The large theatre, though badly pillaged, reveals its plan clearly and evidence of several reworkings. It basically dates from around 440–411 BC, but in the early third century the orchestra area was lowered and a new Hellenistic stage constructed in front of the original one, which then served as its background. There is no *diazoma* (horizontal aisle). A vaulted passage under the stage buildings gave access directly into the public area behind. An interesting feature is the underground tunnel leading from below the stage at an angle into the centre of the orchestra. This is probably the device called by the ancients 'Charon's Steps', for the sudden rising of infernal beings as if from Hades.

Near the side of the theatre is a temple, probably of Dionysos. Farther on is the West Gate, the best preserved anywhere in Greece from Archaic times, leading towards Chalcis. The walls it pierced ran for miles in a great loop around the city and acropolis and down to the sea. Sections of Pelasgic construction on the acropolis are much earlier than the towers, which are of the Classical period.

Some of the houses are large and elaborate, like that near the West Gate, and are virtual palaces. A Hellenistic gymnasium has been excavated east of the theatre. Far off to the southeast, towards the harbour, are a fountain-house, a circular tholos much like that in the Agora at Athens, an Isis sanctuary, sports palaestra, and baths. An elaborate Heroön

1 Theatre   3 Temple of Dionysos   5 Building over Heroön
2 Stage buildings   4 West Gate   6 Houses

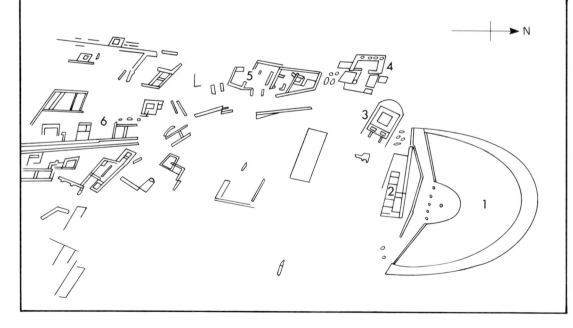

shrine was built over earlier graves of the Geometric period. In the hills that lie to the west of the theatre is a Macedonian tomb with marble couches that are decorated with painted designs.

The important Archaic temple of Apollo Daphnephoros is in the middle of the site, overlying a Geometric apsidal building that may also have been a primitive temple. In its early period the Apollo temple was Ionic in plan and very long: 100 × 20 Ionic ft with 19 wooden columns along the sides, six across the front and back. When rebuilt c. 510 in Doric style, the side columns were reduced to 14, and two rows of eight each were inside the cella. Fine Archaic statuary from it includes a beautiful Theseus and Antiope group.

Philoxenos, who painted the famous portrayal of Alexander's battle at Issus, came from Eretria.

Festos/**Phaistos**

A few months after Sir Arthur Evans began uncovering the palace at Knossos, Italian excavations at Phaistos near the centre of southern Crete started revealing a palace similar in size, plan, and architectural brilliance. More recently, from 1950 to 1965, Doro Levi has explored considerable remains of an earlier palace on the site going back to Middle Minoan I, c. 1900 BC (as does the First Palace at Knossos), constructed in three stages. This was larger than the Second Palace, extending more to the southwest and northeast. When destroyed c. 1700, its ruins were levelled and covered with a cement fill and the new building was constructed over it with a more expansive West Court setting for its principal façade. When this too was destroyed, c. 1450, it was left unoccupied for a century, after which at least the nearby town was again in use to Hellenistic times. An Archaic Greek temple was built with a different orientation over part of the palace ruins at the southwest corner.

Phaistos' setting is superb: on the southeast edge of a long hill some 230 ft above the great Messara plain, four miles east of the gulf on the southern sea towards Egypt. This airy eminence enjoys a splendid view of Mt Ida to the north and Mt Dikte far away to the east. Art was as much appreciated here as the scenery, and magnificent examples have been recovered from the site.

The formal approach was from the west, across a broad paved courtyard with raised walkways. The theatral area on the north side of this court has several rows of seats in parallel straight tiers for witnessing sacred dances, processions, and the like – a more developed plan than the one at Knossos. A monumental broad staircase, 45 ft wide, leads up to the Great Propylaea with its spacious vestibule and inner Propylon porch and light-well beyond. The inner porch had a tall column at the middle front and three at the back. It is likely that the second or third storey above, for which stairs are traceable, was a great stateroom with an Egyptian-style balcony over the door in the façade below, looking out over the West Court. This room may have extended southward over the series of adjacent storerooms on the lower level, and must in any case have been of truly royal scale.

Among the complex of rooms to the south on the lower storey are shrines, crypts and lustral baths, indicating a special cult area. The great Central Court had a colonnade on its east and west sides and was open to the air. As elsewhere, it was probably the scene of the Bull Games, its lower doors blocked off for safety, and with spectators looking down from the upper rooms round about. A square room with internal pillars reaching up through the second storey and with a gypsum-paved floor and wall-base may have had a special use in the ritual of the games, perhaps including the sacrifice there of the conquered bull. The north entrance to the Central Court had a half-column embedded on each side of its high door, apparently extending upwards beyond a third storey – perhaps like the banner-poles at the entrance to Egyptian temples.

A great Peristyle Court, unique in Minoan architecture, lies north of the Central Court, and was probably a formal stateroom. The

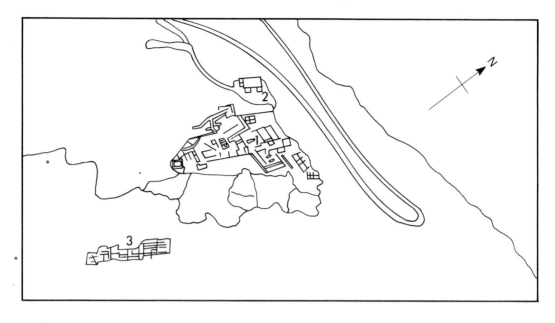

1 Palace
2 Modern tourist pavilion
3 Houses of the town (Minoan to Hellenistic)
4 Theatral area
5 Stairs

6 West Court
7 Great Propylaea
8 Storerooms
9 Remains of the First Palace
10 Cult area
11 Central Court

12 Peristyle Court
13 Royal quarters
14 Workshops
15 Other residence area (princes' apartments?)
16 Ritual room for Bull Games?

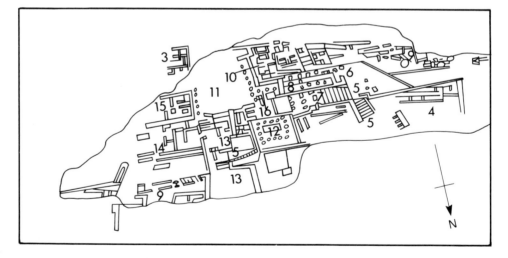

royal dining hall was possibly on the storey above it. To the north and east of this were the residences of the king and queen (her quarters having a private bath), each with a porticoed terrace and stairs to an upper storey. There was a fine view northward to Mt Ida and it was open to the cooling breeze. Other residential quarters that lay to the east of the Central Court may have been for younger members of the royal family.

This palace was clearly of a highly sophisticated design and with elegant appointments.

1 Towers
2 Round tower

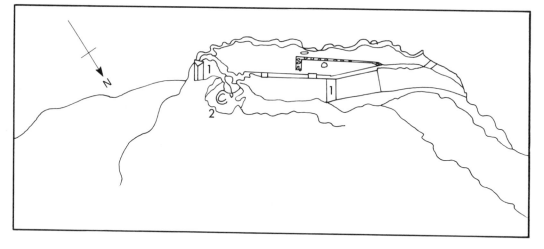

Fili/Phyle

Athens had a series of outlying forts in various directions to protect its approaches by land. Phyle is a good example of one of these. It is constructed on a triangular platform that falls sheer on all sides, especially precipitous on the west and north. Located in a complex of deep valleys on the south slope of Mt Parnes at an elevation of over 2100 ft, it is visible for miles around and from it the view commands nearly the whole of the Attic plain. It sits astride the short route from Athens to Thebes in the northwest and to Tanagra in the north. The site was of obvious strategic importance for a small holding force. Pisistratus' foes held Phyle against his autocratic power, and Thrasyboulos seized the pass early in 403 BC with 70 fellow exiles, coming down from Thebes to oppose the Thirty Tyrants after Athens' defeat in the Peloponnesian War. His forces grew to 700 there, and from Phyle he wrested control of Piraeus in his effort to restore democracy to Athens. The Macedonian king Cassander kept a garrison here, but later Demetrius Poliorcetes dismantled the fortification for the benefit of Athens. In subsequent earthquakes, part of the walls on the west and southwest fell into the gorge, and the slow pressure of invading bushes loosened and tumbled more. The considerable remains were excavated by Skias in 1900 and have been thoroughly studied by Wrede and others for the better understanding that they give of Attic fortification techniques and structures.

The extant walls are dated by most experts to c. 400 BC, though some ascribe them to the later fourth-century occupation by the Macedonians. The plan is a loose pentagon with two entrances and five towers – one of them round. Assailants had to expose their right sides (unprotected by their shields) when forcing the entrances. The walls were constructed of carefully dressed rectangular blocks, averaging 9 ft thick and 19 inches high per course, of which from 6 to 20 levels still stand in the surviving sections. The upper part had buttresses of stone and stone parapets – perhaps the earliest examples in Greek fortresses – designed to withstand the shock of new battering-ram techniques. The walls were capped with a stone paving layer as an added element of strength and advantage to the defenders. The interior, some 300 ft across, had several rooms used as an armoury as well as for food and water storage, and perhaps as barracks for those on duty.

There are ruins of houses below the fort, and a small town lay nearby to the northeast close to a spring. It is argued whether Thrasyboulos' fort was here or was an earlier one on the site of the extant fortified citadel, which the Macedonians certainly used.

Not far away is an interesting grotto of Pan, where many ancient votive offerings were found during Skias' exploration of it. Here was set the opening of Menander's play *Dyskolos* ('The Grouch'), whose text has been recovered from a papyrus copy in Egypt.

Filippi/Philippi

It was here that Christianity entered Europe, when St Paul arrived from the Troad via Philippi's port Neapolis (modern Kavalla) in AD 49. His *Epistle to the Philippians* shows his devotion to his converts there, and he visited the city again six years later.

Philippi had already changed history in another way, when the Roman Republic died on its plains in 42 BC. Caesar's assassins Brutus and Cassius were crushed here in October by Antony and Octavian – the latter becoming sole ruler as Augustus. Horace was on the losing side and fled, as one of his poems wryly records. The city thereafter acquired a Roman flavour and many new buildings. It had been founded from Thasos in the sixth century BC and recolonized in 361 BC, but five years later Philip of Macedon (Alexander's father) took it over as a bastion against Thrace and changed its name from Krenides to one echoing his own. Prosperity grew from its proximity to the gold mines in nearby Mt Pangaios and from the surrounding rich agricultural area, especially after the construction of the great Roman military

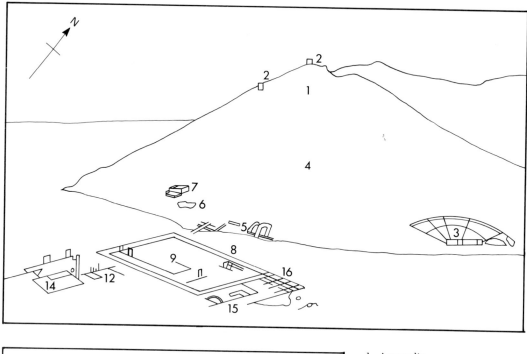

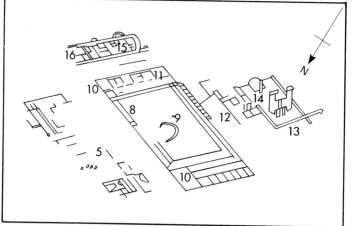

1 Acropolis
2 Byzantine towers
3 Theatre
4 Sanctuary of the
   Egyptian gods
5 Basilica A
6 Basilica
7 Museum
8 Via Egnatia
9 Forum
10 Temples at the forum's edge
11 Library
12 Agora (part)
13 Palaestra (part)
14 Basilica B ('Direkler')
15 Octagon Church
16 Baths

road, the Via Egnatia, which passed through it, linking Italy to Asia. The extant ruins are mostly Roman and early Christian and have been excavated by French and Greek archaeologists, primarily since 1920.

The large theatre was originally Greek, cut into the lower slopes of the conical hill that dominates the site. It was radically remodelled in the second century AD and again in the third to accommodate wild beast and gladiatorial contests. It bears relief carvings to Mars,

Victory, and the gladiators' patron Nemesis. Above the theatre, on a terrace half way up the hill, was a late sanctuary of the Egyptian gods. The heights were turned into a fortified acropolis by Macedonian walls, on which Byzantine ones rest.

The Roman forum is a vast rectangle through whose northern edge runs the Via Egnatia. Porticoes framed its other three sides and the open court was paved in marble. At the east and west corners on the north side were

matched temples and behind the East Stoa a library. This balanced elaboration of the forum dates from the reign of Marcus Aurelius (AD 161–180). The South Portico seems to have been part of an earlier Greek agora, or on its site; the rest, as well as most of a Roman palaestra farther south, was absorbed into the huge Basilica B (long visible towering above ground and called *Direkler*, 'Pillars', in Turkish), which cannibalized their parts. This enormous sixth-century church collapsed before it was completed, the weight and expanse of its dome being too ambitious for the design. Its surviving pillars and capitals, however, are highly impressive.

Another massive church has been recently uncovered to the east of the forum, with an internal octagon within a square and columns on seven of its sides. Beneath this a vaulted Macedonian tomb has yielded fine gold treasures. North of the church was its baptistery, and a complex of baths, with an elaborate Propylon leading in from the Via Egnatia.

Still another large basilica lies north of the forum, across the road; and remains of a fourth have been found farther west. These clearly evidence the importance of Christianity at Philippi in late Roman and early Byzantine times. The Octagon Church is the first example known of this design in Greece.

Gla/Gla

The remarkable fortified citadel of Gla (or Gha) probably derives its peculiar name by corruption of the Albanian word for castle: goulas. It is a unique site, formerly an island in the now dried-up Lake Copais. The entire circumference is crowned by a massive defence wall some 18 ft thick and nearly two miles in length – forming a huge enclosure that is ten times the size of Tiryns, seven times that of Mycenae. The palace level is 220 ft above the surrounding plain (an ancient lake bottom). Situated two miles from the eastern shore of the former lake, it may have been fortified and used by the Minyans, a tribe mentioned by Homer and others as dwelling in nearby Orchomenos in Mycenaean times. The wall and structures within it seem to date from the fourteenth century BC, and were in use at least as late as the early twelfth century BC, when the Mycenaean world collapsed. Its inhabitants evidently controlled the water-level and pattern of the swampy lake by a series of dikes and drainage canals which are still traceable.

The great wall is pierced by four gates. Of these, the southern is the most elaborate and apparently served as the main entrance into the citadel. It is approached by a long paved ramp and has a paved courtyard within; two towers guard the entrance. Between these the heavy wooden doors had attachments of bronze, part of which survive. There was a guardroom at the base of the western tower.

Similar guardrooms and paved courtyards are found inside the other gates, and in addition the Northeast Gate had twin square towers. The wall is mostly constructed of huge rectangular stone blocks laid in horizontal courses, and is thus different from the Cyclopean ramparts of Mycenae and Tiryns.

An L-shaped palace was built along the north edge of the island, its northern section forming part of the rampart wall, its eastern wing raised on a massive stone terrace. It seems to be two distinct palaces of similar plan, each with a megaron hall and an oblong waiting room at the outer end and dwelling rooms towards the centre. There is evidence of a second storey to each, built in sun-dried brick. To the west is a long narrow structure of uncertain purpose and there was probably an open court between the palace wings.

South of the palaces is a large rectangular area approximating an agora of later cities. It has its own enclosure wall, with a gate to the north towards the palaces and a more developed one to the south with a street leading to the main South Gate of the outer ramparts. Within this peribolos are two long structures something like stoas in Classical and Hellenistic agoras. The western one had inner columns in its southern half. Each 'stoa' had four long rooms off its southern end, two off the northern. The eastern 'stoa' is considerably narrower than the other. The rooms of both were possibly for

1 Palace
2 Northwest building
3 'Agora'

4 South Gate
5 Southeast Gate

6 Northeast Gate
7 West Gate

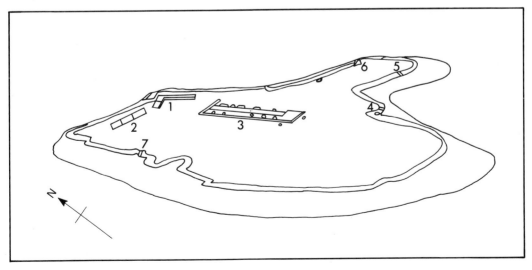

1 Palace
2 Northwest building
3 'Agora'

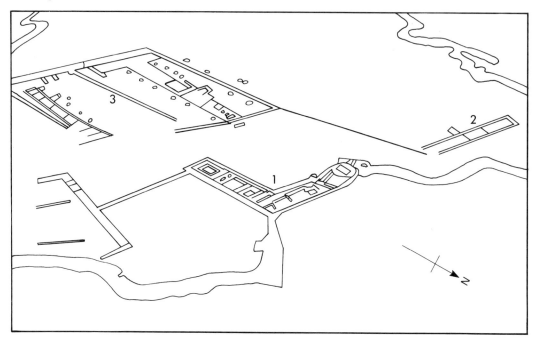

workshops and storage, but some think they may have served as stables for horses and chariots. The open space between the two long buildings may have been for assemblies.

Since there is no evidence of any public dwellings in the large fortified area, it is possible that this island citadel was a common refuge and defended storehouse for several distinct settlements around the lake – another aspect of its uniqueness.

Gla, first excavated by De Ridder in 1883, was further cleared by Threpsiades in 1955–61.

Gortis/Gortyn

Ancient Gortyn, located south of the centre of Crete, about ten miles inland from the sea, became the largest city on the island and was its official capital in Roman times. Homer speaks of it as 'walled', but nothing has been found of a fortified circuit. There are Neolithic remains on the acropolis and evidence of habitation in post-Mycenaean times. A temple of the eighth or seventh century BC, built over an earlier Geometric megaron, has been discovered, with

1 Odeion, with Law Code inscription
2 Site of the agora
3 St Titus basilica

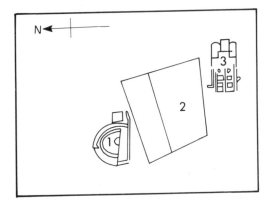

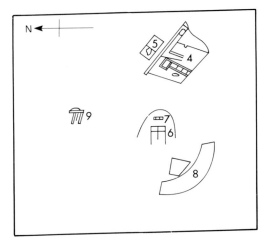

1–3 (see p. 81)
4 Praetorium
5 Nymphaeum
6 Python: temple of Apollo
7 Altar
8 Roman theatre
9 Sanctuary of the Egyptian gods

an Archaic altar nearby that is over 40 ft long. A late Minoan villa or farm survives at the southern edge of the large city area. The main importance of the city, however, was in Classical and Roman days, and many of its major buildings date from the second century AD. The Saracen occupation in the ninth century AD brought ruin and desolation. Italian excavations in the 1880s and since 1954 have so far uncovered only a small portion of this extensive site.

The most interesting structure is the Roman Odeion, southeast of the acropolis hill. This dates from about AD 100 in the reign of Trajan. It is built over an Archaic tholos which carried on its circular wall a long inscribed text of local laws on social status, property rights, gifts, wills, inheritance, divorce, crimes of violence. This is a major document of ancient legislation written c. 500 BC in Doric dialect in letters that proceed alternately from left to right and vice versa in successive lines (the *boustrophedon* or 'plow-turn' technique of Archaic times). It was carefully incorporated into the Roman building. The orchestra in front of the curved rows of seats is paved with black and white marble.

In front of the Odeion is the area of the ancient agora. Beyond lies the sixth-century AD basilica of St Titus built in honour of St Paul's disciple whom he left here as first bishop of Crete and to whom his epistle, written from Nicopolis, is extant.

Southeast of the agora lie several buildings from various periods. The sanctuary of the Egyptian gods (Isis and Serapis) was dedicated by a Roman lady, Flavia Philyra, and her sons. The complex to the south comprises the Python: a temple and altar of Apollo from the Archaic period, built over an earlier Minoan structure. A pronaos porch with six columns was added in the Hellenistic age, and the Romans in the second century AD put a double row of columns inside the cella and added an apse. A treasury is located inside the northeast corner, and a Hellenistic Heroön adjacent to the temple. The ruined brick theatre nearby to the southwest is Roman, and presumably functioned in the Python's ritual in later times. (Another ruined theatre for dramatic purposes lies on the south slope of the acropolis.)

The Roman Governor's palace, the Praetorium, is to the east of the Python. It dates from Trajan's era, with a paved hall added in the fourth century AD. Next to it is a Nymphaeum fountain-house, dating to the late second century AD. Farther to the southeast is a Roman amphitheatre, and on the edge of the city a stadium and Roman baths.

Pliny and Varro describe a famous plane tree at Gortyn that never shed its leaves. Hannibal may have taken refuge in the town in 189 BC.

Gournia/Gournia

Nothing is known of the history of Gournia except as deduced from archaeological evidence, and even its ancient name is unrecorded. The site is of special importance however as an illustration of a Minoan town – the only one yet excavated for practically all its extent. It was uncovered in 1901–04 in the pioneering days of Cretan archaeology by a venturesome team of three American women under the direction of Harriet Boyd Hawes with the assistance of Richard Seager. The finds were elaborately published along with essays on general aspects of Minoan civilization, daily life, art, and religion. The ruins have recently been partially reconstructed.

The setting, on an oval hill overlooking beautiful Mirabello Bay in the ruggedly mountainous eastern sector of Crete, is very attractive. The town seems to have been a fishing, trade, and small-industry centre for neighbouring agricultural communities, under a lord or governor but presumably without a king of its own. The earliest remains date from the Early Minoan period before 2000 BC, but most of the buildings are of the end of Middle Minoan and beginning of Late Minoan, in the seventeenth to fifteenth centuries, with partial re-occupation in Late Minoan III after 1400 BC.

The town plan is accommodated to the contours of the hill, with two main paved streets running north-south along the sides of the central ridge. Parallel and cross streets are narrow and often crooked, and the town must have been rather crowded. Houses are commonly of limestone on the lower courses, with crude brick and wood above. Many had five or six rooms on the ground floor, mostly oblong, but interconnecting corridors are rare. Stairways surviving in several houses indicate a second storey, and in some instances there was

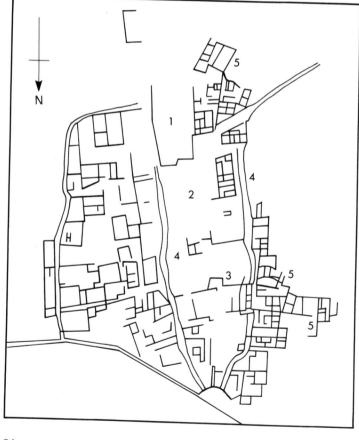

1 Agora/courtyard
2 Palace
3 Shrine
4 Streets
5 Late houses of artisans

an entrance to the upper level from a street higher than that passing the ground floor entrance. Pilasters supporting the upper rooms were rectangular in earlier houses but later were more commonly round. A few late houses along the west side apparently imply partial re-occupation of the site after a ruinous earthquake – probably the cataclysmic one of the mid-fifteenth century that destroyed so many greater Minoan settlements. Objects found in these houses show that they belonged to artisans – parts of potter's wheels, a carpentry shop with bronze saws, axes, drills, chisels, a coppersmith's forge, oil presses, fish hooks, etc.

The palace on the hill-top is only one-tenth the size of that at Knossos but shares characteristic features of palatial design: a main court bordered with alternating columns and square pillars, an ashlar façade with set-backs (as at Mallia), a small theatral area, and surrounding elongated storerooms. Adjacent to the south is a large public court, the equivalent of a later agora, and this is joined to the palace by a set of steps.

On the summit just north of the palace is a small one-room shrine without a porch, in which a clay snake-goddess idol and a tripod altar were found.

Halieis/**Halieis**

Near the southern tip of the Argolid is the bay of Porto Cheli. Along its circuit was the ancient city of Halieis, inhabited from the eighth century BC till the end of the fourth. It prospered most in the fifth century BC after the arrival of many refugees from Tiryns when that town, long faded from its former greatness, was conquered and destroyed by Argos. The Athenians coveted the city for defence against Sparta but their attempt to seize it in 460 BC was repulsed. Sparta took control c. 435 BC, facing Athenian raids in 430 and again in 425

ACROPOLIS
1 Circular tower
2 Defensive rooms
3 Site of stairs to tower
4 Fortification wall
5 Dining room
6 Retaining wall for terrace
7 Altar
8 Industrial terrace
9 Dye works

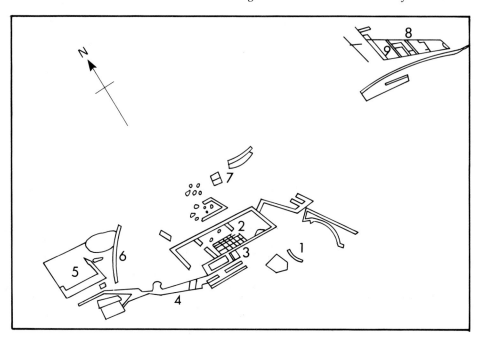

during the Peloponnesian War. An Athenian garrison was established there finally in 423 BC, but after Athens' defeat the city became an ally of Sparta in the fourth century. Extensive fortification walls were later constructed and the city spread widely from the acropolis and adjacent hill all along the bay. American excavations since 1962 have uncovered some of the upper city and explored and cleaned much of what is now under water along the coast. Considerable submerged remains are clearly visible from the air.

The fortification walls, probably built in the fourth century BC and incorporating remains of earlier ones, ran from west and east of the acropolis in broad sweeping arms to meet to the north in an ingenious Sea Gate open only to the west to allow access to the fortified harbour within. A massive gate to the northeast protected the way out to Hermione, the other major city in the southern Argolid. This gate and adjacent houses and wall are now under many feet of water, as are other sectors along the former coastline. Outside the Hermione Gate is a rectangular building with two rows of three square pillars each, like a small stoa. Much farther out are a stadium, baths, and an Apollo sanctuary. Though the lower levels of

NORTHEAST QUARTER
10 Hermione Gate
11 Stoa
12 Bomb crater from World War II

13 City wall (northeastern sector)
14 Houses

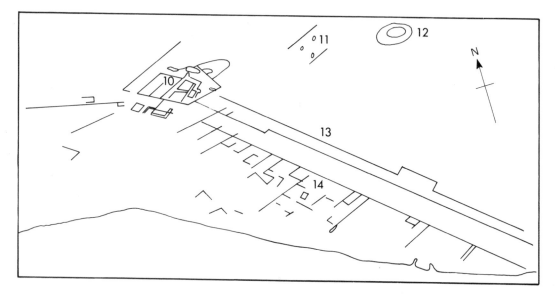

the walls were of stone laid in horizontal blocks, the upper section was in mud-brick covered with roof tiles.

The acropolis hill was used mostly for defence. Excavations have uncovered a good stretch of the wall there and a circular tower, next to which is an oblong structure with three divisions – probably a barracks and magazine. Remains of a stairway have been found leading up into the tower. The western edge of the hill was worked into a terrace with a retaining wall, beyond which is a square room that, judging from all the pottery found in it, must have served as a dining hall. North of the centre of the acropolis complex is an altar, its core composed of two upright poros blocks. It seems to date from the sixth century BC.

On a lower hill to the northeast is a sort of industrial terrace that incorporated workshops, houses, and storerooms. Although these were of flimsy construction traces of red and white paint have survived on the stuccoed walls. At the west end, basins and other ruins indicate a dye works.

Some distance away the Franchthi Cave has yielded Palaeolithic and later remains dating from 7500 BC – some of the earliest habitation evidence in Greece.

Halkis/Chalcis

The second largest of the Greek islands (after Crete), Euboea extends for over 100 miles along the coast of Locris, Boeotia, and Attica, nearly touching the mainland at its capital city, Chalcis. Here the famous Euripus Narrows, less than 140 ft across, have been bridged since the fifth century BC over the mysterious swift current in the strait which reverses itself many times each day – a phenomenon that greatly puzzled Aristotle and is not adequately explained even today. Aulis is only a short distance to the south, and Eretria some 12 miles to the east along the island's southern shore.

Chalcis was admirably located at the crossing of many commercial routes by sea and land, and prospered early. Its name reflects its industrial fame – either from *chalkos* (bronze) or *chalke* (the murex shell producing purple dye). In the eighth century BC it sent out many colonies to northern Greece – so many to the three-branched peninsula between Thessalon-ike and Amphipolis that the region was called Chalcidice. It also colonized abroad: Cumae and Rhegium in southern Italy, Naxos and Zancle (Messina) in eastern Sicily. Early adopting the alphabet, it passed on this great tool of commerce and learning to Europe via Cumae, which was the first Greek town in the West and a pioneer beach-head of civilization.

Chalcis and Eretria were interminably at war over the control of the Lelantine Plain, a fertile region lying between them. After the seventh century BC, Chalcis was the dominant power here. In 506 BC it became subject to Athens and supported her against Xerxes in 480 with ships and men. It was greatly damaged by the Roman conquest in 146 BC.

There is practically nothing visible today of the ancient city, which is wholly covered by the lively modern town. Its museum houses finds from all over Euboea. The dramatic setting earns its inclusion in this aerial survey of Greece.

Heraion/Argive Heraion

On the slopes of Mt Euboea, a few miles east of Argos and southeast of Mycenae, was an ancient common sanctuary of the Argives to their special patronness Hera, queen of the Olympian gods. The site, known as Prosymna, has tombs from Neolithic times and from the pre-Greek era of the Early Bronze Age. A sanctuary, with streams providing water for purification rites, must have existed here from the Mycenaean period. It was at the Argive Heraion that the Greek chiefs gathered to pledge loyalty to Agamemnon in the great expedition against

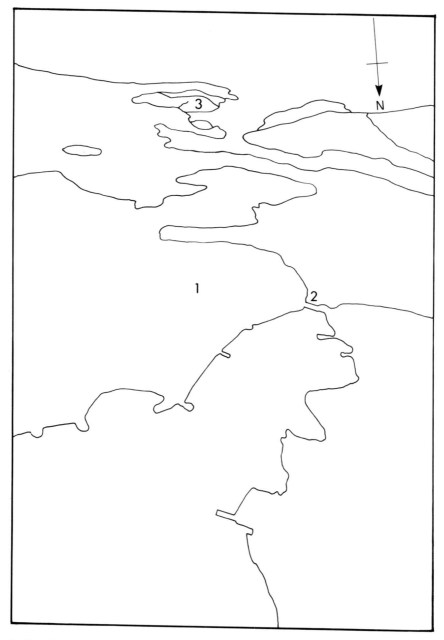

1 Site of ancient Chalcis
2 Euripus strait
3 Aulis

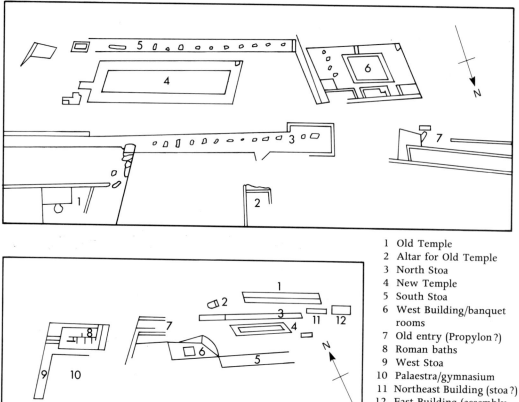

1 Old Temple
2 Altar for Old Temple
3 North Stoa
4 New Temple
5 South Stoa
6 West Building/banquet
rooms
7 Old entry (Propylon?)
8 Roman baths
9 West Stoa
10 Palaestra/gymnasium
11 Northeast Building (stoa?)
12 East Building (assembly
hall?)

Troy, and there that later Cleobis and Biton (as Herodotus tells) pulled their mother in a cart to the festival and were rewarded for their piety by speedy release from the miseries of this life.

The Heraion of Archaic and Classical times is a complex of buildings on three terraces. It was discovered in 1831 and excavated in 1836, 1892–95, and later, most extensively by Charles Waldstein. Blegen explored the prehistoric remains of the area.

The Archaic temple is on the uppermost terrace, which was skilfully levelled and bolstered by a massive retaining wall imitating Mycenaean construction. The Old Temple, no doubt replacing yet earlier shrines to Hera, appears to date from the first half of the seventh century BC and is the earliest example in the Peloponnesus using stone along with wood. Its stylobate rests directly on the terrace rock, without a foundation layer. There are 6 × 14 columns, an archaic pattern, in Doric style.

The upper elements were probably of brightly painted wood. It seems to have faced west, if the structure on that side of it was its altar (some think it a cistern). The temple burned down in 423 BC, when an aged priestess, Chryseis, negligently fell asleep and a blazing lamp set it afire. (She subsequently fled for sanctuary to Tegea.) The stepped supporting walls lower down are also archaic.

In the sixth century BC, two or more stoas were built on the middle terrace – the earliest known Doric examples of a structure later very common in Greece. A large square building (the 'West Building') is also a pioneer, with a peristyle colonnade around an inner court. It has three rooms along the north side, which may have served as a banquet hall for honoured pilgrims. In the middle of the fifth century BC the South Stoa was added on the lowest terrace, and off to its right the 'East Building', with three interior rows of columns – a hypostyle hall probably used for sacred assemblies.

The New Temple on the middle terrace was built during the Peloponnesian War, probably between 420 and 400 BC. Its architect was Eupolemos of Argos and it is Doric, but with an unusual 6 × 12 column design. Some decorative sculpture fragments are of very fine quality. Inside stood a splendid large statue of Hera by the great Polyclitus, in gold and ivory, crowned, holding a pomegranate in one hand and in the other a sceptre on which perched a cuckoo – a bird sacred to Hera. Nero left for the goddess a purple robe, and Hadrian gave a golden peacock with jewelled feathers. An ancient pearwood statue of Hera was also kept in this temple.

To the west is an L-shaped stoa and, above it, Roman baths. These indicate the long duration of this very ancient cult.

Heronia/**Chaeronea**

Situated in the northwest section of Boeotia, Chaeronea lies on a fertile plain amid low mountains and rolling hills. Neolithic finds nearby show that it was early chosen for habitation. The river Kephissos flows nearby – not the one of the same name at Athens. The ancient acropolis was on the double summit of Petrachos hill, where some of its walls are visible. Nothing of the city remains except the theatre cut into the rocky northern slope of the hill. Although this is probably the smallest theatre in Greece, of mediocre design and execution, it did have a good view at least over Lake Copais. It seems to have been constructed late in the fifth century BC, with some considerably later rows of seats higher up. A relief to Apollo Daphnephoros and Artemis is cut into the upper rock wall. The city was noted for its production of perfumed ointments from various flowers.

On the southern spur of the acropolis is a sanctuary to the Muses and a temple of Apollo Thourios. Some distance away in the plain near the Haimon stream is a small Doric temple containing at least two Corinthian columns.

About a mile to the east, near the Haimon stream and the defile of Kerata a famous battle took place which radically affected subsequent Greek history. There in 338 BC Philip II of Macedon, with notable aid from his son

1 Acropolis on Petrachos
2 Theatre

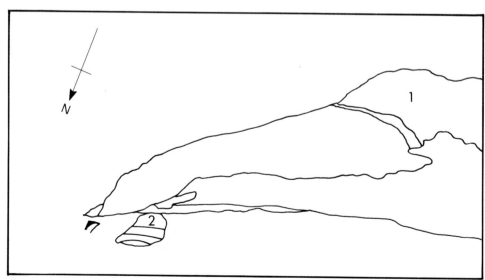

The lion monument is off to the left, out of view (*see p. 96*)

Alexander, then aged 18, decisively defeated a coalition army of some 30,000 Greeks gathered from Athens, Thebes, Megara, Corinth, and other cities by the fiery oratory of Demosthenes calling on all central Greece to defend its liberty against the encroaching despotism of Philip. Demosthenes himself was in the battle and shared the bitter allied defeat. Alexander here had his first major battlefield experience and liked it all too well. His father thereafter controlled most of Greece, and Alexander went on to subdue much of the world in a meteoric ten-year campaign. The Macedonian dead were buried under a large mound (*polyandreion*) near the stream. Philip sent the ashes of the Athen-ians home to Athens. The brave Sacred Band of Thebans, who died to a man opposing Alexander's thrust, were buried under a memorial lion monument which stands today outside the village. It was made in three sections of hollowed-out Boeotian marble, and stood some 18 ft high atop a rectangular plinth, squatting on its haunches. A low wall formed a sacred peribolos around. Its fragments were reconstructed during the Greek excavations of the area in the early twentieth century.

In 86 BC the Roman general Sulla defeated on the same battle site the army of Pontus under Mithridates' commander Archelaos – a major event in Sulla's fierce career.

More useful perhaps to the world was the birth here of Chaeronea's most famous son, Plutarch, about AD 46. He was a learned and polished writer of refined philosophical and religious ideals, a biographer of great men and a tireless essayist. He held a lifetime priesthood at Delphi but retired to Chaeronea for his final years. At the Renaissance he had a marked influence on many writers including Shakespeare.

Isthmia/**Isthmia**

The Peloponnesus is joined to the rest of Greece by a land-bridge or isthmus east of Corinth, four miles wide. The ancients dug a scooped-out path (*diolkos*) along which their wooden ships could be laboriously pulled, to avoid the long and risky circuit of the peninsula. Nero tried to make a canal here, but only in 1893 by modern methods was a usable one excavated. There was a defensive wall across the Isthmus, perhaps going back to the Spartans' plan to stop the Persian advance in 480 BC and later added to, especially in the days of Justinian around AD 550. The best preserved section, which lies to the east of the theatre and temple, includes a fortress loop; many blocks originally used in the ancient sanctuary buildings are incorporated in it.

Near the Isthmus' eastern edge was the sanctuary of Poseidon renowned throughout Greece. Games and contests were held here every other year in the spring, second only to those at Olympia in importance and arrangements. From their inception around 582 BC the Isthmian Games were under the supervision of nearby Corinth, but passed to Sicyon's after Corinth's destruction by the Romans in 146 BC until its revival by Julius Caesar. Pindar wrote Isthmian Odes to celebrate victors in these competitions. During the Games of 336 BC Alexander was designated avenger of Greece on Persia and launched on his amazing career. The liberty of Greece was publicly proclaimed there by Flamininus in 196 BC after his defeat of the Macedonians at Cynoscephalae, and Nero flamboyantly reaffirmed Greek independence in AD 67 in Isthmia's theatre, after singing for the audience.

The chief monument in the sanctuary was the great temple of Poseidon. A peculiar Archaic predecessor has been traced beneath it, seemingly 7 × 19 columns with one interior row of nine plus three more in the pronaos. An unusual feature is a series of paintings on the outer wall of the cella behind the peristyle of columns. Fragments recently found indicate geometric and figured patterns in panels divided by vertical bands; purple, grey, orange, yellow, blue, and brown colours were used. This temple burned down c. 475 BC. Its replacement was Classical Doric, 6 × 13 columns with a double row of six inside the cella plus an engaged pilaster at the east end of each row at the back of the pronaos porch, re-roofed after a serious fire in 394 BC. The Romans added a temenos wall in the second century AD and surrounded the sacred preserve with stoas on the east, west, and south sides. An enormous altar stretched across the whole east front in Greek times and a smaller, later, one was at the southeast corner of the temenos, near the Propylon formal entry gate. Outside the South Stoa was a Roman shrine to Palaemon/Melicertes, in whose honour the Isthmian Games were instituted.

The stadium in early days ran southeast from near the temple's southeastern corner; its starting-line has been discovered, with incised grooves for the cords pulled by an official to topple the starting-gate bars for the runners' release. The later stadium was farther to the southeast in a grove along the hillside, at right angles to the former one.

The theatre is poorly preserved but is an intelligible structure. Near it are interesting rooms hollowed out of the hill, probably for ritual banquets of the actors before a performance. A great pit or well south of the temple has also been cleared. Excavation of the sanctuary by Oscar Broneer from 1952 into the 1960s is being supplemented by P. Clement, mostly in the area of the walls.

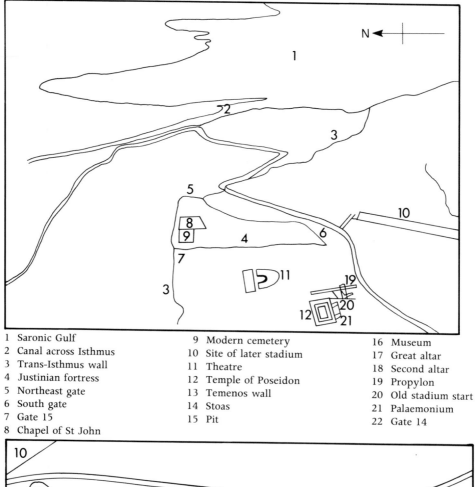

1 Saronic Gulf	9 Modern cemetery	16 Museum
2 Canal across Isthmus	10 Site of later stadium	17 Great altar
3 Trans-Isthmus wall	11 Theatre	18 Second altar
4 Justinian fortress	12 Temple of Poseidon	19 Propylon
5 Northeast gate	13 Temenos wall	20 Old stadium start
6 South gate	14 Stoas	21 Palaemonium
7 Gate 15	15 Pit	22 Gate 14
8 Chapel of St John		

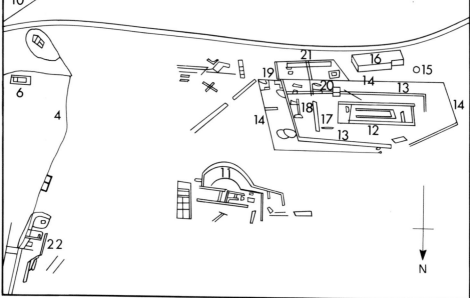

Ithaki/Ithaca

In the *Odyssey*, the hero's homeland – from which he was so long away, at Troy and in fabulous adventures on the way back – is Ithaca. It is described as an island on the sea-route along the northwest coast of Greece, rough, steep, with many inlets, unsuited to horses but good for goats and the vine, without great plains or pastures, commanding two seas, near Doulichion, Same, and Zacynthos, and close to land (or whatever *chthamale* means). Homer describes many details of the island: Odysseus' great palace, a town a short way off, a harbour with an island outside it, Mt Neritos, a grotto of the Naiads, Eumaeus' pig-sties a day's walk from the palace with a spring nearby, and various other features.

It has been generally assumed since Classical times that the poet is referring to the island still called Ithaki between northern Kephallonia and Epirus. Dörpfeld and some others have argued that only Leukas, a bigger island to the north, fits the Homeric data, and they have sought to identify there the places and features mentioned in the poem. But there are serious problems with this, and British excavations on Ithaki since 1930 have greatly strengthened the arguments for its being Homer's Ithaca.

It is unsound to demand precise geographical details in the epic account. Rather, only a general setting is to be expected: a definite context for the story, with some specifics put in to lend it interest. Homer is writing heroic poetry, not history or geography. He probably did not know this part of the world at first hand but drew on accounts of contemporary and earlier sailors and Mycenaean traditions. What he

1 Polis Bay
2 Cave of Tripods

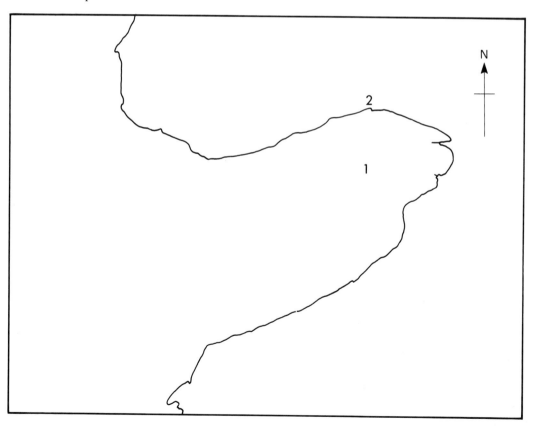

actually says about Ithaca will not exactly fit any island; but Ithaki fits well enough, and its name from ancient times is a powerful argument in its favour. Excavations there have shown clear commercial contact with the mainland and Ionia from the ninth century BC onwards, and numerous Mycenaean sherds of the straight-stemmed kylix type common at the time of the Trojan War have been recovered. Heurtley acutely reasons that large stone blocks still to be seen in some houses at Pelikata and the ancient wall around the nearby heights must come from a Mycenaean structure (presumably Odysseus' palace) since they were saved for re-use instead of being cast into the fill at the site like the rubble of older pre-Mycenaean buildings. He and others think many *Odyssey* sites can be located in Ithaki.

Polis Bay on the northwest coast would have been the harbour of the Mycenaean town, which was probably where Stavros now is on the slopes and heights to the northeast. The palace would have been at Pelikata, a mile north of Stavros, judging from meagre finds there of Mycenaean type. Vathy Bay could be Homer's Phorcys, and the Phaeacians may have put the sleeping Odysseus ashore at nearby Dexia Bay. Eumaeus' farm was likely in the Marathia area southeast of Mt Stefano where equivalents to Homer's Arethusa spring and Korax cliff can be found. The Grotto of the Naiads where Odysseus worshipped and hid his treasure from Phaeacia must be a conflation by the poet of one in the hills above Dexia (too far from the sea), and one on the edge of Polis Bay far to the north, where excavators found twelve

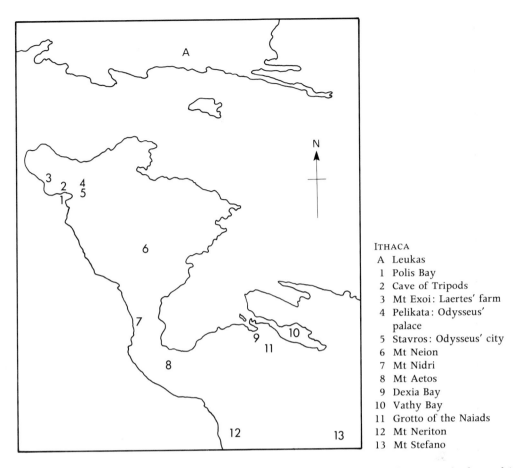

ITHACA
A Leukas
1 Polis Bay
2 Cave of Tripods
3 Mt Exoi: Laertes' farm
4 Pelikata: Odysseus'
  palace
5 Stavros: Odysseus' city
6 Mt Neion
7 Mt Nidri
8 Mt Aetos
9 Dexia Bay
10 Vathy Bay
11 Grotto of the Naiads
12 Mt Neriton
13 Mt Stefano

bronze tripods from the Geometric period, recalling those which Odysseus hid, later Greek sherds inscribed 'To the Nymphs', and a broken clay mask from the first century AD bearing Odysseus' name. All this seems connected with a continuing cult of the great hero – Odysseia Games there are recorded in the third century BC, and an ancient stadium may be located in the long hollow at the edge of Polis Bay.

In such a mountainous stony island with little soil it is fortunate that this much has survived from heroic times. Ithaca, however, will always be safely enshrined in an immortal poem.

Kabirion/**Kabeirion**

The ancient cult of the Kabeiroi had many mysterious and confusing aspects and apparently seemed strange even to the Greeks. It possibly was imported from Phrygia (some think Phoenicia). Its chief centres in Greece were Samothrace, Lemnos, and this Kabeiric sanctuary a few miles southwest of Thebes. The name comes from the Semitic root *kbr* meaning 'mighty'. Greek religion usually referred to these divinities as 'The Great Gods'. Four were named: Axierus, Axiocersa, Axiocersus, Cadmilus. They were assimilated to various aspects of Demeter, Hermes, Hephestus, and Dionysos (sometimes renamed Cabirus), and were honoured as patrons of fertility and of sailing.

The sanctuary near Thebes was discovered and partly excavated by Dörpfeld and Judeich

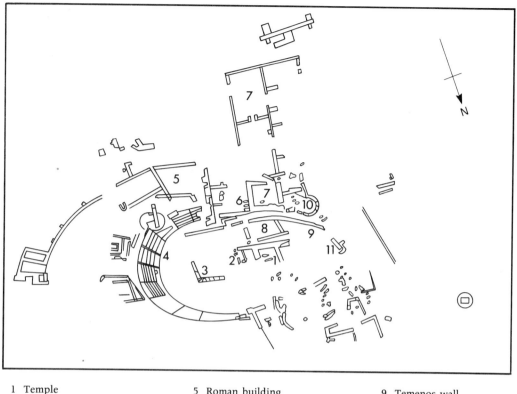

1 Temple
2 Altar?
3 Altar?
4 Spectators' seats (theatre)

5 Roman building
6 Steps
7 Hellenistic stoa
8 Rectangular building

9 Temenos wall
10 Round building
11 Offering pits

in 1887. German exploration of the site has recently been resumed by Gerta Bruns and is as yet incomplete.

The central temple is very long for its width, divided into three sections: a cella, a porch with four columns across its breadth, and a separate room at the back in which were two pits for offerings, covered over like graves. The temple seems to date from the fourth century BC, and is a rebuilding of one from the previous century. Whether its altar was immediately in front, as Dörpfeld thought, or farther out into the orchestra of the theatre is not clear from the insufficient remains extant. A rectangular building next to it, of uncertain use, is probably of the mid-fifth century BC; the circular structure slightly to the west is later. A long stoa (some 130 ft in length) running

southward from the 'rectangular building' is Hellenistic in date. Steps and a path led from it to the theatre's orchestra. A Roman building, with mortar construction, farther east testifies to the continuing use of the sanctuary in Imperial times.

A semicircle of seats for spectators of the ritual forms a small theatre to the east of the temple. It had no stage structure, but looked directly on the altar and temple front where, no doubt, mystic pageants were performed for the cult's adherents. These rituals were known as the *Dromenon*, a reference to their being acted out.

The temple of Demeter Kabiria referred to in ancient accounts has not been definitely identified. It may be the 'rectangular building' or one of those to the north of the temple.

In the excavations a remarkable group of vases was found, unique in decorative style and of great interest. They are in black-figure technique, with some over-painting, and seem to have been made locally or in nearby Thebes in the fifth century BC. Many have scenes of outrageously grotesque and irreverent caricature, of real humour and boldness. They apparently reflect the farces performed in the sanctuary and reveal their Dionysiac facet.

Kalidon/Calydon

Many popular myths were located at Calydon: its early king, Oeneus, was the first to plant the vine when Dionysos introduced it to Greece; his son Tydeus was one of the Seven against Thebes and father of Diomedes, the great warrior at Troy; his other son Meleager slew the fierce Calydonian Boar after a famous hunt participated in by Atalanta and many heroes; his daughter Deianeira was the wife of Hercules and the unwitting cause of his death. Calydon had a comparatively insignificant role in history, however, and diminished after Augustus forced most of its citizens to move to his newly-founded Nicopolis; famous art treasures were then sent to Patras across the Gulf of Corinth.

Greek and Danish excavations between 1926 and 1938 have revealed little of the ancient town except part of its acropolis walls and gates, but important religious monuments have been uncovered on an outcropping plateau southwest of the city at the end of a Sacred Way to the shrines.

A small Archaic temple constructed about 575 BC has left fragmentary remains near the southern edge of the site. It was probably dedicated to Apollo Laphrios, but there are good arguments in favour of ascribing it to Dionysos, whose cult naturally flourished at Calydon.

To the west is the much larger temple of Artemis Laphria, identified from inscriptions. Perhaps her brother Apollo shared it with her, as often happened elsewhere. Only part of the foundations survive, but there is evidence enough from abundant terracotta decorative figures and roof tiles to date the final structure to the fourth century BC, probably around 360,

replacing two earlier temples on the site from the sixth and seventh centuries (c. 570 and c. 620 respectively). The temple is built out on the west end of a spur of rock in an eminently commanding position. It is Doric, with 6 × 13 columns in the Classic pattern. One innovation is rain-spouts in the form of hounds' heads instead of the usual lions – in honour of Artemis the huntress, its patron. Official entrance to the sanctuary was by a special Propylon gate to the north. Over by the other temple is a small columned hall that probably served as display centre for ex-votos left by pious worshippers.

Farther north a long stoa was added in Hellenistic times, probably near the start of the second century BC.

Some distance to the east of this stoa is an interesting Heroön, a cult-shrine to a certain Leon of Calydon, as an inscription indicates, dedicated in his honour by his wife Krateia, seemingly around 100 BC. It is therefore often referred to

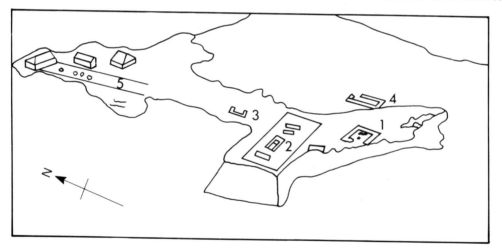

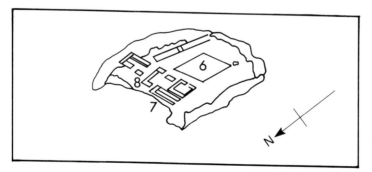

1 Temple of Apollo Laphrios (or Dionysos?)
2 Artemis Laphria temple
3 Propylon (entrance gate to sacred area)
4 Hall of ex-votos
5 Hellenistic stoa
6 Heroön (Leonteion): peristyle court
7 Underground cult–crypt and upper room
8 Entrance (Prostasis) to corridor and peristyle court

as the Leonteion. The hero was revered as 'a new Hercules', but is not otherwise known to history. The structure is basically rectangular, around an open court with a colonnade on all inner sides. A special entrance (prostasis) on the north leads into a long corridor on the east side of the peristyle court. The various covered rooms around the open court were probably for gatherings, musical ceremonies in the hero's honour, and ritual banquets. Near the centre of the north front of the whole complex is a cult-room, with interior stone stairs leading down to a funeral crypt below, where the stone bed, neatly carved into the rock, is still visible. This was, no doubt, the hero's burial chamber and centre of his cult.

Another smaller Heroön has been located more recently to the west of the stoa.

Kea/Kea: Ayia Irini

Westernmost of the Cyclades, only 13 miles east of Sunium, the oval island of Kea was early colonized by Ionians. In Classical times it was the birthplace of the poets Simonides and Bacchylides, the sophist Prodicus, and other noted intellectuals. Little remains now of its major cities Ioulis, Karthaia, and Poiessa. An important Bronze Age settlement has been excavated since 1960 by Professor John L. Caskey at Ayia Irini on the northwest coast. This has revealed long habitation from the Early Bronze Age to Roman times. Cycladic, Minoan, and Mycenaean cultural patterns are all evidenced in its period of greatness, which reached

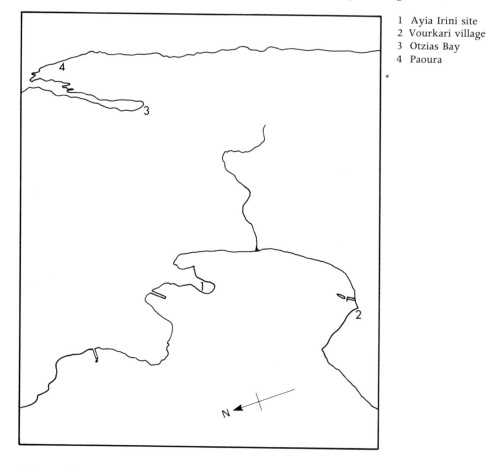

1 Ayia Irini site
2 Vourkari village
3 Otzias Bay
4 Paoura

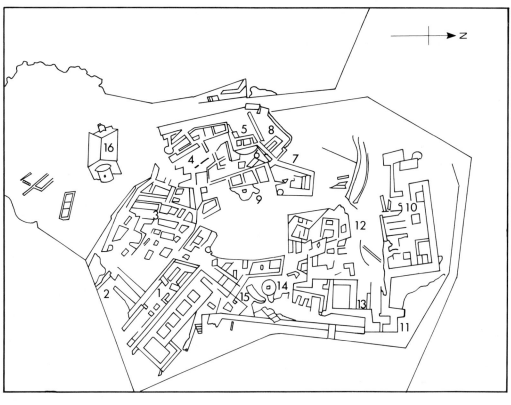

1 Temple
2 Area B
3 House A
4 Area C
5 House E
6 Early wall and tower

7 Late defence wall (west)
8 Spring
9 Area F
10 Area N
11 Late defence wall (north)
12 Area L

13 Area M
14 Late tomb/tumulus
15 Area G
16 Ayia Irini church

a peak of prosperity in the Late Minoan and Early Mycenaean eras, c. 1600–1400 BC. Great earthquakes in the middle of the fifteenth century BC and later, probably connected with the cataclysmic upheavals of Thera, did extensive damage, but the ruins now unearthed are still massive and imposing.

The site is small, on a narrow promontory jutting southward into the bay opposite Vourkari village a mile northeast of Koressia, the ancient harbour of Ioulis, chief town of the island. Inside the substantial circuit walls put up in the Middle and Late Bronze Ages the buildings crowd one another, with very tight passages between. Some of the houses, notably House A, are quite elaborate complexes of rooms, with deep cellars (used for storage and treasures) cutting into earlier habitations beneath. An extensive drainage system protected these cellars from flooding. Some narrow streets, stairs, and public benches have been found. A large tomb in the eastern sector seems to have been a prominent tumulus near the main street, obviously of some important person or ruler, probably of the Late Bronze Age. A potter's kiln has been identified, and much fine pottery recovered with a great variety of styles and from many periods, including imports from Crete and elsewhere. Fragments of wall frescoes with floral and figured designs testify to elegant interiors.

A remarkable temple structure, perhaps the earliest yet found in Greece, shows use and rebuilding from the fifteenth century BC

to the Roman period. It is located near the south of the town and is long and narrow, with its innermost room divided into two oblong compartments which presumably were the sacred *adyton*. Here were found many unusual and striking large terracotta figures of goddesses with long skirts, open bodices, and detailed heads. These indicate centuries of worship within this unique building.

Outside the western wall was a fresh-water spring, to which covered access was provided from the early times of the settlement. Considerable ruins outside the walls are now under water, the sea-level having risen since antiquity.

Kenchree/**Kenchreai**

The eastern harbour of Corinth, on the Saronic Gulf towards Athens, Asia, Egypt, and the Levant, lies six miles east of Acrocorinth, which is easily seen from its shore. It was said to be named after Kenchrias, a son of Poseidon and Peirene, a nymph of Corinth. Its fine deep natural bay was further improved by added stone moles, probably in Greek times though the extant remains are substantially Roman — as are all the ruined buildings along the water-

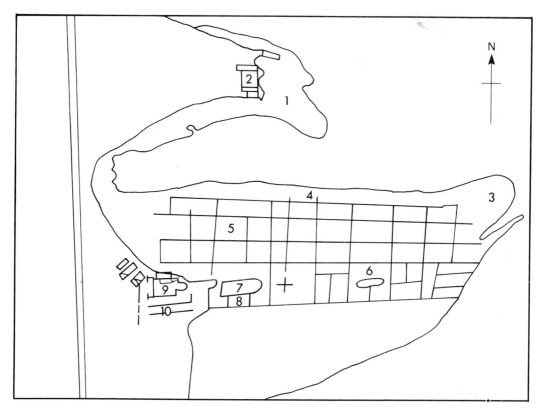

1 Northeast mole
2 Roman brick building
   (sanctuary of Aphrodite?)
3 South mole
4 South pier
5 Warehouses

6 Piscina ('Channel Complex')
7 Submerged apsidal structure
8 'Temple'
9 Christian church (on site of
   sanctuary of Isis)
10 'Marble Hall'

front. Evidence of the Greek town has been found on the hill to the northwest, but the site has not yet been extensively excavated. Some buildings are visible there, including a fuller's establishment, and coins from the sixth to the third centuries BC testify to its early and enduring commercial activity. Pausanias mentions a famous bronze statue of Poseidon here, and a temple to Artemis.

In Roman times, Corinth prospered more than any other city in Greece, and its eastern harbour was very busy, leading to considerable building of shipping and warehouse facilities. Most of these are now under water, due to subsidence of the coast. Excavations and clearance were undertaken in 1963 and later by Professors Scranton and Ramage and others from co-

operating American universities. This involved new underwater techniques, and led to the discovery of unusual glass-mosaic panels representing Homer, Plato, waterbirds, harbour buildings, etc., found in crates under the sea.

Near the northeast mole is a large Roman building of brick with marble decoration which, from numerous terracotta finds, seems to have been a sanctuary of Aphrodite, perhaps connected with that on Acrocorinth. It is some 120 ft square, with a mosaic floor and a peristyle of four columns on each side of the main room.

The south mole protects an extensive pier with a complex of rooms obviously used as warehouses for the varied merchandise brought to Corinth from all over the eastern Mediterranean world and beyond. The southeast

segment of rooms has a special arrangement which suggests a 'piscina' for keeping live fish – called the 'Channel Complex' in early reports because of the interconnecting corridors. In the southwest corner are two apsidal buildings, one of them completely submerged now, which probably constituted a sanctuary to Isis and was later adapted as a Christian church with mosaic floors. Next to the outer one is a rectangular structure that may have been a temple. South of the inner apsidal building is the 'Marble Hall' with fine paving and wall revetment. A long building beside and parallel to the central shore was explored but was afterwards covered over again and so is not visible in the photo.

Kerkira/Corfu: Palaiokastritsa

There is a steadily growing body of evidence suggesting that the Homeric poems are rooted in historical realities, however much this factual core may be elaborated by bardic tradition and the epic poet's lively imagination. In northwest Corfu in the Palaiokastritsa area, Victor Bérard and others have plausibly found a region that seems to correspond with the Scheria of the *Odyssey*, the land of the kindly sea-faring Phaeacians on the edge of the Greek world not far from Ithaca. In this theory, Alcinous' palace is to be thought of on the heights of Kattro Point below the modern town of Lakones. Nausicaa, the young Phaeacian princess who finds the shipwrecked Odysseus (perhaps at Ermones inlet farther south along the coast) and directs him to the palace, says that her father's lofty-walled city has a fine harbour on each side, with narrow entry (*Odyssey* 6.263–5), with a garden nearby luxuriant with every kind of tree and fruit. Port St Spiridion on the west would fit one of

1 Kattro Point (site of Alcinous'
  palace?)
2 Port of St Spiridion

3 Port Alipa
4 Kosleri Point
5 Vigla islet

6 Liapades Bay
7 Kolivi island

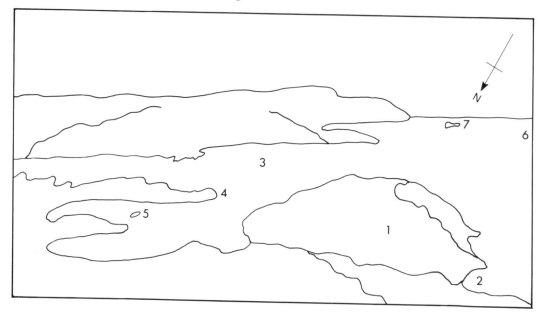

these harbours, Port Alipa to the east the other, opening out from its narrow entrance into a triple cove between the lofty promontory and Kosleri Point. Though no ruins from the Heroic Age have been found on Kattro Point, the whole site is admirably suited to the needs of a fortified centre for a sea-loving people – which may be justification enough for the poet's putting them there on the basis of ancient traditions. Further, the small islet, Vigla, in the eastern cove, could well be imagined to represent the Phaeacian clipper ship 'swift as a darting hawk' which Poseidon turned to stone in the harbour on its return from bringing Odysseus home to Ithaca. Whether or not Homer actually had this particular place in mind makes no difference to the poetry, which in any case is a world of its own created with supreme art. So apt a correspondence, however, as this site provides for the setting of books six to eight of the *Odyssey*, can help us enter more fully into the poetic story. The name Scheria implies a rocky cliff, as here.

The historic city on the island is farther south on the east coast where the long island's centre projects towards the mainland. It was called Kerkyra (Latin: Corcyra), a name which also embraced the whole island. Corfu is an Italian corruption from 'the city of the heights' (*Koryphon*). It was a Corinthian colony from the eighth century BC, which rebelled for its freedom in the first Greek naval battle, 665/664 BC, and prospered from its commerce. When it later called in Athens to protect it from Corinth, it triggered off the disastrous Peloponnesian War. Corfu continued to be important in both Roman and Byzantine times.

The remains of ancient Kerkyra are too meagre and scattered to be meaningful from the air. They lie south of the modern city, mostly in the Palaeopolis peninsula and farther on in the grounds of the royal villa Mon Repos. Most important is the Archaic temple of Artemis, of which little survives except some striking sculptures of the pediment, grouped around a colossal Gorgon/Artemis with a belt of snakes. An Archaic tomb of Menekrates had a snarling lion crowning it, now in the museum. Nearby a small temple has been found at Kardaki close to the sea. There are some pre-Greek remains on the northwest edge of the island at Cape Kephali and at Aphiona.

Knossos/**Knossos: The Context**

The sensational discoveries by Sir Arthur Evans at Knossos since 1900 not only uncovered the greatest of all Minoan sites but revealed details of a splendid civilization in prehistoric Crete that had been long forgotten. Subsequent excavations, at Knossos and elsewhere in the island, have greatly supplemented knowledge of Minoan culture but many mysteries remain, including its origins and its language – of which many documents survive in the as yet undeciphered 'Linear A' script.

Habitation in the area goes back to Neolithic times, possibly as early as 6000 BC. Around 2600 BC, a new group of people moved into Crete, apparently from Asia Minor, perhaps Luvians. They established settlements at new sites as well as earlier ones like Knossos and Phaistos, and introduced the Bronze Age culture with its advanced styles of pottery, implements, and jewellery. Evans divided this Bronze Age into three basic periods, Early, Middle, and Late Minoan, each of which then was subdivided into three phases, and fitted into a parallel chronology in Egypt. Platon's new system of Pre-Palatial, Proto-Palatial, Neo-Palatial, and Post-Palatial is preferred by many, being determined by data from Crete itself. The first great palaces appear in Middle Minoan Ib, *c*. 1900 BC, when foreign commerce and Cretan art began to flourish. Around 1700 BC a catastrophe, probably a massive earthquake, reduced these palaces to ruins. They were soon rebuilt (in MM III), and this Neo-Palatial period is the acme of Cretan glory. Some other disaster in the last half of the fifteenth century again destroyed the palaces. Only Knossos was promptly rebuilt. The final stage of the palace shows evidence of control by Mycenaean Greeks, though there is dispute at present over the dates of this period which may have lasted to about 1190 BC; after that the palace was abandoned, though not the town.

1 Palace
2 Viaduct
3 Site of 'caravanserai'
4 Royal villa

5 Makryteichos village
6 Little Palace
7 Amnisos beach
8 Dia island

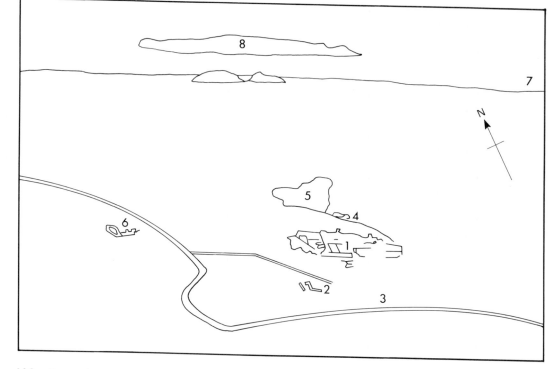

The palace has a fine setting, some three miles inland from the sea near the centre of the island's northern coast. A shallow curving valley leads to the harbour of Katsamba just east of modern Heraklion. Five miles eastward along a fine sandy beach is the other ancient port, Amnisos, at the foot of a low hill (hidden in this photo by the highlands at top right). An elegant two storey villa with fine frescos, and harbour buildings, have been found there – all dating from around 1600 BC when the Great Palace at Knossos was rebuilt. To that period also belongs the Little Palace which is slightly to the west of the Great Palace. It had a peristyle court surrounded on two levels by spacious rooms. At least some of its columns were fluted.

There was a lustral area, a shrine, and several crypts with pillars. Fine works of art were found among the ruins and some Linear B tablets found here indicate, as do those from the Great Palace, occupation by Mycenaean Greeks during the last period of use. Northeastward, a contemporaneous royal villa, similar but on a smaller scale, has its own throne behind a balustrade.

The town of Knossos, adjacent to the palace, seems to have had at least 40,000 inhabitants. With easy access to the sea nearby and to Phaistos via the Messara Plain and the southern coast towards Egypt, Knossos for centuries had a powerful commercial empire. Basically peaceful and sports-loving, the Minoans were great pioneers of Western culture.

Knossos/**Knossos**: **The Palace**

When the early Greeks came into contact with Knossos (perhaps as mercenary warriors brought on Cretan ships to Egypt to help drive out the Hyksos), they were amazed at the complexity and splendour of its Great Palace and brought home stories of a 'labyrinth' guarded by a fearsome monster, the Minotaur. The Athenian hero Theseus eventually slew him, with the help of Minos' daughter Ariadne. Daedalus, the inventive craftsman who had built the Labyrinth, meanwhile fled with man's first wings to Cumae in Italy, his son Icarus falling on the way after flying too close to the sun.

These primitive legends reflect Greek awe at Cretan civilization, especially the vast and complex palace, a veritable labyrinth of rooms and corridors on four levels – the royal residence quarters seem to have had two storeys above the Central Court level and two below, built down the slope. The massive ruins now uncovered and partly reconstructed are essentially from the second palace, built even more magnificently than its predecessor around 1700 BC. Its heart was the Central Court, probably also used for the celebrated Bull Games, a specialty of Cretan daring and perhaps the first organized spectator sport. Around the court spread a maze of rooms, of all sizes and varieties of rectangle, intricately interconnected by corridors, passages, doors, and stairs. Most

of what is visible from the air on the west side of the court is of the upper storey, which had a formal Propylon entrance at the head of stairs at the south and a series of rooms, storerooms, and spacious pillared halls. Below were smaller rooms, shrines, crypts, and a great series of storage magazines for food and supplies. Off the northwest corner of the court is the famous 'Throne Room' complex with its gypsum throne and benches on either side of it, frescoes on the walls, and a square pit with steps leading down and columns around, probably open to the sky above – perhaps a pond for exotic fish in the Egyptian manner, or possibly a lustral basin for ritual use. This area was probably used by the Priestess of the Goddess of the Labyrinth for ceremonial purposes; the king's actual throne room was more likely to be one of the larger rooms in the royal residential quarters on the east side of the court.

The Queen's Room, with its lively dolphin fresco and rosettes and adjacent bath, is on a lower level to the east. On ground level and above in the northeast sector of the palace were more storerooms, shrines, artisans' workshops, and the servants' quarters. North of the court's centre a long corridor and entrance-way, with a striking painted relief of a great bull charging into the woods, led to an oblong room with many pillars – an imposing hypostyle hall that was an impressive entrance into the Great Palace from the north. To the west is the theatral area of stepped seats for watching the ritual dances, etc. as referred to by Homer. A platform at the side was probably a royal loggia or box. A long row of steps at the other side of the palace led down to the East Bastion and the valley below.

A stepped portico at the southwest edge of the palace complex brought one to a viaduct over the southern stream bed and to an outlying group of buildings (the 'Caravanserai') where travellers could rest and bathe before entering the palace area. Some houses have been found at various places in the surrounding country-side. A dwelling with several storeys and a pillar-crypt sanctuary, at the southwest of the palace compound opposite the Corridor of Processions (with its Cup Bearer fresco), was probably the house of the High Priest.

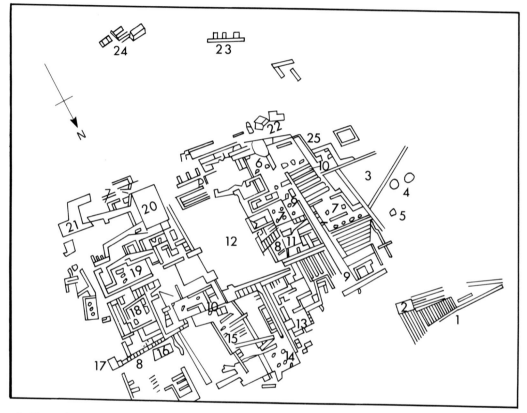

1 Theatral area	11 Rooms over the Throne Room	18 Workshops
2 Royal loggia?	12 Central Court	19 Royal residence quarters (four storeys?)
3 West Court	13 North entrance (with Charging Bull relief)	20 Shrine of the Double Axes (under roof)
4 Offering pits	14 North hypostyle hall	21 Southeast house
5 Altar	15 Servants' quarters	22 South house (High Priest's)
6 Upper Propylon	16 Room with great pithoi jars ('Magazine of the Giant Pithoi')	23 Viaduct
7 Halls with pillars		24 'Caravanserai'
8 Stairs	17 East Bastion	25 Corridor of the Processions
9 Upper long corridor		
10 Storerooms ('West Magazines')		

Korinthos/Corinth: The Central Area

Most of Corinth's ruins are dated to the Roman period after the destruction by Mummius in 146 BC. Some Greek monuments are traceable however, most notably the great Archaic temple on the terrace north of the agora. This is one of the oldest temples extant in Greece, dating from the mid-sixth century BC, and replacing an even older shrine of the seventh century. Presumably it is the famous Apollo temple referred to by ancient authors, but no sure proof of its dedication has yet been found. Archaic features are the high platform under the stylobate (more than the usual two steps), the long plan with 15 columns down the sides, six across the front and back (spaced a bit more widely apart), the thick squat contour of the columns and their upper elements, and their monolithic construction. The cella had two independent sections like the later Parthenon: the western room square, the eastern oblong; each with a double interior colonnade to support the roof, and a door to its own porch.

The Sacred Spring is also early, its bronze lion-head spouts showing fifth-century style; later in the Roman era it was below ground level. The more elaborate Peirene Fountain goes back to a pre-Greek period, its facilities having been rebuilt time and again. Water was brought to it from a mountain source via a long tunnel in the rock leading to four oblong reservoirs in front of which was a low wall (later adorned with Ionic columns) over which urns were let down to draw water. There was an outer courtyard with an open-air fountain added in early Roman times and later the inner façade was redone in marble, with vaulted apses at the sides. Another Peirene atop Acro-corinth was ascribed to Pegasus' alighting there, as a water source at the summit of a high mountain needs some explaining.

The nearby peribolos of Apollo is likewise pre-Roman but was later reconstructed. Its large court with surrounding Ionic colonnade enclosed a bronze statue of the god under a canopy, and earlier a small temple of the Classical period. The adjacent baths are probably those donated by Eurykles of Sparta in the first century A D, and praised by Pausanias as the finest in Corinth. The broad paved Lechaion Road ran direct to the port on the Gulf. The North Basilica on its western edge covers an old Greek market of the fifth century B C. The Roman market north of this had a semicircular design.

At the point where the Lechaion Road enters the agora was a Propylon entry gate, replaced in the Roman period with a triumphal arch bearing gilded chariots of Helios and Phaethon. Just west of this was the 'Captives' Façade', a row of Corinthian columns at ground level and on the upper storey figures of barbarian captives substituting for pillars. Behind, a square open court bordered the North Basilica's end. In the Classical Age a race track ran across the later agora's centre. Some of the starting line from the fifth century B C arrangement is visible in front of the Julian Basilica (a Roman law court), as is the later Hellenistic course, which has a different orientation required by construction of the South Stoa. A circular monument nearby is of unknown purpose. State archives were probably kept in the 'Southeast Building', near which were various offices whose mosaic floors are under a protective

1	Offices, with mosaic floors (covered)	12	Julian basilica	25	Northwest shops
2	South basilica	13	Altar	26	Sacred Spring
3	Fountain-house	14	Roman temples and Babbius monument	27	'Captives' Façade'
4	Bouleuterion	15	West shops	28	Peirene Fountain
5	South shops	16	Museum	29	Peribolos of Apollo
6	New excavations (Byzantine and Frankish ruins)	17	Temple E (Octavia?)	30	Lechaion Road
7	South Stoa	18	Odeion	31	North basilica
8	Central shops	19	Glauke Fountain	32	Semicircular market
9	Bema	20	Temple C (Hera Akraia?)	33	Baths (of Eurykles?)
10	Circular monument	21	North Stoa		
11	Southeast building (archives?)	22	North market		
		23	Archaic temple (of Apollo?)		
		24	Northwest Stoa		

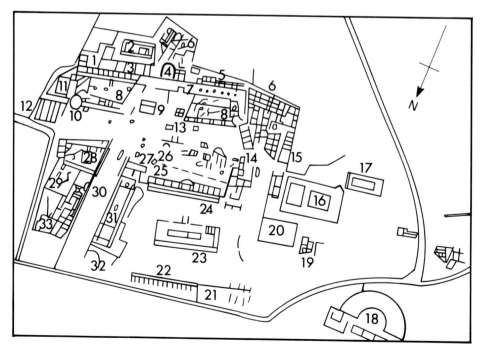

roof; the Agonothetes, who supervised the Isthmian Games, had their offices here as did the Roman Governor. An elegant marble fountain-house adjoined the South Basilica; west of it the apsidal Bouleuterion was for City Council meetings.

Behind the Central Shops the terrace is 13 ft higher than the rest of the agora. Beyond the Bema, a speakers' platform for public gatherings, lies the South Stoa, the largest secular building in Greece. Along the western edge of the agora was a row of six Roman temples, all small, one of them oriented to the south. The Glauke Fountain once had a porticoed façade and north of the Roman Odeion was the theatre, with its Greek cavea still extant.

Korinthos/Corinth: The Demeter Sanctuary and the Gymnasium Area

Few sites in Greece were so favoured as Corinth's. At the base of the Isthmus it was the inevitable crossroads of commerce between central Greece and the Peloponnesus and for all shipping to the east or west. Behind towered Acrocorinth, one of the finest natural citadels in the world. A prehistoric settlement dated before 4000 BC lay closer to the Gulf, as probably did Homer's Corinth (Ephyra) where Sisyphus and Bellerophon reigned and Medea slew her children. The Dorian city at the foot of Acrocorinth remained the developed site, however, though modern Corinth has moved several miles northeast to the coast. American

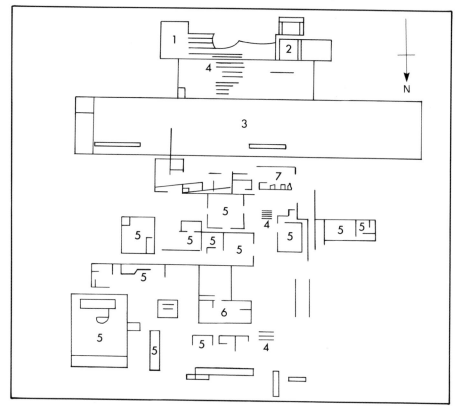

DEMETER SANCTUARY

1 Sanctuary of Demeter: theatral area
2 Demeter cult room/temple?

3 Terrace/stoa
4 Rock-cut steps
5 Ritual dining halls

6 Dining hall T
7 Building A

GYMNASIUM AREA

G Site of gymnasium court
8 South Stoa
9 East Stoa corner
10 To the Asclepieion and Lerna Fountain
11 Tombs of the Christian era
12 Domed building (part of baths?)
13 Bronze foundry
14 Apsidal building
15 Roman ruins and wall with column fragments
16 'Fountain of the Lamps'
17 Modern irrigation channel

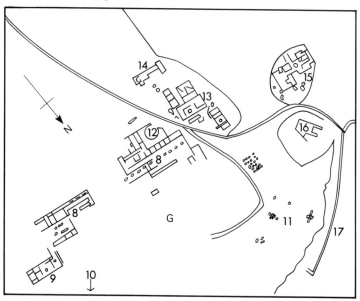

excavations since 1896 have uncovered and elucidated only key sectors of the ancient city's great expanse within its Long Walls which looped from Acrocorinth to Lechaion on the northern Gulf. The other harbour was Kenchreai on the Saronic Gulf to the east. The population rose to over half a million at its peak.

Corinth's greatest age was in the seventh century BC under the autocrat Kypselos and his son Periander, when its commerce was international and its fine pottery sought everywhere. It colonized Syracuse and Kerkyra and was the official centre for resistance to Xerxes' invasion. Irked by Athens' commercial ascendancy, Corinth sided with Sparta and helped defeat the Sicilian Expedition, but later joined Argos, Athens, and Thebes in opposing Spartan power. The Roman general Mummius ruthlessly destroyed Corinth in 146 BC because it was the capital of the Achaean League. A century later however Julius Caesar revived it as a Roman colony. It became the capital of Roman Greece and rose to unrivalled prosperity and notorious luxury and vice. St Paul chose it as the centre of his apostolate to the pagans because it was then the leading city of Greece and full of merchants and sailors from all over the Mediterranean world. Barbarian assaults by Herulians and Alaric were compounded by devastating earthquakes in the sixth century AD, reducing once-glorious Corinth to ruins.

Recent and still continuing excavations in outlying districts are here illustrated for their interest, though neither is yet sufficiently complete to allow full interpretation.

Pausanias mentions a sanctuary to Demeter and Kore on the north slope of Acrocorinth, with statues not visible to the public. Exploration in 1961 and subsequently has re-vealed an extensive complex of buildings that fits this reference, with confirmation from the many finds of terracotta statuettes, pottery, and coins. The sanctuary seems to have existed here since Archaic times and to have been reorganized in the late fourth century BC, finally being restored in the Roman period after the destruction by Mummius. The remains are in a bad state of preservation and identification is largely problematic. An unusual number of dining-quarters points to a ritual banquet as central in the cult. One structure ('T') has seven inter-related rooms. All dining areas have stone couches around the walls; some have wash basins and drains, some also small kitchens or service rooms. There are sacrificial pits and votive deposits. Rock-cut steps lead up to a theatral area with rows of seats and a cult structure or small temple. In the Roman period there is evidence of chthonic worship. All is nicely terraced.

A quarter of a mile north of the theatre, near the edge of the first plateau above the Gulf, is the Fountain of Lerna and the adjacent Asclepieion of the fifth century BC or earlier. Just south of these the Roman gymnasium, probably replacing a Hellenistic one on the site, is being excavated. Covering a considerable area, it had stoas surrounding its open court, with Doric exterior columns paralleled by a thin Ionic inner colonnade. A domed structure to the south is probably part of the Hellenistic baths, to the west of which apparently was a bronze foundry. In the apsidal room south of this was found a terracotta mask and a Roman curse-tablet of lead. Near the cliff edge a fountain-house ('of the Lamps') has been explored, revealing an underground fountain and a room with wash basins, swimming pool, and water-supply tunnels. Nearby, a Bronze Age village had utilized the spring.

Kos/Cos

Colonized in the Mycenaean Age by Achaeans and Carians from nearby Asia Minor, Cos was later taken over by Dorians who reputedly came from Epidauros. It was part of the Dorian Hexapolis of allied cities in the eastern Aegean but after 477 BC was dominated by Athens, then by Macedon and Rhodes and finally by Rome. Ptolemy II was born there during a sojourn of his mother Berenice. The influential elegiac poet Philetas was a native of Cos and Theocritus came here for some years to associate with him. The island also claimed Apelles the

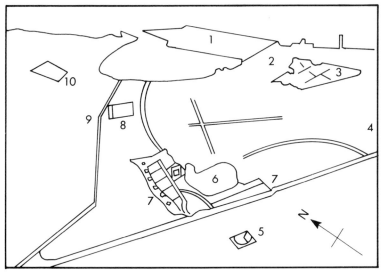

CITY
1 Castle of the Knights of Rhodes
2 Plane tree
3 Agora and harbour sector
4 Hellenistic temple precinct
5 Odeion
6 Acropolis
7 Roman sector
8 North baths (Roman)
9 Site of the stadium
10 Harbour baths (Hellenistic)

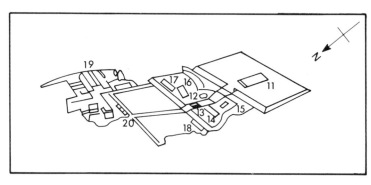

ASCLEPIEION
11 Temple of Asclepius
12 Exedra
13 Altar
14 Ionic temple (Greek)
15 Roman building (priest's house?)
16 Roman temple (Ionic) for Imperial cult
17 Lesche?
18 Fountain
19 Roman baths
20 Entry Propylon

great painter as one of her sons, and most famous of all, Hippocrates, the Father of Medicine, whose clinic and widespread fame attracted persons from all over the Greek world. Besides this cultural eminence Cos was known for its wine and fine silk – its special see-through garments were a source of envy and scandal among the Romans. During the late Middle Ages the island was controlled by the Knights of Rhodes but eventually fell to the Turks, then to the Italians. It became part of Greece again in 1948.

Originally the main city was at the southwest edge of the island, but when that was devastated by the Spartans during the Peloponnesian War it never recovered. A new city was established in 366 BC at the northern tip of the island. Despite several ruinous earthquakes it recovered and was for centuries a great commercial and cultural centre. Italian excavations since 1928 have uncovered parts of the Greek and Roman city in scattered areas of the present one.

Behind the castle and the 500-year-old plane tree 'of Hippocrates' lie the ancient harbour quarters and main market or agora. Greek structures from the fourth to the second centuries BC have been excavated along with many of Roman date. A fine Propylaea entrance has been found, some stoas, and several temples. Notable is a precinct of Aphrodite with a peristyle court enclosing twin temples and altars, apparently dedicated to the goddess under two different titles: Pandemos and Pontia – of the people and of the sea. To the south is a Hellenistic temple and nearby a large altar of Dionysos. Around the old acropolis hill to the southwest are mostly Roman ruins: a fine paved street, houses, baths, and gymnasium. Other baths and a stadium lie to the north, and to the south a neat Odeion which has been carefully restored. These constructions are from the second and third centuries AD. At some distance on a hillside is a Greek theatre dating from early Hellenistic times.

The most striking antiquity is some two miles to the south on a substantial hill: the Asclepieion. This was built a hundred years after Hippocrates in the late fourth century, but in honour of his great contributions to medical theory and humane practice it was dedicated to the healing god Asclepius. It was added to and reworked in later periods. The dramatic ascent up four terraces through formal gates amid fine buildings on both sides brings a splendid view from the top terrace of the whole complex and of the city and sea beyond. The main temple at the summit was Doric with 6 × 11 columns, its bottom step made of black marble. A great altar on the terrace below was flanked by an Ionic temple on the west (dating from the late fourth century BC, and the earliest on the site) and a later Roman temple on the east, also Ionic. In the former were famous paintings by Apelles which were eventually carried off to Rome. A public bench (*exedra*) and club hall (*lesche*) are also on this terrace, while that below was left open so as to give an unimpeded view as one ascended to the upper levels. The Asclepieion at Cos is one of the most imaginative and effective creations of Classical architecture.

*Lerni/*Lerna

On the western shore of the head of the Gulf of Argos, facing Tiryns and Nauplia, Lerna was well situated to control access to the rest of the Peloponnesus. It lies at the foot of Mt Pontinus near the sea, some ten miles south of Argos. Abundant water flows from a series of springs at the mountain's base, often flooding the road and keeping the area a swamp. Here Hercules performed another of his benefactions, by controlling the unruly waters – transformed in myth into the fearsome monster Hydra ('Water Beast') with many heads. Here too was supposed to be an entrance into Hades, where Dionysos descended to bring out Semele and where Pluto disappeared with Persephone. Mysteries in honour of Lernaean Demeter were celebrated to commemorate that symbolic event. It was here that Zeus pursued Io and disguised her as a cow to evade Hera's jealousy. Because the daughters of Danaus had thrown the heads of their murdered husbands into the nearby Alcyonian Lake they were condemned in Hades

1 Mt Pontinos

2 Myloi village

3 Hydra springs and swamp (Amymone)

4 'House of Tiles', etc.

5 Gulf of Argos

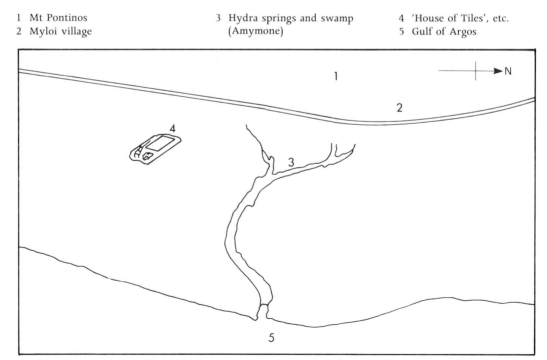

to perpetually carry water in leaky buckets. The lake was reputed to be bottomless, and Nero tried unsuccessfully to plumb its depths.

This wealth of local legends reflects memory of Lerna's antiquity. Professor John L. Caskey's skilful excavations between 1952 and 1958 have produced evidence of habitation here from the Neolithic period, at least as far back as 4000 BC, down into the Mycenaean Age.

The prehistoric settlement just south of the springs contains ruins of a Neolithic house and a remarkable Early Helladic fortification wall, a rare occurrence in Greece. A large house of that period at the north end of the site is perhaps an early palace. Over it c. 2200 BC was built a much more massive and important structure, called the 'House of the Tiles' from the many roof tiles that fell into its foundations when it burned down sometime before 2100 BC. This is the most impressive building from pre-Greek times that has been found in Greece. It is 80 ft long and 38 ft wide, with a neatly symmetrical ground plan unusual for its period. Small rooms surround larger ones in the interior, with long corridors and effectively positioned doors. The main entrance was on the east side and stairs led up to a second storey. The walls are three feet thick, of sun-dried brick on stone foundations, and covered with plaster or stucco; benches ran along the lower outside walls on the north and south sides and the floors of the rooms were of packed yellow clay. This unrivalled example of Early Bronze Age architecture is now under protective roofing.

The great palace was destroyed by fire – perhaps by lightning interpreted as wrath of the gods, for it was not rebuilt but buried under a convex mound of earth surrounded by a circle of round stones, seemingly a sign of fear or awe. Other houses, both rectangular and apsidal, were constructed nearby. Two Late Helladic I shaft graves, like those at Mycenae, suggest that the site was taken over by early Greek kings by 1600 BC. Evidence of later habitation here has been eroded away.

Lindos/**Lindos**

The striking acropolis of Lindos, perched between two bays of rich blue water, above the white houses of the town below, is one of the most memorable scenes in Greece. The great cave under the southern edge of the hill is especially impressive from the air or sea, being difficult to see from the acropolis itself.

There is evidence of habitation in the area before 2000 BC and of a cult on the acropolis from Mycenaean times. Pindar says that the city was founded by Kerkaphos, descendant of the Sun. Colonists from Athens and the Argolid seem to have settled here in the thirteenth century BC, about the time of the Trojan War. Lindos helped colonize Gela in Sicily in 688 BC, and Parthenopea, which later became Naples. It was the chief city of the island of Rhodes in early times, and is mentioned by Homer along with Ialyssos and Cameiros. It joined with them and Cos, Cnidos, and Halicarnassus in the Dorian Hexapolis of the fifth century BC. Cleoboulus, one of the 'Seven Sages', was its benevolent and progressive leader in the sixth century BC, when the city especially prospered. Because of its geographical position and two harbours, it was for long an important centre of sea trade. The Byzantines built a fortress on its heights which was taken over by the Knights of St John and later by the Turks. Excavations were primarily carried out between 1902 and 1914 and in 1952, with considerable reconstruction of some of the ancient monuments.

Dominating the acropolis at the southern point, some 350 ft above the sea, is the temple of Athena Lindia, evidently the original site of the ancient cult of the goddess near the great cave in the eastern cliff over the sea. The temple built here in the days of Cleobulus in the early half of the sixth century burned down about 348 BC. Its replacement soon after was Doric, 75 × 25 ft, with four columns across the east and west ends but none down the sides. Little now remains of its square forecourt with surrounding columns and an altar, but it is established that the colonnade was Ionic, apparently added c. 200 BC. In front was an earlier Propylon, imitating that on the Acropolis at Athens, dated to *c.* 300 BC. An enormous stoa was built in front of this about a hundred years later, with 42 columns; eight of these in each of its projecting wings reach forward to frame the majestic approach. In the middle was a broad staircase over 60 ft wide. Above the colonnade, nearly 20 ft up, ran a Doric frieze, while below among the pillars were many statues left by devotees of Athena. This whole U-shaped complex functioned as the formal Propylaea to the upper sanctuary. In Roman times a small temple was added at the southeast edge of the acropolis, for the cult of the Emperor. On the opposite side of the eastern section of the hill are the ruins of the Governor's Castle that was built by the Knights, and of a chapel of St John adjacent to it.

Part of the way down the steep descent to the town is an ancient relief of a ship's stern and rudder. Built into the deck was the base for a statue to Hagesandros, a devotee of Poseidon, as the inscription indicates. Part of the ancient Sacred Way up to the acropolis passes this relief. The cult of Athena Lindia enjoyed widespread fame in the Greek world. Its setting is awe-inspiring still.

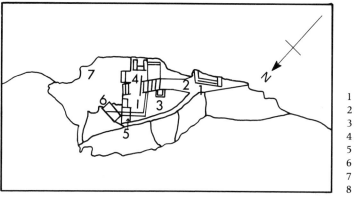

1 Temple of Athena Lindia
2 Site of forecourt
3 Propylon
4 Propylaea
5 St John's chapel
6 Knights' castle
7 Site of Roman temple
8 Cave in the cliff

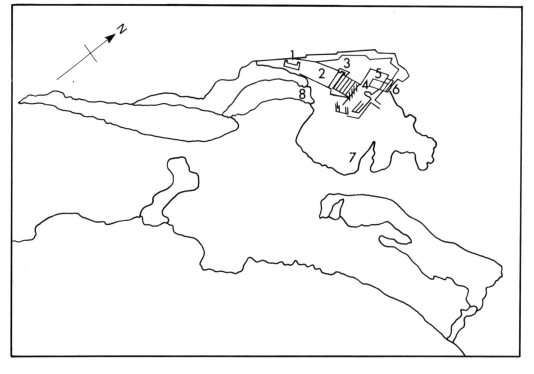

Malia/Mallia

Unlike Phaistos and Knossos, the palace at Mallia is on a level plain not far from the sea. It was originally built, like them, in the early Middle Minoan period c. 1900 BC, then rebuilt and somewhat altered two centuries or more later, after the destruction that had struck the other palaces also around 1700 BC. About the same size as Phaistos and of basically similar plan, it has the advantage of not being cluttered with the ruins of other later structures built over it. First discovered and partly cleared by Hazzidakis in 1915, it has been thoroughly studied by the French School since 1922, with excavations of houses and tombs still in progress in adjacent areas.

The large oblong Central Court has a sunken altar or sacrificial hearth (eschara) in the middle and porticos on the north and east sides – the eastern side's pillars were alternately round

and square, the northern one's rested on bases and were apparently interconnected by a grill fence. Rooms on the western edge of the court were apparently for religious and cult use; at the southwest corner was an offering table with a large round depression in the centre and 34 small pits around it to hold libations and other sacrificial offerings. There is a pillared crypt in the cult area, and a raised platform looking out over the court – perhaps a royal box. Groups of storerooms occur at the east and west edges of the palace complex and eight large circular containers at the southwest corner functioned as a granary. Outside are remains of earlier storerooms from the first palace period. A long corridor running north-south leads to what was probably the residential area of the royal family. The King's Megaron was also here, and nearby was a somewhat smaller one for the

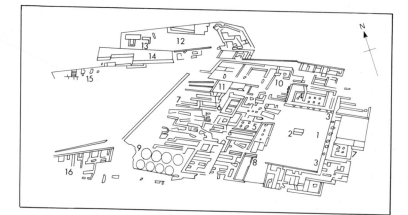

1 Central Court of the palace
2 Altar/sacrificial hearth
3 Portico
4 Pillared hall
5 Cult rooms
6 North-south corridor
7 Storerooms
8 Offering table
9 Granaries
10 North Court
11 Royal residence, megarons
12 Agora
13 Bent Portico
14 Hypostyle crypt (covered)
15 Houses
16 Proto–Palatial storerooms
17 Houses (southern sector)

queen. The King's Room was paved, with four pillars along three of its sides (not the western). The North Court may have been primarily a domestic area for the preparation of food, etc. A room with six pillars north of the court may have supported a banquet hall above it, with the kitchen nearby to the east. There is evidence of a second storey over much of the palace, with stairs leading up from the Queen's Room and other locations.

Northwest of the palace is a cluster of rooms around an open area that was probably a market or agora. On the west side is a structure named the Bent Portico and close to it a raised platform. South of this, now under protective roofing, is an interesting hypostyle crypt with a complex of walls and pillars with some of their plaster coating preserved. Houses have been uncovered nearby, and in other large sectors farther to the south and east of the palace. Many contain bathrooms, light-wells, paving, and frescoes.

A paved Minoan road leads from the palace and agora to the sea. The ancient cemeteries located near the coast have yielded many objects of great artistic interest.

Mantinea/Mantineia

Though there was a high hill nearby where an early settlement was established, Mantineia is one of the rare Greek fortified cities situated on a plain. Its elliptical circuit of walls, some two and a half miles around, is one of the best examples of Greek defensive works and is generally well preserved, especially along the northern and eastern sides. Built about 370 B C, at the same time as the great fortifications at Messene and perhaps under direction of the same architects from Thebes, the walls of Mantineia are in the double-shell or sandwich technique, the space between the outer courses of large rectangular or polygonal blocks holding a fill of field stones and earth, generally to a total width of 14 ft. At regular distances of about 85 ft are square towers, some 120 of them in all. There are ten gates, most of them designed so that the entry runs parallel to the wall for several feet, not with direct access, giving an added defensive advantage. The northwest gate, however, has a simple direct entrance, with extra strength built around the opening. A fine example of the gate and tower arrangements is seen on the south where the Tegea Gate connects with the road to that city. A special feature at Mantineia is the diversion of the river Ophis ('snake') to flow around the fortifications on all sides except for a short distance on the southeast, forming a supplementary moat whilst also protecting the city from flooding, as used to happen.

Within the walled oval near the centre, French excavations by Fougère in 1887–89 have uncovered part of the ancient civic sector.

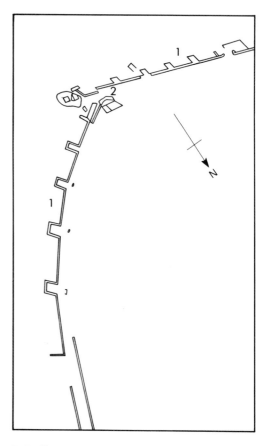

1 Walls
2 Tegea Gate

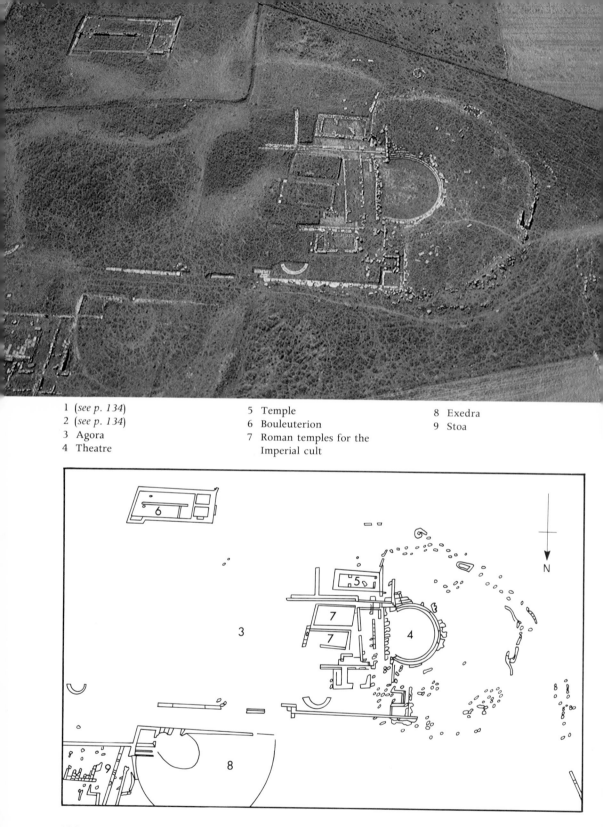

1 (see p. 134)
2 (see p. 134)
3 Agora
4 Theatre

5 Temple
6 Bouleuterion
7 Roman temples for the
   Imperial cult

8 Exedra
9 Stoa

The agora was a large rectangle, with the council hall (Bouleuterion) to the south and in Roman times on the opposite side a North Stoa and large semicircular exedra. At the west end are four rectangular structures, the southernmost being a temple of uncertain ascription. Next to it are two temple-shrines dedicated to the Imperial cult in Roman times. The agora is some 490 × 278 ft, with a street running eastward to the walls.

The theatre, to the west of the agora, is poorly preserved and rather undistinguished. It is built on level ground, not cut into a hillside in the usual manner. The cavea of seats had to be made on banked up earth; it has seven wedge-shaped sections, with eight sets of stairs – some of which were later blocked off or relocated. The seats were mostly of limestone, with some of marble; there was no *prohedria* row of special backed thrones of honour. The stage buildings are out of alignment with the theatre plan, apparently as a result of hasty reconstruction at some later time; the proscenium is also late. Most of the theatre was built after the walls c. 360 BC.

Mantineia was founded c. 500 BC by the incorporation of five adjacent villages. It was politically opposed to Tegea, its rival for the domination of southern Arcadia and for control of the drain-pits that made the great plain usable. Mantineia was against Sparta until the Persian Wars, then she helped Sparta to suppress the helots. She opposed Sparta again, on Athens' side, in the Peloponnesian War – one of whose battles occurred at Mantineia in 418 BC, ending in Spartan victory. Sparta demolished the city in 385, but after the Theban triumph at Leuctra in 371 BC it was repopulated and the present great walls were constructed. The famous battle at Mantineia in 362 BC ended Theban power in the Peloponnesus. The city was destroyed in 223 BC by the Achaean League but was soon refounded as Antigoneia, a name that it retained into Roman times.

Marathon/**Marathon**

The name of Marathon is one of the most honoured in Western history. Here, in the late summer of 490 BC, a brave band of Greeks (probably about 9000 Athenians with 1000 Plataeans) decisively defeated and threw back a much larger Persian force sent by Darius to punish Athens for aiding the Ionian Revolt. The shrewd strategy of Miltiades and the historic courage of the Greek hoplites (aided for the first known time by slaves) demolished the assumption that the fearsome imperial power of Persia was invincible and helped spur Greece to new confidence and patriotic enthusiasm and pride in political freedom.

The 192 Athenian warriors who fell in the battle were buried on the spot under a mound of earth 30 ft high and some 600 ft around the base. Memorial tablets with the names of the fallen, arranged by tribes, were embedded in the mound but have since disappeared. The tumulus (*Soros*) was partially explored in 1890. Ashes of men and the burned bones of sacrificed animals were found, and black-figure pottery of the early fifth-century BC style (now on display in the Athens Museum). The stone arrowheads found here earlier are probably prehistoric – though Herodotus reports such use by the Ethiopian archers in the Persian army.

The battle took place primarily in the plain where the *Soros* stands, and along the nearby marsh and shore. The Persian dead were probably buried by the victors in an open pit. The Plataean dead were given their own tumulus, built about two miles west of the Athenian *Soros* – perhaps the one recently explored and opened near the region called Vraná. An Athenian trophy monument has also been discovered about the same distance northeast of the *Soros*, in what was probably the location of the Persian camp before the battle. Miltiades had his own monument somewhere nearby.

Between the Athenian and the Plataean tumuli a Mycenaean tholos tomb has been excavated and a golden cup found among its contents. In its dromos two horses had been sacrificed and buried.

Tradition placed the landing of Deucalion after the flood at Marathon – an indication of memories of primitive habitation in this fine plain. Prehistoric remains and Bronze Age tombs

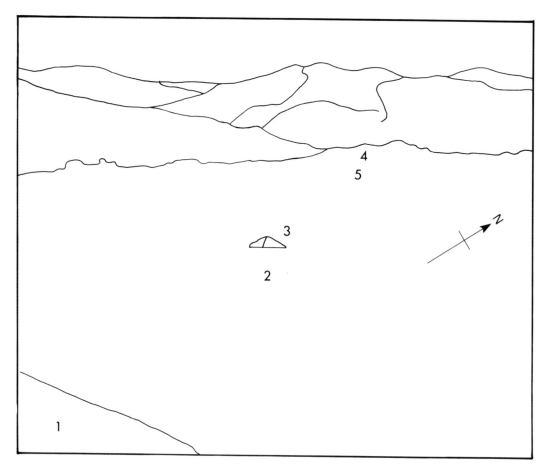

MARATHON
1 Sea
2 Battlefield

3 Athenian mound (*Soros*)
4 Site of the Plataean mound?
5 Site of Mycenaean tholos tomb

in the area witness the long history of the site. A cave of Pan, mentioned by Pausanias, has been located in the lower slopes of the mountains to the northwest of the plain.

It was at Marathon that Herodes Atticus was born about AD 100. He used his great wealth from land-holdings to construct many notable buildings around Greece. He was an outstanding orator and writer of the time, becoming a Senator at Rome and even Consul in 143 AD. His vast estate at Marathon is still partly traceable.

Megalopolis/**Megalopolis**

After the victory of Thebes over Sparta at Leuctra in 371 BC, the Theban leader Epaminondas created a new city to be the capital of his Arcadian Confederacy. It was meant, along with Mantineia, Argos and Messene, to restrict Spartan dominance to Laconia. The circuit of its walls was nearly five miles in length, yet the city was built within four years and populated by forced migrations from villages and towns of the region. Three times it repulsed Spartan attempts to capture it, in 353, 331, and 234 BC but internal dissensions weakened it and it was

sacked in 223 BC, most of its citizens fleeing to Messenia, but returning two years later after another Spartan reverse. The town was rebuilt in 194 BC and existed in Roman times, though by Pausanias' day it was mostly in ruins. Megalopolis was the birthplace of Philopoemen (253–183 BC), 'the last great leader produced by Greece', and of the historian Polybius who was a friend of the Scipios during Rome's great struggle against Carthage. The city was divided into two districts by the river Helisson: the federal city to the south, known as Oresteia, the municipality of Megalopolis across the river to the north.

British excavations in 1890–93 revealed the agora of the northern town and around it the sanctuary of Zeus Soter, the portico of Philip, the perfume market, Roman baths, and traces of a stoa and council hall (Bouleuterion) – but now these are hardly visible owing to ploughing and planting of the terrain. South of the river Helisson (which flows into the Alphaeus on its way to Olympia and the sea) the ruins are impressive, as the photograph shows.

The theatre, according to Pausanias, was the largest in Greece, and could hold over 20,000 spectators in its 59 rows of seats. There are two horizontal aisles (diazomata) and ten radial stairways. The orchestra area is nearly 100 ft across. The cavea of seats is built into a hillside overlooking the river and northern town. Its fourth-century stage was of wood and could be dismantled and stored, along with scenery, in the special skenotheke room at the western

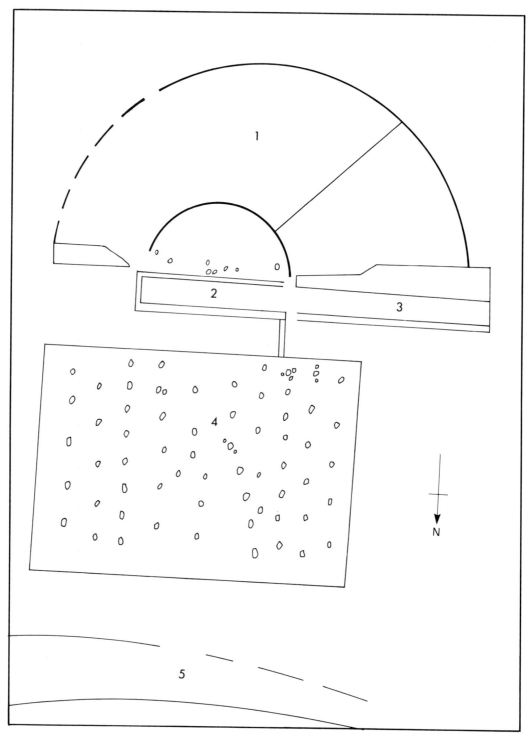

1 Theatre
2 Stage building/porch of
   Thersilion
3 Skenotheke (property room for
   theatre equipment)
4 Thersilion
5 River Helisson

entry to the stage area. This was in order not to encumber unnecessarily the access to the Thersilion nearby. After the destruction of that building, however, in 222 BC, the stage was rebuilt in stone with 14 marble columns, taking over from the porch of the Thersilion as a formal backdrop to the orchestra.

The Thersilion, named after its donor, was a remarkable structure – a sort of rectangular theatre roofed over to serve as meeting place for the Assembly of Ten Thousand who, with the Council of 50 federal representatives from associated states, governed the Arcadian League. It was 218 ft broad and 172 ft deep; its 67 Doric columns were ingeniously arranged in rows radiating from the speaker's platform south of the centre to provide a maximum unimpeded view. The floor seems to have sloped like a theatre's to improve both seeing and hearing the speaker. A porch on the south side, with 16 Doric pillars, faced the theatre.

Altars have been located on each side of the Thersilion, and to the west is a stadium near a spring sacred to Dionysos.

Messini/**Messene**

The fertile area and great plain of Messenia west of Sparta was early taken over by the Dorians when they settled in Greece. Sparta struggled fiercely to hold it under her control and exploitation, leading to the three Messenian Wars in the eighth, seventh, and fifth centuries BC. The natives had to seek refuge on the heights of Mt Ithome, where the young Zeus was supposed to have lived for a time, and where many helots fled from Spartan serfdom, often obtaining freedom from Zeus' priest.

When Thebes defeated Sparta at Leuctra in 371 BC, Epaminondas established a new capital of Messenia, naming it Messene, on the lower slope of Mt Ithome. This was part of his strategic plan to contain Spartan power, along with allied strongholds at Mantineia, Megalopolis, and Argos. The Spartan tyrant Nabis was thwarted by Philopoemen in his attempt to seize Messene in 202 BC, but Philopoemen was later trapped by local rebels against the Achaean League and poisoned. His successor at

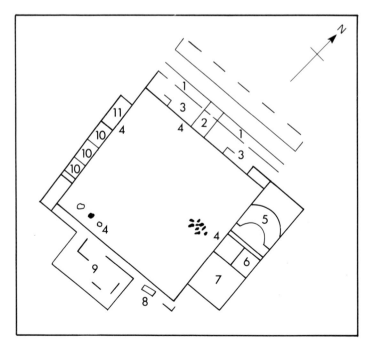

1 North Stoa (late)
2 North Propylon
3 Sebasteion
4 Porticoes of temple court
5 Small theatre
6 East Propylon
7 Synedrion?
8 Heroön
9 Prytaneion?
10 Cult rooms
11 Artemis Orthia shrine

1 (see p. 142)
2 North Propylon
3 Sebasteion
4 Porticoes of temple court
5–9 (see p. 142)

10 Cult rooms
11 Artemis Orthia shrine
12 Temple (of Asclepius and
   Hygieia?)
13 Ramp

14 Altar
15 Exedra

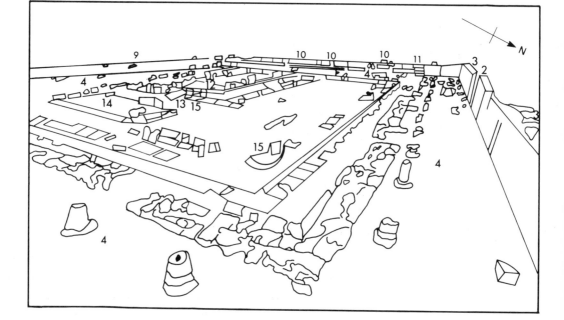

Megalopolis, Lykortas (the father of the historian Polybius), avenged him soon after. Little is known of Messene's history thereafter. Only a small portion of its considerable area has been excavated, the recent work in the Temple Square proving, however, exceptionally rewarding.

The famous walls of Messene, over five miles in circuit, are considered the finest example of fourth-century Greek fortifications. Though some date them later, they were most likely constructed around 360 BC at the early stage of the city's existence. The masonry is most neat and careful in the extant portions. Square and semicircular towers were set at intervals down the length. Of the several gates, the Arcadian is the most notable, with a circular inner court between outer and interior towers.

Until very recently it was assumed that the excavated square within the city area, surrounded by colonnades and small buildings, was the ancient agora. But Orlandos, in completing the excavation of the area between 1969 and 1972, has revealed a fine temple in the centre. A wide-angle ground photo, taken in November 1972, is included here to show this interesting find.

The temple is Doric, some 91 × 44 ft and with 6 × 12 columns, apparently of Hellenistic date. The west porch has two columns between anta walls, but the east porch opens directly on the peristyle without intervening columns.

There is evidence of an earlier temple below, dating from the fifth or fourth century BC. A ramp at the east end leads to a large altar directly opposite the East Propylon in the surrounding double colonnade of Corinthian style. Several exedras served as public benches.

North of the East Propylon is a small theatre. It is probable that this was primarily for sacred ritual gatherings like the one in the Asclepieion at Pergamum. Because of it, and the finds in the room south of the Propylon (which may have been the Synedrion assembly hall) of a relief showing a knight before Asclepius, together with an inscription referring to rooms built in Asclepius' honour, it is probable that the whole complex is a major Asclepieion and the temple was in that god's service, perhaps in conjunction with Hygieia.

There are several small cult-rooms on the west side, the northernmost of which was a shrine of Artemis Orthia, also worshipped at Sparta. An Heroön contained four family tombs of honoured citizens. Emperor worship was practised in Roman times in the Sebasteion rooms to the north, between which the North Propylon gave entry into the square via steps at the south end.

Portions of a theatre and stadium and a large temple have been located elsewhere in the city area, and on Mt Ithome's slopes is a temple of Artemis and on the summit an altar of Zeus.

Mikine/Mycenae

Because of Homer, 'well-built Mycenae, rich in gold', where Agamemnon ruled and met his shameful death at his wife's hand on his triumphant return from Troy, has a unique mystery and appeal. Its great setting suits its fame and its role as chief city of early Greece: a triangular hill-top over 900 ft high, at the edge of a deep gorge with twin conical mountains behind, commanding a view and control of much of the Argolid. It was the eponymous dynamic centre of the brilliant first stage of Greek civilization, the Mycenaean, that flourished c. 1600–1200 BC throughout southern and central Greece, and which is so vividly described in the *Iliad* and *Odyssey*.

Legends of its founding by Perseus, the son of Zeus and Danae, and later conquest by the dynasty of Pelops under Atreus and his son Agamemnon, reflect the subjugation of the native Pelasgians by the Danaoi c. 1900 BC, coming from Asia Minor via Egypt, and the take-over by the Achaeans – the first true Greeks, whom Homer immortalizes – in the seventeenth century BC. After 400 years of violence and splendour, the Mycenaean world collapsed not long after the Trojan War in the late thirteenth century BC and the Dorians seized its centres of power. Mycenae was destroyed by 1120 BC. It revived on a small scale in Classical times, but was demolished by

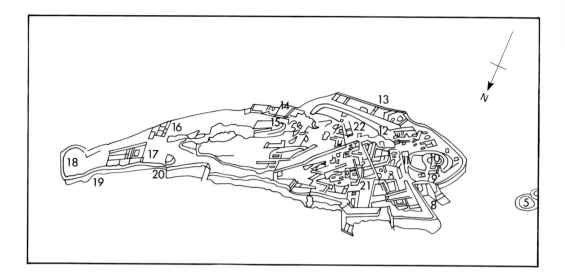

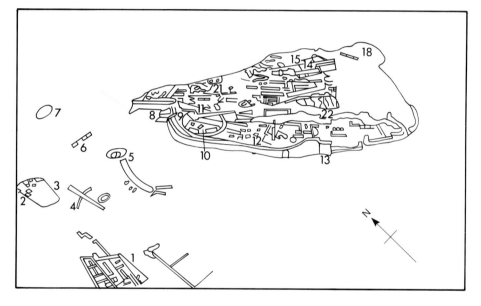

1 House of the Oil Merchant, etc.	8 Lion Gate	16 House of Columns ('Little Palace')
2 Grave Circle B	9 'Granaries'/guardrooms	17 Northeast houses
3 'Clytemnestra' tholos	10 Grave Circle A	18 Northeast extension
4 Hellenistic theatre fragment	11 Ramp	19 Secret cistern entry
5 'Aegisthus' tholos	12 West houses	20 Postern gate
6 Perseia fountain–house	13 Polygonal South Tower	21 Northwest houses
7 Lion tholos	14 Palace	22 Cult area (altars, etc.)
	15 Temple area	

Argos some ten years after the Persian Wars. Schliemann excavated the ruins in 1874–76, with sensational finds, followed by Stamatakis, Tsountas, Wace, Papadimitriou, and Mylonas. The great treasures of gold from the Shaft Grave Circles are in the Athens Museum.

The mighty citadel walls, in places 45 ft wide and as much as 56 ft high, date in their extant form from the fourteenth century BC, with an earlier stage and a massive reworking and extension – which Wace dates to *c.* 1340, and Mylonas a century later. The Lion Gate, postern, and northeast extension belong to this later period of regal magnificence, as also does the palace in its full development. The secret cistern, an engineering marvel with 79 steps cut into the solid rock in a descending curve to a safe basin for water storage, is also of this period.

The principal entry through the citadel fortifications is the famous Lion Gate at the northwest corner, protected by a salient wall and bastion of huge 'Cyclopean' blocks, its lintel 15 ft long and 6½ ft thick, weighing a hundred tons. Holes for the door pivots and blocking bar are still visible, as are the ruts in the threshold below. Above the gateway was a triangular relieving gap fronted by a grey limestone slab with two lions (or griffins?) standing with front feet resting on joined altars supporting a pillar of Minoan type – narrower at the bottom than top. Inside the gate on the right are rooms that served either as granaries or as a guard-post. The great Grave Circle A with its six shaft graves surrounded by a circular fence of stone slabs, where rich royal treasures were found by Schliemann, dates to the sixteenth century BC, long before Agamemnon. Another Grave Circle, B, outside the walls, discovered in 1951, is even earlier, *c.* 1650 BC.

A wide ramp led towards the palace on the citadel's heights. The royal megaron and living quarters are at the eastern end, with a court and throne room to the west. North of the palace was the temple area, rebuilt many times. A great number of elaborate houses are located inside the citadel; those to the southeast were perhaps a Little Palace; others, like the Oil Merchant's, are outside the walls.

Beyond the citadel to the northwest are three large tholos tombs of 'beehive' shape, and several more are farther off, including one ascribed to Atreus, which is the largest and finest of them all.

Naxos/**Naxos**

Largest of the Cyclades and noted for its varied scenery, fine marble, wine, and citrus fruit, Naxos has been celebrated in art and music as the island where Ariadne was abandoned by Theseus on his way home after slaying the Minotaur at Knossos. She was found there and loved by Dionysos – who in some accounts had been born there from the thigh of Zeus, after his mother Semele had been consumed by lightning. There is evidence of habitation on the islet Strongyle, modern Palati, from Proto-Cycladic times before 2000 BC, and of extensive Cycladic and late Mycenaean settlements nearby just north of the modern town and, presumably, under it. There was an organized walled city there; its tombs were of both the pit and chamber type, with many dating from the Geometric period. Part of the Classical city has also been found at the end of the torrent bed that separates the modern town and Haplomata hill.

In the Archaic period of the seventh and sixth centuries BC, Naxos was at the peak of its power and importance in the ancient world, controlling the Cyclades by its fleet, acting as protector of Delos, engaging in widespread trade, and flourishing as a centre of sculpture and early Ionic architecture. Its despot Lygdamis (*c.* 550–524 BC), a friend of Pisistratus at Athens and Polycrates of Samos, contemporary 'tyrants' of notable energy and cultural interests, promoted commerce and public building but was hated for suppressing individual freedom. The island was involved in the Ionian Revolt against Persia, and for that act of daring was demolished by Datis in 490 BC on his way to Greece (to be frustrated at Marathon). Forced to join the Athenian confederacy after the Persian Wars, Naxos tried to rebel in 466 BC but was firmly conquered. In Roman times, Marc Antony gave the island

1 Strongyle/Palatia islet
2 Ionic temple
3 West door
4 Causeway

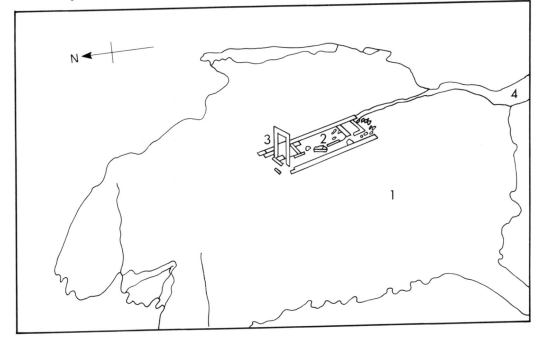

1 Strongyle/Palatia islet
2 Ionic temple
3 (*see p. 149*)
4 Causeway

5 Harbour
6 Excavation sites
7 Haplomata hill
8 Kastro/acropolis

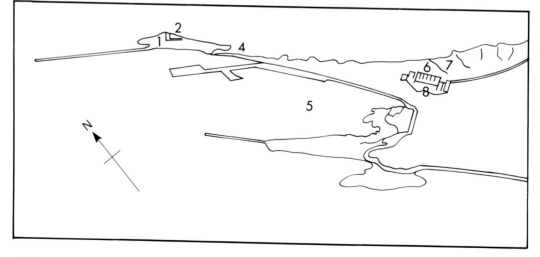

to Rhodes. After long Byzantine control, Naxos was taken by the Venetians in 1207 and its independent Duke Marco Sanudo rebuilt it on a grand scale. The Turks conquered the island in 1566, and the Russians held it from 1770–74. Its picturesque villages retain much antique flavour.

The most notable monument from Classical times is the Archaic Ionic temple on the islet Strongyle at the edge of Naxos city near the centre of the western coast. It seems to date from the days of Lygdamis and was left unfinished after his fall from power. A pioneering example of Ionic style, its cella had two interior rows of four columns each supporting the roof. Besides a porch at each end, with two pillars between projecting anta walls, there was a special hall at the west end, between the cella and opisthodomos, 31 ft deep and with access only from the west. The great door to this room, nearly 20 ft high with triple inset surface and egg-and-dart moulding, is all that now stands erect. There is controversy whether the temple had surrounding columns, and it is not certain which god was worshipped in it – presumably Dionysos but perhaps Apollo. It is oriented southeast/northwest and in all probability had a Propylon near the causeway facing the city.

Beyond the Venetian castle and Sanudo Palace some of the Classical city is being unearthed. A square stoa has been partly cleared in the agora area, and other structures are under excavation. Elsewhere on the island is a Demeter/Kore sanctuary, and giant Archaic *kouros* statues lie abandoned in the quarries.

Nemea/**Nemea**

Situated in a pretty valley between Sicyon and Argos, with a fine view of Mt Kyllene to the west and of the mountains of Arcadia to the south, Nemea is best known for its legendary lion finally slain by Hercules. A festival grew up there very early, becoming the Panhellenic Games which ranked with those at Olympia, Delphi, and Isthmia, and at which Pindar wrote victory odes for contestants. The Games were originally supervised by Cleonae, but were later taken over and reorganized by Argos in 573 BC, after which they were held every second summer in July. Argos replaced the claim of their institution by Hercules with the story that Adrastus, king of Argos and leader of the Seven against Thebes, established them in honour of Opheltes, child of Nemea's king Lycurgus, who was slain by a dragon that Adrastus subsequently killed. The prize at the Games was a crown of wild celery, and national glory.

The chief monument at Nemea is the fine temple of Zeus, built in local grey limestone, still partly standing, and with most of its other parts lying about in massive display. It was built towards the end of the fourth century, c. 325 BC, in Doric style but showing some departures from tradition – it was contracted at the back by the omission of the usual opisthodomos porch, and had only 12 columns along the side, not 13, with the regular six across the front and back. These columns are unusually slim and lofty. There were two others between the projecting walls of the front porch, and inside the cella two rows of six, with four across the back. These were on two levels, the lower course with Corinthian capitals, the upper row smaller and Ionic. Behind this interior colonnade was an unusual *adyton* with a crypt to which five steps led down. This was said to be the Tomb of Opheltes, and was incorporated from an earlier temple. At the front a ramp led down to a huge altar over 130 ft long and 8 ft wide.

The rectangular building south of the temple is of undetermined purpose. It had square pillar bases inside, and parts of two other long structures parallel to it have been uncovered which may have marked the southern limit of the sacred temenos.

Farther south is a rectangular complex in two parts, with interior columns, probably a palaestra for athletic uses. Its western section was, at least later, baths. A small museum now stands over part of these. The long building east of the palaestra was at first considered to be the gymnasium, but recent finds of cooking utensils, food remains and coins suggest it was

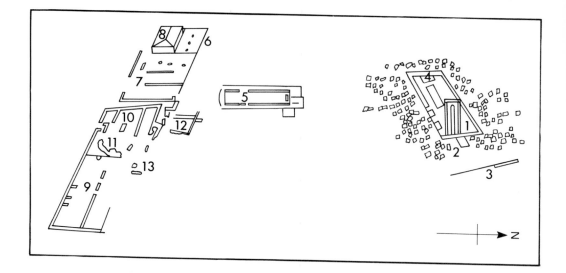

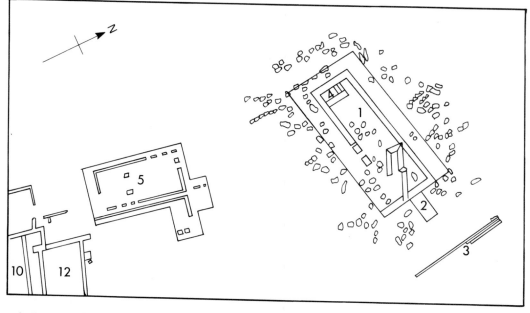

1 Zeus Temple
2 Ramp
3 Altar
4 Adyton/crypt
5 Rectangular buildings
6 Baths
7 Palaestra

8 Museum
9 Hotel
10 Church
11 Apse of the church
12 Baptistery
13 Kiln for temple tiles

more likely a hotel (*xenon*) for special people at the Games. It has five entrances along the south side, with inner vestibules. Under it was found an ancient kiln, apparently for making the temple's roof-tiles. These buildings are all of the late fourth or early third century. Over the hotel was built a Christian church with an apse and a baptistery, uncovered by American excavations in 1924–27 and in 1964.

Some 500 yards southeast of the Zeus sanctuary a stadium was built into a hollow in the hillside. A poorly preserved theatre is also there and, nearby, the reputed den of the Nemean Lion.

Nikopolis/**Nicopolis**

Although essentially a Roman city, Nicopolis was in some respects accommodated to Greek traditions. It was founded by Octavian (Augustus) to commemorate his decisive naval victory over Antony and Cleopatra at nearby Actium in early September, 31 BC. The new 'Victory City' was populated by forced transfer of the inhabitants of a wide surrounding region, along with veterans from the war. St Paul wintered there, probably in AD 64, writing his epistle to Titus whom he had left as bishop at Gortyn in Crete. Pope Eleutherios was born there in the following century, and later the city was an important Christian centre, as its four great basilicas testify. The Vandals of Genseric sacked Nicopolis in 475 AD, and Totila's Huns again in 551 AD. Justinian rebuilt the city with new walls forming a

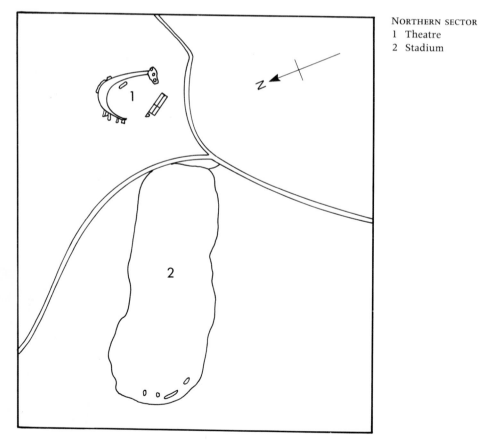

NORTHERN SECTOR
1 Theatre
2 Stadium

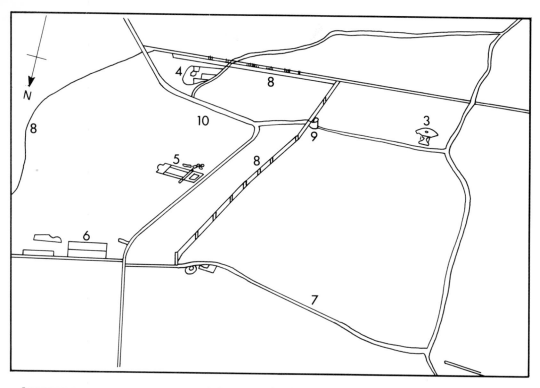

fortified citadel much smaller than Augustus' circuit. It fell to the Bulgarians in 1040. Today its ruins are abandoned and lonely.

At the northern part of the large site is Mikhalitsi hill, where Octavian had camped and where he erected trophies and a temple to his patron Apollo. (He gratefully honoured Mars and Neptune also with a hillside monument for their help in his victory). On the lower slopes of the hill, overlooking Mazoma lagoon, is the huge Roman theatre, cut into the hillside in Greek fashion but built of bricks and mortar – probably in the second century A D. Much of the high stage building and some of the stone seats still remain though most have been carried off for re-use in later buildings. Holes for awning poles to shade part of the auditorium can be identified. A large depression to the west reveals the site of the stadium, to which the Actian Games were transferred. It is rounded at both ends – a rare feature in Greece but common enough in Asia Minor. The natives

refer to this ruin as Karavi, the 'ship'. There was also a gymnasium nearby.

In the southern, walled, sector of the city is a small theatre or Odeion, and to the east a large structure sometimes called Hadrian's Palace, but which is more likely to be the Bouleuterion where administrative meetings took place. The Augustan walls are extensive but in a badly ruined condition. Along their western stretch ran a superimposed aqueduct bringing in cool mountain water from the distant Louros torrent. A great gate at the centre of the western wall corresponds to the West Gate in the contracted citadel of Justinian, whose massive Byzantine ramparts survive in long high sections. Some baths lie north of the enclosure.

Within the citadel area three large Christian basilicas have been found, and a fourth church outside the walls has recently been uncovered. They have been studied by Greek excavators since 1913 and in recent years. Near the centre is a huge church with five aisles and a threefold

transept, named after Bishop Alkyson (who died in AD 516), whose mosaic portrait is preserved in an adjacent building that may have been a catechetical school. Farther south is the large Doumetios Basilica, with fine floor mosaics, dated to around 540 AD, and a triple nave. Basilica C along the north wall can now barely be discerned. In Basilica D outside the citadel area is preserved an elaborate mosaic with a peacock design.

Olimbia/Olympia : The Setting

Olympia is famous for its charming scenery as well as for its Games. It was not a city but a sanctuary of Zeus and Hera to which pilgrims came from all over the Greek world, especially every four years for the great Panhellenic festival. At the foot of the distinctive conical hill Kronos or Kronion, near the confluence of the river Kladeos with the much more important Alpheios, the sanctuary developed into a dense architectural complex that was eventually crowded with perhaps 3000 monuments to victors in the Games, to princes, and to various cities commemorating their achievements. The site was important even in Mycenaean times, when the cult of Zeus displaced that of the Pelasgian divinity Kronos and Hera took over from the primitive chthonic worship of Ge (Earth), echoing the Dorian conquest of the Peloponnesus.

Originally the festival celebrations here were simple and Hercules was claimed as founder. In 776 BC a formal competition was organized, involving a foot-race of a stade's length (some 600 ft) as well as religious

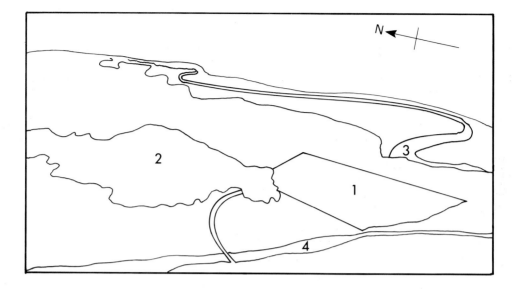

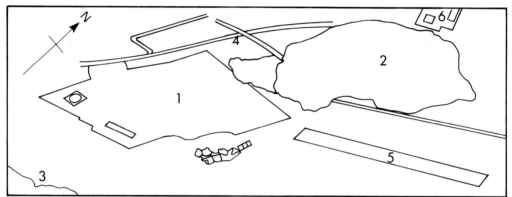

1 Sanctuary
2 Kronion hill
3 Alpheios river

4 Kladeos river
5 Stadium
6 Museum

ceremonies. This sacred contest was subsequently held, with few exceptions, every four years and the Greeks came to date events by the Olympiad in which they occurred. The Games steadily grew in fame and extent so that in Classical times they lasted for five days and also included two-stade and long-distance races, wrestling, boxing, a race in armour, horse and chariot races, and the Pentathlon (long jump, one-stade race, javelin throw, hurling the discus, and wrestling). Some of the competitions were open to boys, but none to foreigners until Roman days. Victors were crowned with wreaths of wild olive and thereafter greatly honoured by their native cities. They could erect a memorial in the sanctuary area, but only if they had won three times could it be their portrait. Pindar wrote splendid odes for 14 Olympic winners. There were also other events to entertain the crowds: musical concerts, lectures by writers and rhetoricians, public reading of new literary works – as, for example, those by Herodotus. Special heralds travelled throughout Greece in advance of each festival to announce its exact time (usually in August or September during the period of full moon after the summer solstice), and other officials supervised the training of the athletes, who had to

come to Olympia ten months early for continual practice. A Sacred Truce prevailed during the period of the Games, when Greeks everywhere stopped warring among themselves and people flocked to Olympia from all over the country with a sense of national unity otherwise largely dormant. The crowds camped out in tents and provision had to be made for feeding them. A doctor was on hand and souvenirs were peddled. Athletes and officials from competing cities had special accommodation. The Games were held for 1200 years, until they were stopped in AD 393 by decree of Theodosius I.

The site was rediscovered in 1766, partly excavated in 1829, and fully uncovered and studied by German scholars in three major campaigns: 1875–81, 1936–41, 1952– onwards.

The stadium has been recently cleared and restored. Its earthen banks could seat some 40,000 spectators. The marble starting and finishing lines, 600 Olympic feet apart, survive in places. There was a stone curb around the course and a water channel, and special stone seats on the south for the judges. Originally starting within the sanctuary near the Pelopion, the stadium was moved outside to the east during the fifth century BC. The vaulted entry supported the later additional banks of seats. The parallel hippodrome has since been washed away.

Olimbia/Olympia : The Sanctuary

The best preserved building at Olympia is also the oldest, the temple of Hera. An important example of Archaic Doric, it replaced earlier temples of wood and initially itself had mostly wooden columns and entablature. The extant structure dates from *c.* 600 BC. Its columns (16 along the sides, six across front and back) were successively replaced in stone and their proportions and style vary greatly. The upper walls were of sun-dried brick, the ceiling of wood. The cella had interior columns (a later addition), every second one engaged to the wall and thus forming five chapels on each side, in one of which stood Praxiteles' statue of Hermes. At the back were Archaic cult statues of Zeus and Hera on thrones; the fine head of Hera survives.

To the south was the Pelopion, a small wooded mound with an altar to Pelops,

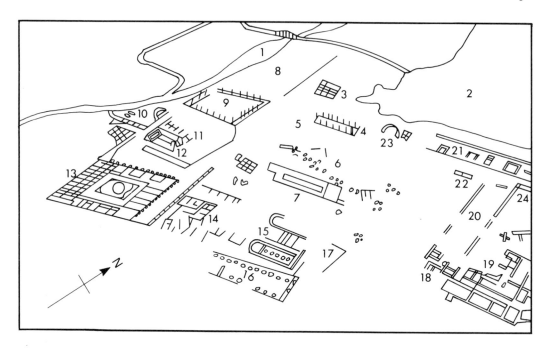

1 Kladeos river	9 Palaestra	17 Trapezium court
2 Kronion hill	10 Baths	18 Hellanodikeion
3 Prytaneion	11 Theokoleon? (priests'	19 Nero's house
4 Temple of Hera	residence)	20 Echo Hall
5 Site of Philippeion (under	12 Phidias' workshop	21 Treasuries terrace
trees)	13 Leonidaion	22 Metroön
6 Pelopion	14 South baths	23 Exedra of Herodes Atticus
7 Temple of Zeus	15 Bouleuterion	24 Entrance to stadium
8 Gymnasium	16 South Stoa	

enclosed in a wall with five sides and a Doric Propylon at the southwest end added later. Nearby, not identifiable now with certainty, was the altar of Zeus, the heart of the sanctuary, where sacrifice was offered daily. The Metroön farther east honoured Rhea (mother of Zeus) and Cybele.

The great temple of Zeus was one of the largest in all Greece. It was built of porous shelly limestone in need of marble stucco surfacing and is Classical Doric in design, 6 × 13 columns, with a great access ramp on the east and famous sculpture (largely preserved) in the pediments and on the metopes. Built between 470 and 456 BC, it was demolished by a great earthquake in the early sixth century AD. The stylobate measures 200 Olympic ft, the cella 94 × 43½ ft. There were interior columns on two levels, and an upper gallery from which people could admire close up the colossal Zeus by Phidias, seven times life size. This statue was counted one of the Seven Wonders of the World. Flesh parts were of ivory, the rest plated with gold. Even though seated on a throne, the god towered 40 ft above the pedestal. He held a Victory in his right hand, in his left a sceptre on which an eagle perched. Precious stones were embedded in his robe, beard and hair, and in the ebony and ivory throne. The ancients greatly admired its grandeur and majesty. Phidias' workshop, of the same size as the temple cella, has been identified to the west, overlaid by later structures.

Farther south, just beyond the walls of the Altis (as the core sanctuary area was called) was the Bouleuterion, headquarters of the Olympic Senate administration, where contestants took the oath of fair play. It had two wings, each ending at the west end in an apse divided into two rooms (special offices ?), with a row of columns down the centre and an Ionic portico across the whole front (a third-century BC addition). An enclosed square courtyard between the wings was open to the sky. To the south was a stoa, and to the east the Hellanodikeion, official residence of the festival presidents. Adjacent is a huge house built for Nero's flamboyant visit in AD 69 when he sang for the bemused throng and won seven prizes.

The eastern edge of the Altis was framed by the Echo Hall, built in the fifth century BC when the stadium was moved farther east, and repaired in the days of Alexander the Great. The northern border was a terrace with a dozen treasuries, small temple-like display shrines erected by various cities, many of them colonies abroad. At the western end Herodes Atticus contributed an exedra, a semicircular public bench which had in front a welcome source of fresh water piped in from a spring. The Prytaneion nearby was the magistrates' residence and banquet hall for Olympic victors. The gymnasium was for training in races, the palaestra for wrestling. The huge Leonidaion square with 138 surrounding Ionic columns and a peristyle central court (with a garden inside in Roman times) was a hotel for honoured guests and visiting officials.

Olimbos/Olympus

According to Homer and Hesiod, Mt Olympus was a delightful abode of the gods, without snow or rain, where the immortals enjoyed an endless banquet of ambrosia and nectar among the pleasant grass and streams and looked down on human doings with mixed amusement and dismay. From here Zeus hurled his thunderbolts to punish evildoers or the blasphemous – when not pursuing mortal maidens or wrangling with Hera or off to a banquet 'among the blameless Ethiopians'. From these heights Apollo, Artemis, Aphrodite, Ares and the other Olympians witnessed or participated in the Trojan War and other affairs of men. In Greek mythology, Olympus was sacred and inaccessible. When Zeus nodded the whole mountain shook.

The reality is properly awesome and majestic but less glamorous. Olympus is the highest mountain in Greece, towering 9570 ft above the sea which lies nearby to the east. It is a long range with greatly diversified aspects – sometimes smooth and rolling, elsewhere rugged, abrupt, and precipitous. On the lower slopes oak and beech and plane trees grow abundantly; higher up only pine. The final heights are cold and barren, holding snow in crevices all year round. To the south is Lower Olympus and beyond that Ossa and Pelion, which the impious Giants once sought to heap together to storm Olympus. On the west the slopes are gentler, reaching down towards Achilles' homeland, Phthia. To the north is Pieria, abode of the Muses. The mountain has an aura of mystery and legend, and is usually shrouded in cloud, even when the rest of the sky is clear, for 'Zeus the cloud-gatherer' is a poetic visualization of a continuing climatic fact. It is very rare that the summit is entirely clear, as in one of these photos.

The most impressive facet of Olympus is on the east towards the adjacent sea. There the vast and fearsome Mavrolonghos Gorge falls endlessly downward from the summit in a wild jumble of rough slopes past Litochoron village to the coastal plain. Above it the quadruple peak stands out afar: Skolion, Skala, Mytika, and Stephani the 'Throne of Zeus' – a great curving hollow sweep of limestone fit to enthrone in majestic grandeur and sublime isolation the Father of gods and men.

1 Throne of Zeus
  (Stephani)
2 Mytika
3 Skala
4 Skolion
5 Toumba
6 Lower Olympus

N

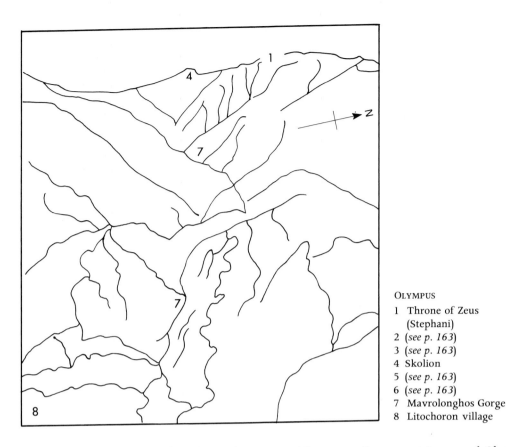

Climbing to the summit has always been a rare and risky event, though often accomplished in the present century. There are now alpine shelters and organized ski areas in the upper regions, below the sheer ultimate peaks where the air is clear, chilly: not really meant for men.

There are other mountains named Olympus elsewhere in Greece and in Asia Minor. But when the word is mentioned it is this one which leaps to mind, as much from its own world-renowned grandeur as from Homer's immortal account.

Olinthos/Olynthos

A few years after its destruction, Demosthenes said of Olynthos that later generations would scarcely believe a city had been on the site. Nevertheless the report on the American excavations between 1928 and 1934 fills 14 large volumes. Much of the site was left unexcavated even so, though exploratory soundings provided evidence for estimating what was there. The exposed ruins are now partly covered over again and their pattern is less clear – though it is notably more intelligible from the air.

There was a Neolithic settlement from c. 2500 BC at the southern tip of the south hill. This hill was resettled c. 800 BC, but farther to the north, by a Macedonian tribe. A civic centre developed, with an early fifth-century BC Bouleuterion, a fountain-house, etc. Xerxes forced the city to provide him with men and ships when passing through in 480 BC to attack Athens, and on their way back from humiliation at Salamis the Persians burned the town and turned its territory over to others. Perdikkas of Macedon re-established Olynthos in 432

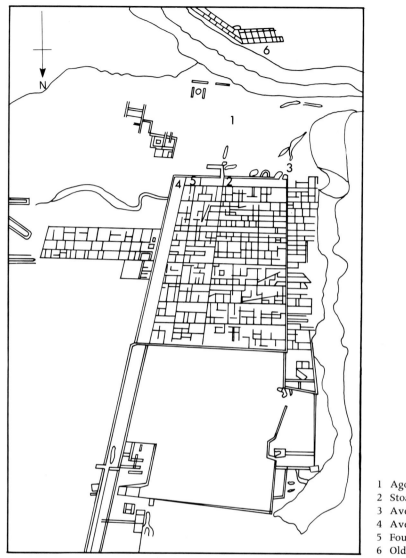

1 Agora
2 Stoa
3 Avenue A
4 Avenue B
5 Fountain-house
6 Old civic centre

BC and brought in many thousands from other cities, so that it became the most important town in the Chalcidian peninsula, growing to a population of perhaps 30,000. The northern hill was developed with an orderly grid of streets forming blocks of housing uniformly 300 × 120 ft (a ratio of 5:2), the broadest avenues running north-south. Olynthos is a rare example of an extensive residential district surviving from Classical times and a valuable evidence of ancient town-planning.

Most of the houses had three or more rooms opening onto a portico behind an airy court –

which was often surrounded by columns as in the later houses on Delos. Some evidently had a second storey. Walls of mud-brick (effective insulation against heat, cold, and noise) were plastered and painted; many of the floors were surfaced with decorative mosaics made of pebbles – among the earliest specimens of this art yet found in Greece.

The commercial district was kept separate from the residential at the southwest corner of the hill, opposite the old civic centre whose function it took over. This new agora had a simple stoa along its southern end, and con-

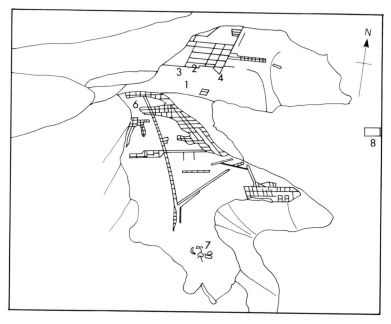

1 Agora
2 Stoa
3 Avenue A
4 Avenue B
5 (see p. 166)
6 Old civic centre
7 Neolithic site
8 Villa of Good Fortune

tained a fountain-house with a façade like a small Doric temple, its water piped in from a spring nearly ten miles distant. Terracotta conduits for water have been found in tunnels under some of the streets.

Beyond the twin hills to the east several elaborate villas have been excavated (many of them since reburied). The South Villa, the Villa of the Bronzes, and the Villa of Good Fortune – named after invocations in its mosaics – are the most notable. The last of these may have been an inn or club. Its wine store has been found, and three fine pebble mosaics,

which have survived, were laid on its floors, one depicting Dionysos in a chariot, another Thetis with the armour of Achilles, and two Pans leaning on a large wine-jar.

Though Philip II of Macedon swore unending friendship to Olynthos (the treaty text has been found), he ruthlessly demolished the city eight years later, in 348 BC, and it disappeared from history. Its desolate ruins have been especially instructive for the dating of styles of art and architecture in the late Classical period immediately preceding the new patterns of the Hellenistic age.

Pella/**Pella**

Pella, Alexander the Great's birthplace, was not definitely located until recently. Though references in Herodotus, Thucydides, Xenophon, and Livy gave a general clue, excavations in the area in 1914–15 had little success. In 1957 however new evidence led to the site and Greek archaeologists have since uncovered part of the city where tiles stamped PELLA have been found as well as some splendid floor mosaics. The prehistoric settlement Phakos is on a hill to the south, which in ancient times was an island in the surrounding swampy lake. This site continued in use through Roman times, but c. 410 BC king Archelaos of Macedonia moved his capital from Aigai (modern Edessa) to twin hills on dry land north of Phakos – the 'rocky land' implied by the new name. He built a splendid palace there which has not yet been discovered – it was perhaps located on the western acropolis, where a complex Hellenistic building has been partly disclosed in Area III and a stoa-like structure nearby in Area II. This palace had famous paintings by Zeuxis and to it came other great lights like the poets Agathon and Euripides (whose *Bacchae* was first staged in Pella's theatre, as yet unlocated), and later Aristotle to tutor the young Alexander, born here in 356 BC. Pella grew into the largest city in Macedonia, and was connected to the sea 14 miles away by a navigable canal. It was seized and partly destroyed by Aemilius Paullus after the Roman triumph at Pydna in 168 BC, and faded in importance while Thessalonike became pre-eminent in Macedonia.

The current excavations are only partial but have produced notable art finds and clarified some of the city's plan. It is evident from the alignment of streets, running north-south towards Phakos and the acropolis or at right angles to these, that a grid pattern was followed. There is reason to suspect that the agora was near Area VI, where a peculiar circular structure with three adjacent round tholoi with mosaic floors may have been a cult shrine or Heroön. The houses in Areas I, IV, and V probably are near the centre of town. The temple of Athena Alkidemos has not yet been found; it is likely to be on the western acropolis but possibly on the other acropolis to the east under the modern village.

The most fully excavated sector, Area I near the modern road from Edessa to Thessalonike, contains some splendid large houses or public buildings – House I for instance has yielded no items of domestic usage, its great court and Ionic peristyle and richly decorated outer rooms perhaps serving civic purposes. There and in House 5 striking floor mosaics were discovered; some still remain in place, others are in the new museum. These mosaics are early examples from the late fourth and early third centuries BC, later than those found at Sicyon and Olynthos but before the marble-cube mosaics on Delos. They are made in natural pebbles of white, black, and red colour, with lead or clay mullions outlining details for clarity. In House 1, besides scenes of centaurs, a griffin attacking a stag, Dionysos

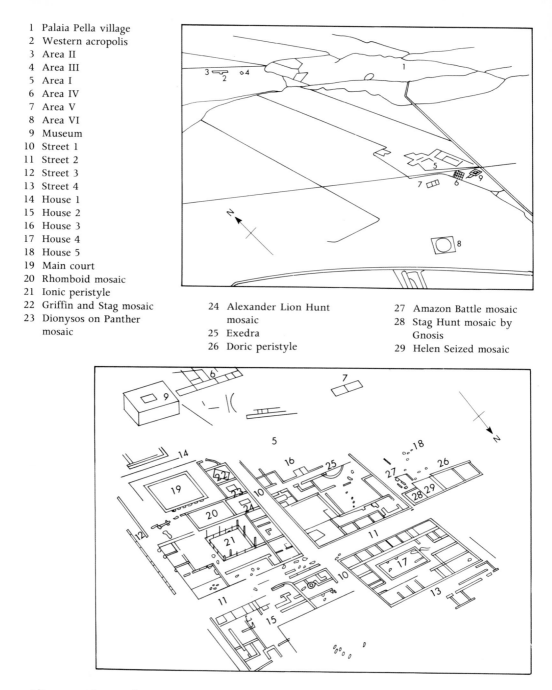

riding a panther, and geometric patterns, there was a vivid Lion Hunt – which probably represents Alexander (wearing a special princely cap) saved by Krateros at a recorded hunt near Soussa. House 5 preserved fine mosaics of an Amazons battle, Helen and Deianeira being carried off by Theseus and Phorbas, and a Stag Hunt signed by the artist Gnosis. Street drains are also preserved, and clay tubes with filter basins for drinking-water distribution throughout the residential area.

1 Temenos of Hera Limenaia sanctuary
2 Temple of Hera Limenaia
3 Sacred Pool
4 Classical cistern and drain
5 Hellenistic cistern
6 Hellenistic house/ritual dining hall
7 Stoa
8 Stairway
9 Geometric temple of Hera Akraia
10 Triglyph altar
11 Archaic temple of Hera Akraia
12 Agora/west court
13 Harbour
14 West bay
15 Hellenistic house
16 Modern lighthouse

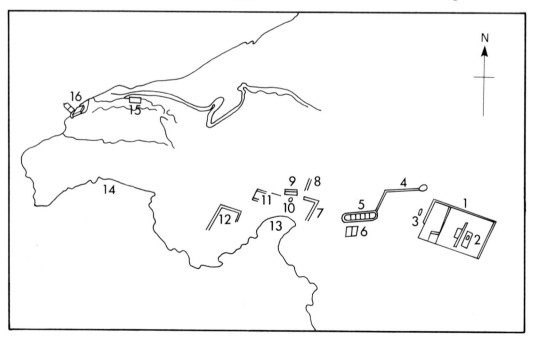

Perahora/**Perachora**

Across the Gulf from Corinth 'the distant site' (*Pera-chora*, or *Peraia*) of an oracular sanctuary of Hera has a memorable location at the tip of a long promontory pointing westward down the Gulf of Corinth and providing from its heights, a little to the east of the Heraion, a magnificent view past Helicon and Parnassus to Naupactus and into the Peloponnesus as far as Mt Kyllene in Arcadia. In Mycenaean times the area was under the control of Megara, but later Corinth took it over. In the Geometric period of the ninth and eighth centuries BC a popular cult of Hera flourished here, as votive finds from many cities indicate, complementing and rivalling the great Heraion near Argos. The Spartan king Agesilaos captured the sanctuary in 390 BC, the historian Xenophon being among his officers and describing the quick campaign. The area was abandoned in early Roman times and was brought to light by British excavations in 1930–33.

To the east of the sanctuary was a fortified acropolis at the loftiest point of the promontory; the tip where the modern lighthouse stands also shows remains of walls. The rather open bay below must have supplemented the very limited harbour facilities provided by the pretty but tiny cove directly adjacent to the lower temple.

Around this miniature harbour, on levelled areas at the foot of the steep cliffs, were most of the sanctuary buildings. Most important was the temple of Hera Akraia. It is a long structure, of which little remains except at the west end, and seems to have been built around 530 BC, replacing a much older temple of apsidal plan to the east which goes back to Geometric times. This may date from 850 BC and was destroyed *c.* 710 BC. In front of its east end in later times was an altar decorated with triglyphs and metopes like a Doric frieze at ground level. There was an Ionic column on each side, and two others farther to the north where stairs led up to the higher land. This unusual altar seems to date from *c.* 500 BC. Perhaps the Ionic columns supported a canopy above the altar. To the east an inverted L-shaped building is a late Classical stoa from *c.* 320, balancing the temple area and probably taking over the functions of the older agora across the cove which was destroyed in the middle of the fourth century BC. This stoa had two storeys, the lower one Doric, the upper Ionic – an unusually early example of such an arrangement. There were ten columns in each of these façades. The floor was of pebbles embedded in cement. The 'agora' on the west side of the harbour is pentagonal in shape, a little less than 80 ft across, enclosed (except for part of the eastern section) by a wall of upright stone slabs on a foundation of rectangular blocks. It had a colonnaded porch on the south and west sides, and a bench along the wall at the south-south-east corner. Dating from the late sixth century BC, with revisions into the mid-fourth, it may have been a kind of stoa with an open market in the centre. In the second century AD a long Roman house with five rooms in a row was built diagonally across its ruins.

To the east is a fine Hellenistic cistern of long oval shape with interior supports for the roof. The building just south of it may be a late house, or perhaps a ritual dining hall.

The temenos of Hera Limenaia is at the eastern end of the site on a higher level. Its rectangular temple, with a sacrificial pit near the centre, is dated to the eighth century BC. The oracle mentioned by Strabo may have been located at the Sacred Pool nearby, as phiale cups found in it would suggest.

Pilos/**Pylos**

Although little can now be seen from the air of the excavated palace at Epano Englianos because of the protective roofing over the ruins, the perspective is nevertheless illuminating for the geographical and scenic setting and confirms the ancients' shrewdness in choosing the site. It is safely inland from sea-raids but close enough to the sea for commerce and travel, presumably using as a port the charming sandy cove Bouphras or Voidokilia a few miles

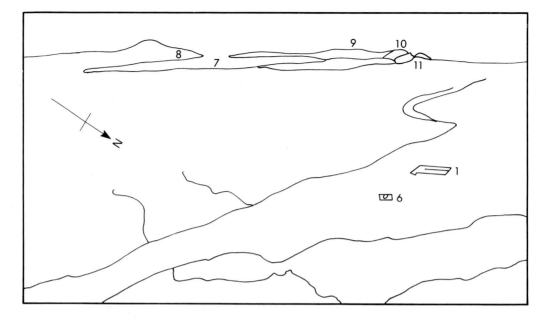

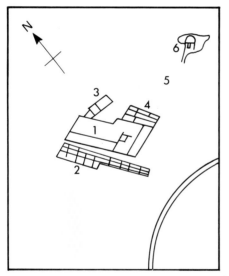

1 Main palace
2 Earlier palace
3 Wine storage magazines
4 Workshops/armoury
5 Site of wall and gate
6 Tholos tomb
7 Navarino bay
8 Modern Pylos
9 Sphacteria island
10 Classical Pylos
11 Bouphras/Voidokilia cove

to the southwest and just north of Sphacteria. The view across the long valley and the lowlands to the great bay and the glistening blue sea is particularly fine, worthy of a king.

Archaeological evidence indicates that the site was already occupied by the early second millennium BC in the Middle Bronze Age, and fortified in the sixteenth century (part of a wall and gate survive northeast of the palace). Early in the thirteenth century BC these walls and the houses within were demolished and the hill-top levelled and a palace built on it. This probably reflects the tradition of Neleus taking control on arrival from Iolkos, south of Mt Olympus. His son Nestor, the garrulous old man in the *Iliad* who returned from the Trojan War to rule on in Pylos many more years 'like an immortal', seems to have built a new palace just to the east which is comparable in size and wealth with Agamemnon's at Mycenae, and similar in plan to that at Tiryns. This was destroyed by fire *c.* 1190 BC, probably in a raid by the usurping Dorians. Blegen discovered the buried ruins in 1939 and after the war excavated them from 1952–65. It is the best preserved of all Mycenaean palaces and certainly the most instructive.

The older palace to the southwest, in more ruinous condition and not under the new metal roof, had a megaron hall facing onto a square

room with three columns, and a complex of other rooms to the west, presumably both residential and storage quarters. Its kitchen has been identified. Fresco fragments showing a scene of battle probably depict Neleus' conquest of the fortified settlement.

The later main palace is considerably more extensive and sophisticated. Its heart is a great megaron room with a raised circular hearth at the centre, its fire providing light, warmth, and cooking facilities. Four wooden pillars, each with 32 flutes (as their marks in the floor stucco show) supported a roof over the megaron except for an opening above the hearth. There were balconies around on an upper level and bedrooms off them. Remains of stairs indicate a second storey over much of the palace, with the ground-floor rooms lofty – ceilings 10 or 11 ft high. At the northeast edge of the megaron are depressions where the royal throne stood with a libation pit next to it. There is a vestibule at the megaron's only entrance on the southeast and beyond that a porch with two columns and an open-air courtyard. This corresponds closely to Homer's description of the palace of Odysseus on Ithaca. Fine long corridors on each side of this complex of central rooms led to storerooms at the sides and back, in which thousands of clay drinking cups were found and many huge storage jars (*pithoi*) for wine and oil. An archives office near the front entrance yielded great numbers of clay tablets inscribed in the Linear B, pre-Homeric Greek script. A second smaller megaron with adjacent rooms was probably the queen's quarters. The king's rooms nearby include a bath-tub which is still in place. Several tholos tombs have been found in the vicinity.

Pireefs/**Piraeus**

Until the fifth century BC, Athens used Phaleron beach for its harbour, as it was both close by and extensive, but when Themistocles developed a major Athenian fleet to oppose the Persian threat he made its base Piraeus and in 493 BC began an ambitious project of fortifications around most of the area, with connecting Long Walls all the way to Athens, some five miles away to the northeast. Pericles completed the undertaking and by 431 BC the system included a wall from Athens' circuit to the eastern edge of Phaleron Bay and two parallel courses to the Piraeus circuit running about 600 ft apart, with a military road between them. These were dismantled at Sparta's insistence on Athens' defeat in the Peloponnesian War but were rebuilt with some changes in the middle of the fourth century BC, mainly after Conon had destroyed Sparta's naval ambitions off Knidos in 394 BC. The Macedonian successors of Alexander kept a garrison at Piraeus to control Athens, but Sulla demolished the town in 86 BC and it remained unimportant until recent times. It is now a major city and the chief port of Greece, with most of its ancient remains engulfed or long since gone.

Parts of the old walls can be seen here and there, especially along the south and west edges of Akte hill, and part of the Asty Gate, with its round and squared towers, is visible near the terminus of the electric railway to Athens – whose tracks follow the course of the southern Long Wall. The modern street pattern corresponds closely to the ancient one which was designed for Pericles by the famous town-planning expert Hippodamos of Miletus, who fitted a grid of streets to the terrain of Akte and Munychia hills and the three ports, with a large agora east of Zea. A fifth-century theatre to the east of the agora, mentioned by Thucydides, has been traced but is now covered over. A smaller theatre northwest of Zea, next to the present museum, is Hellenistic from the second century BC, with 13 wedges of seats in the lower section and 26 above the *diazoma*; these upper ones were not cut into the hillside but were supported on radial sub-structures. Its stage front had 26 columns across the proscenium, five of these on each parascenium wing. Masons' marks in alphabetical sequence on the lower bank of seats probably served as guides to assigned locations in the upper rows.

The main harbour, as today, was Kantharos, with Eetioneia Point and the north shore of Akte reserved for the navy, commercial shipping being centred on the south and east

1 Akte peninsula
2 Kantharos harbour
3 Eetionia Point

4 Site of Aphrodision
5 Inner harbour
   (*Kophos Limen*)
6 Long Stoa

7 Market area
8 Asty Gate
9 Site of Dionysion
10 Hippodamos' agora
11 Theatre in Zea
12 Zea harbour
13 Arsenal
14 Phreattys?
15 Site of Asclepieion
16 Serangeion?
17 Stalida islet
18 Munychia harbour
19 Munychia hill and
   castle
20 Site of theatre in
   Munychia
21 Site of temple of
   Artemis Munychia

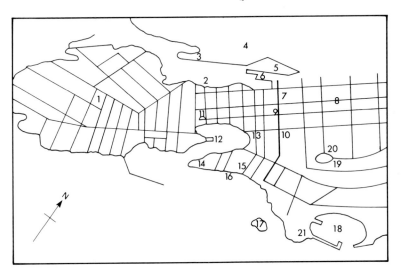

sectors, with five stoas along the dock area and a market nearby. There was a temple to the north in honour of Aphrodite Euploia, patron of fair voyages, and somewhere nearby one to Zeus Soter and Athena Soteira ('Saviours'), reflecting Greek mistrust of the turbulent sea. The harbour entrance on the west was partly closed by two moles, with towers or lighthouses at their tips. Ship-building yards are recorded in Kantharos, and an arsenal for fitting out warships along the edge of Zea; it

has disappeared but the plans by the ancient architect, Philon, survive.

There was room for 196 triremes in Zea, the sheds (still partly traceable) being arranged like the spokes of a great wheel. Another 82 triremes could be berthed in Munychia harbour. The Serangeion near Zea had baths cut out of the rock. Nearby was the Phreattys, the seat of the Criminal Court. The opening of Plato's *Republic* takes place in Munychia, in view of Stalida islet.

Platee/**Plataea**

Plataea was a brave little town in the southeast corner of Boeotia, remembered today not for its own tragic history but for the glorious victory nearby of combined Greek forces over the fearsome Persian army in 479 BC, bringing to a humiliating failure Xerxes' flamboyant invasion of Greece, after his naval disaster at Salamis some months before.

The Persians had sacked Plataea the previous year and burned the Acropolis of Athens. They then took up a position along the Asopus river, facing the pass through Mt Kithairon that separates Boeotia from Attica, in a great plain ideally suited to cavalry manoeuvres. With rare inter-city unity a combined Greek force, dominated by Athenian and Spartan contingents, moved in from Eleusis. Though outnumbered at least three to one and with no cavalry, they managed by daring and initiative to repulse a series of probing attacks, kill the Persian cavalry commander and, in a confused larger engagement, slay the Persian general Mardonius and devastate his army and camp. This victory effectively ended the Persian Wars and launched Greece on an era of splendid cultural flowering and new national pride. A famous monument to the victory was erected at Delphi near the Temple: intertwined bronze serpents holding a cauldron aloft. There was also commemoration every four years for centuries afterwards in the Eleutheria festival at Plataea.

The city itself was in constant jeopardy from Thebes. As early as 519 BC Athens undertook its protection. At Marathon in 490, Plataea sent its whole army, 1000 men, who fought valiantly and earned their own burial mound, recently

claimed found some distance from the greater Athenian *Soros*. In 480 BC, Plataea joined Athens' fleet to resist the second Persian invasion, in which its own area had been pillaged. With Athens' help it fought off a Theban attack in 431, but after a two-year siege fell to the Peloponnesians in 427 BC and was destroyed and most of its citizens slaughtered. Those who survived were granted Athenian civic rights until the town was restored by Sparta in 386 BC – only to be destroyed once more by Thebes fourteen years later. The Macedonians rebuilt it again and the Romans and Byzantines continued to maintain it, on a smaller scale. Its ruins today are meagre and often confused; some structures excavated years ago are hardly visible now. American excavations in 1890–91 and Skias' in 1899 uncovered long stretches of walls and parts of an Archaic temple and fragments of what may have been the Macedonian hostel, used as an agora in Roman times.

The air view shows the core of the ancient city, an enclosed acropolis on a low oval mound. This is probably where the early town was and where it shrank back to in its final period. The present walls surrounding the area are clearly a late reworking from earlier material – a Roman/Byzantine enclosure that seems to follow the Classical circuit. Larger rings swept farther south and east in a rough triangular pattern to enclose a larger area for the Spartan and Macedonian restorations of the city.

The temple and agora are located to the south of the inner acropolis circuit. The site of the battle in 479 BC is at some distance to the northeast on the plain near the Asopus river.

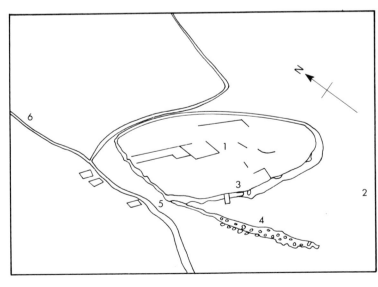

1 Acropolis
2 Agora area (temple, hostel, etc.)
3 Inner circuit of walls
4 Middle circuit of walls
5 Site of Megale Brysis spring
6 Road to Thebes

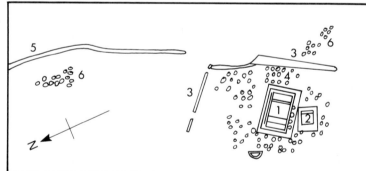

1 Temple of Nemesis
2 Temple of Themis
3 Terrace wall
4 Altar
5 Road to the citadel
6 Ruins of monumental
   tombs

Ramnous/**Rhamnous**

Suitably named after the spiny thorn-shrub that still guards its lonely ruins, Rhamnous was an important fortified outpost of Athens in the fifth century BC, its walls and citadel rebuilt *c.* 412 (when Sunium too was fortified) to guard the route from Euboea and the coastal road to Oropos. The orator Antiphon was born here *c.* 480, among whose students of rhetoric was Thucydides. Study of the ruins began in 1817.

From at least the sixth century BC there was a special cult at Rhamnous of the goddess of retribution, Nemesis, in association with Themis, the personification of law and right custom. Their sanctuary is in a valley south of the acropolis on an artificially constructed platform of large marble blocks along the ancient road to the citadel. A small Archaic Doric temple of the late sixth century BC was presumably dedicated to Themis, whose statue by Chairestratos was found there (now in the Athens Museum) along with two others, and a pair of marble thrones inscribed to Themis and to Nemesis. Only 21 ft across and 35 ft long, it had no surrounding colonnade but two Doric columns between the front porch wings. Its cella walls were of polygonal construction, a rarity in temples. The material used is a local grey limestone.

Almost touching this older temple was another later and much larger one in honour of Nemesis. It seems to have been started in 436 BC but never wholly finished because of the Peloponnesian War – there are no pediment sculptures, for instance, and the fluting of the columns is uncompleted. The architect must have been the same one who also built the contemporary temples of Hephaistos and of Ares at Athens, and of Poseidon at Sunium, as these all share common characteristics, including Ionic touches following the example of the Parthenon. It had only 12 columns along the sides (with six across the front and back), and a porch at each end. The lowest of the three steps below the peristyle was in blue-grey marble to stand out more noticeably. Protective bosses on the stylobate blocks were not smoothed off – perhaps deliberately left on as an interesting variant and shadow-source.

There was a sculptured Ionic frieze above each porch, as on the Hephaisteion at Athens; only the façade metopes were carved. Griffins were used as decorative figures on the roof corners. Inside stood a famous statue of Nemesis, fragments of which have been recovered. Pausanias ascribed it to Phidias (although it was probably by his best pupil, Agorakritos), and said that fittingly enough it was carved from the very block of marble brought by the presumptuous Persians for an expected trophy, on their disastrous invasion of Greece in 490 BC. According to Pausanias' admiring description the goddess wore a crown decorated with deer and small Victories; in her left hand she held an apple bough, and in her right a bowl with Ethiopians engraved on its outer surface.

Ruins of monumental marble tombs line the road northward to the acropolis. A single great gate with four flanking towers gave access through the outer circuit of walls. An inner oval at the summit constituted a fortified citadel from earlier times. Within the walls are meagre remains of a small theatre, which had a square orchestra and no stone cavea seats but five marble thrones of honour with inscriptions to Dionysos, who also had a sanctuary on the heights. Another shrine was dedicated to two physicians, Aristomachos and Amphiaraos. There may have been a Bouleuterion, stoa, and gymnasium too, but the ruins are ambiguous. The town was within the fort. There was no harbour, but a fine open beach.

Rodhos/Rhodes City

At the northeastern tip of the island, Rhodes city was created in 408 BC by the three old towns of Mycenaean days, Lindos, Kameiros, and Ialyssos, to be a new capital. Designed by the famous town-planner, Hippodamos of Miletus, in an efficient grid pattern, it extended from the acropolis northward to the Great Port and grew to house some 80,000 inhabitants. Besides being a major commercial centre and chief naval power of the Aegean it was a famous school of art and rhetoric and contained many thousand statues. Cato, Cicero, Lucretius, Caesar, and the poet Apollonius practised oratory here in the tradition started by Aes-

chines the rival of Demosthenes. Alexander's court sculptor Lysippus made a splendid four-horse chariot of the Sun for the sanctuary of Helios, and Bryaxis, Heliodoros, Philiskos, and the sculptors of the renowned Laocoön group enlarged Rhodes' artistic fame, as did the great painter Protogenes. Here stood the Colossus, one of the Seven Wonders of the World. It was cast in bronze by Chares of Lindos, a follower of Lysippus, between 304 and 292 BC, the funds deriving from the sale of the siege machinery left behind by Demetrius Poliorcetes in admiration of the city's valiant resistance to his attack. The Sun-god towered some 150 ft

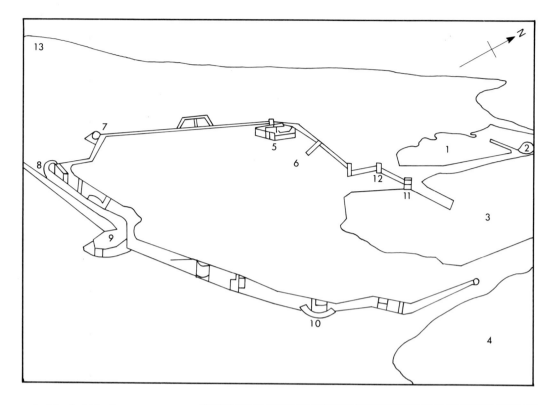

13

7

5

6

12

11

1

2

8

9

3

10

4

1 Mandraki harbour
2 St Nicholas fort
3 Great Port
4 Akandia Bay
5 Palace of the Grand
   Masters
6 Collachium (residence of
   the Knights)
7 Spanish Tower
8 St Mary Tower
9 Koskinou Gate
10 Italian Tower
11 Temple of Aphrodite
12 Sanctuary of Dionysos
13 Acropolis hill (Mt
   Smith)
14 Stadium

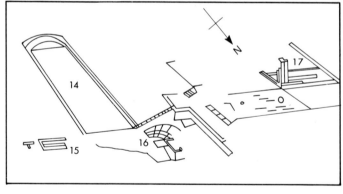

14

15

16

17

15 Palaestra/gymnasium
    edge

16 Odeion/auditorium
17 Temple of Apollo

above the harbour edge (including the 30-ft pedestal), crowned with golden rays and holding his right hand to his brow, perhaps peering into the sunrise. It lay in ruins for eight centuries after being toppled by an earthquake *c.* 225 BC, until the pieces were carried off to Syria in AD 654 on 900 camels to be melted down and sold. It did not straddle the harbour (much too wide), nor did it stand where the St Nicholas fort is – this is too small an area for the huge support- and access-mound needed in its construction.

In the lower town near the harbour was a Doric temple of Aphrodite of the third or second century BC, some of whose poros limestone blocks have been discovered. Nearby

was a Dionysos sanctuary with fine porticoes and famous paintings. A Hellenistic stoa mentioned in ancient sources may have been near the present Koskinou Gate. The theatre was probably near the harbour, and a shrine of Artemis Aristoboule is also mentioned.

The upper town was spread over the acropolis hill; some of its streets and houses have been located, and on the edges of the district are tombs cut into the rock and others built above ground for the leading families.

The stadium, 600 Rhodian feet long (660 ft), is on the lower level of the hill. It was built after the great earthquake of the late third century BC. Six rows of its seats are preserved at the curved end and restored along the side. Northeast of it lay the large rectangular gymnasium and palaestra area, some of whose bordering stoa foundations are visible. Adjacent

to them on the west is a small theatre-like structure built within a square framework and all of marble. It was probably an auditorium for philosophy and rhetoric lectures, holding about 800 people. On the terrace above is the third-century Doric temple of Apollo Pythius, built of poros stone. Farther north at the summit are the meagre remains of another temple dedicated to Zeus Polieus and Athena Polias, with a fine view of the sea.

Rhodes underwent many political reversals, alternately siding with Athens and revolting from the alliance; it was subdued by Carians, Macedonians, and Romans (Cassius plundered it before his disaster at Philippi in 41 BC). The Saracens looted it, and in 1309 the Knights Hospitallers of St John subdued it, later building the vast fortress and fine Gothic palace that are still so impressive today.

Salamis/**Salamis**

As much ink has been spilled over the battle of Salamis as blood was shed in the original engagement. Scholars have debated with vast detail and ingenious arguments the identification of topographical sites mentioned in the ancient sources, primarily Herodotus, Aeschylus, and Strabo. The ancient names have not always continued, and it is likely that the terrain is not entirely the same today, due to changes in sea-level and in the coastline on a small scale. Aeschylus' poetic and highly dramatic account is not safe geography. Herodotus is much more specific and detailed but raises problems, especially what he means by Psyttaleia and Kynosoura. The latter most naturally fits the long 'dog-tail' peninsula projecting eastward from the ancient city site. All data and factors considered, Psyttaleia is most likely modern Lipsokoutali island east of the promontory, though some argue for St George's island inside the strait.

Herodotus tells how the Athenians withdrew to Salamis and the 'wooden walls' of their new fleet when the Persians forced their way through Thermopylae to Athens and burned the Acropolis. (Women and children were sent off to Troezen on the mainland.) The Persian fleet of some 400 ships blocked off the eastern

mouth of the strait between Perama and the promontory, and its Egyptian squadron sealed the western exit near Megara's port of Nisaea. The Greeks, boxed in, boldly took the initiative and attacked at dawn. Having great manoeuverability, they exploited a ramming strategy and sank many Persian vessels, slaying the survivors in the water and on the island of Psyttaleia, which they captured. Xerxes saw the debacle with dismay from a lookout on Mt Aigaleos, probably the hill of Perama near the straits. His scheme of conquering Greece was shattered at Salamis and a few months later he suffered further humiliation in the defeat of his army at Plataea. Aeschylus fought at Salamis, as he had ten years earlier at Marathon, and graphically portrays the enemy's consternation in his *Persians*, one of the few Greek tragedies based on an historical event. The victors set up trophies on Psyttaleia and on the cape near the ancient city.

The island's history goes back at least to Mycenaean times, when it had commercial and political ties with nearby Aegina and distant Cyprus – where there was another town called Salamis. Homer speaks of a contingent from Salamis in the Trojan War, led by Ajax, son of Telamon. Both Megara and Aegina

1 Kynosoura?
2 Atalante island? (Talantonisi)
3 Salamis town: the ancient site
4 St George's island
5 Site of Boudoron fortress
6 Megara spit (Nisaea)
7 Perama
7a Xerxes' tent
8 Mt Aigaleos
9 (see p. 186)
10 Cape of Trophies
11 Battle strait

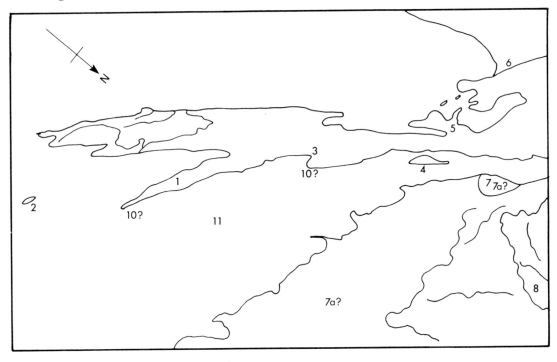

1 Kynosoura?
2 Atalante island? (Talantonisi)
3 Salamis town: the ancient site
4 St George's island
5 (see p. 185)

6 (see p. 185)
7 Perma
7a Xerxes' tent
8 Mt Aigaleos
9 Psyttaleia? (Lipsokoutali island)

10 Cape of Trophies
11 Battle strait
12 Piraeus
13 Phaleron
14 Athens (behind smoke)

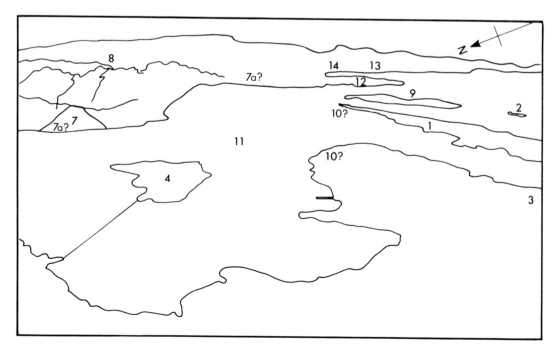

sought to control the island, but Athens took it over in 612 BC, on the urging of Solon, for defence purposes. Cassander of Macedon seized it in the late fourth century but Athens regained it in 229 BC. The original capital was on the south, facing Aegina, but during Athenian domination was at the head of the bay west of the battle strait, at modern Ambelaki. The acropolis can still be identified but only a few ruins have survived – most of them are underwater at the bay's edge. On the west side of the island, near Megara's projecting port of Nisaea, remains of the Athenian fortress Boudoron that once guarded the strait have recently been recognized. The island's coastline is bafflingly complex.

Samos/Samos: The City

In the Archaic period, Samos was a prosperous and powerful city, especially under the rule of Polykrates who seized power about 532 BC until he was cruelly slain by the Persians ten years later. His flair, wealth, and ambition attracted famous poets and artists to his court, among them Anacreon and Ibycus. He built up a naval power that dominated most of the Aegean, in alliance with Amasis of Egypt, and the sea-mole which he constructed to improve the harbour was an ancient marvel, and still supports its modern counterpart. He commissioned Eupalinos, a skilled engineer from Megara, to cut a remarkable tunnel more than half a mile long through Mt Ampelos to serve as safe water-channel in case of siege. This undertaking, scarcely paralleled in Greek endeavour, took fifteen years to complete, with workmen boring from both ends to meet in the middle; it is still an awesome experience to walk inside it. He also rebuilt the Heraion temple on a scale that moved Herodotus to wonder. After him Samos helped the Ionian Revolt but later joined the Persians at Salamis, then turned against the remainder of their fleet in the final Greek victory at Mykale, the promontory of Asia less than two miles from Samos. Athens subdued the island with difficulty, and it subsequently fell under the control of Macedonia, the Ptolemies of Egypt, and finally the Romans. It was plundered by Verres in 82 BC and later by pirates and by Marc Antony. German and Greek excavations have revealed only scattered remnants of the town (now Pithagorio/Tigani) – once the home of such brilliant figures as Pythagoras and Epicurus, Aesop, the versatile artist and inventor Theodoros, the great mathematician Conon, the astronomer Aristarchus who knew that the earth revolved around the sun, and the explorer Kolaios whose daring voyage to the Pillars of Hercules around 650 BC brought him both wealth and renown.

There was a Neolithic settlement here in the third millennium BC near the Castle of the Logothetes, and there are traditions of Pelasgian and Carian occupation. The late Mycenaean town was known as Astypalaia and Ionian colonists took the site over during the eleventh century BC.

Apart from the great harbour mole and Eupalinos' tunnel, the most impressive monument left of ancient Samos is the fortification wall of which there is an especially well-preserved long section on the acropolis, with neatly constructed towers set at close intervals. The theatre, in very poor state, is on the acropolis slope to the south of Spiliani monastery, half way to the eastern exit of Eupalinos' tunnel. The site of the ancient agora is covered by part of the modern town. Roman buildings have been found, especially more to the south. There is a cemetery area in that sector also and an important necropolis on the northeastern flank of the acropolis hill.

The great Heraion sanctuary is about five miles south of the city, along the coast beyond the airfield.

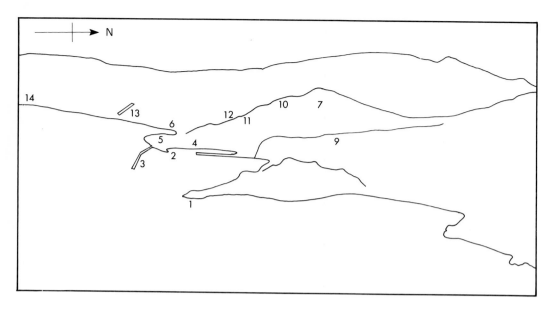

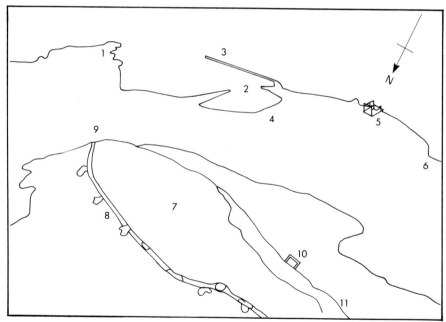

1	Cape Phonia	5	Castle of the Logothetes
2	Ancient harbour	6	Roman ruins
3	Ancient mole (under the	7	Acropolis
	modern one)	8	Fortification wall and towers
4	Site of agora	9	North necropolis

10	Spiliani monastery
11	Site of theatre
12	Eupalinos' tunnel entry
13	Airfield
14	Site of Heraion

Samos/Samos: The Heraion

According to legend, Hera was born and brought up along the torrent Imbrasos near the sea some five miles south of Samos city. This no doubt represents a Greek assimilation of a much earlier local divinity, seemingly a goddess of the lygos tree whose cult must go back to the pre-Greek inhabitants here before 2000 BC. The worship of Hera was brought from the Argolid by post-Mycenaean Ionian settlers around 1000 BC. A sanctuary grew up along the Imbrasos that came to rival the great Argive Heraion. The huge altar by the artist Rhoikos to the east of the Archaic temple is built over a smaller one of the Geometric period next to the stump of a lygos tree (a kind of willow) venerated from much earlier times.

West of this altar there was constructed in the early eighth century BC a long temple with a row of columns down the middle to support the roof. It was 100 ft long by 20 ft wide, and is therefore known as Hecatompedos I. Some time later a line of tree-like pillars was added surrounding the sacred structure, seven along the ends, 17 down the sides. This is the earliest proven example of the essential design of a true Greek temple with surrounding peristyle and ranks with the old temple at Thermon in importance for the history of Greek archi-

tectural development. It was destroyed in a disastrous flood c. 670 BC, but soon replaced by a similar structure with 6 × 18 columns in the peristyle and an extra row inside the east front colonnade. Instead of columns down the interior it had pillars along the inside of the walls to support the ceiling. This is Hecatompedos II, another pioneering step in the growth of Greek temple design. South of it at an angle was a wooden hall, some 230 ft in length, with simple wooden pillars supporting its flat roof. This is the first true stoa, a type of building later to become universal in Greek agoras and sanctuaries.

Around the middle of the sixth century BC the stoa and the adjacent temple were torn down and replaced in a major expansion and development of the sanctuary area. An enormous temple was built by the local artists Rhoikos and Theodoros which was the first fully realized Ionic prototype. It had a double row of columns on all sides and two parallel rows extending into the deep eastern porch and through the length of the cella to support the roof. The great altar to the east was 120 ft long by 54 ft wide, engulfing the Lygos shrine. A new stoa was built at an angle north of the temple.

1 Temple of Hera (built by Polykrates)	2 Site of North Stoa
	3 Houses

4 Temple A
5 Temple of Aphrodite
6 Temple of Hermes
7 Site of Apollo/Artemis temple
8 Geneleos statue group base
9 Sacred Way
10 Rhoikos' altar over lygos tree shrine
11 Roman temple over the end of Hecatompedos II
12 Roman temple
13 Baths
14 Monopteros altar/temple
15 Site of monument to the Ciceros
16 Ship base
17 Hermes/Aphrodite temple
18 Site of South Stoa

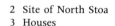

Within 25 years the great temple burned down. Polykrates had it replaced by an even larger one, also in limestone and re-using some column bases and other fragments from its predecessor, but he shifted it some 60 ft to the west. Its stylobate measured 368 ft × 181 ft. There were three rows of nine columns across the west end; three rows of eight across the east front, and 24 along the sides in a double row, all of them over 60 ft high. This vast temple was never fully finished. The Romans added steps across the east front, and built a further temple between them and the altar. Several other temples from Archaic to Roman times are scattered in the area and many statues, including one to Cicero and his brother Quintus. Apparently the ship of the daring explorer Kolaios was also on display.

Samothraki/**Samothrace**

A ruggedly beautiful island far north in the Aegean, Samothrace shared with the mainland to the north a pre-Greek Thracian culture and language, elements of which continued to survive long after Greek colonists settled here in the late eighth century BC. There were special connections with Troy, whose founder Dardanus was said to have come from Samothrace on a raft and whose brother Aetion established the sacred Mysteries on the island by a revelation from Zeus. The Samothracian religion was a peculiar amalgam of Phrygian Cybele; a local chthonic mother-goddess Axieros (assimilated to Demeter); a fertility god Kadmillos; attendant Kabeiroi demons (Dardanus and Aetion, later conflated with the Dioscuri); divinities of Nature and rebirth: Axiokersos and Axiokersa (paralleling Hades and Persephone in the Eleusinian Mysteries); Hekate of the underworld; Aphrodite Kerynthia, and the mystic marriage of the Phoenician Cadmus with Harmonia. From the sixth century

BC onwards, this cult drew pilgrims from afar as devotees and initiates, including Herodotus, Lysander the king of Sparta, and Philip of Macedon and Olympias, the parents of Alexander the Great. The town along the sea, protected by a descending walled ridge, prospered in the Archaic period and sent ships to fight the Persians at Salamis. But it was the nearby Sanctuary of the Great Gods in a gulley to the west that was most important and famous, and it survives today in massive ruined monuments clarified in French, Austrian, Swedish, and American excavations, since 1863.

The oldest part of the sanctuary is a pre-Greek rock altar from around 1000 BC, incorporated in a small Archaic Greek double precinct of the late seventh century BC. Surrounding this primitive sacred area is the great Rotunda of Queen Arsinoe, the largest round building of ancient Greece, over 65 ft in diameter. Constructed c. 285 BC by the wife of King Lysimachus of Thrace, its cylindrical wall of Thasos marble was crowned by a circular row of pilasters on a projecting balustrade with a Doric entablature above, while inside, against the upper wall, were Corinthian half-columns topped by an Ionic cornice. Sacrifices were conducted here amid gathered representatives (*theoroi*) from Greek cities.

A rectangular 'Hall of Lords' (*Anaktoron*) to the west was used for nearly a thousand years, from the sixth century BC to the end of the pagan cult, for the first stage of initation into the Mysteries around a wooden platform at the

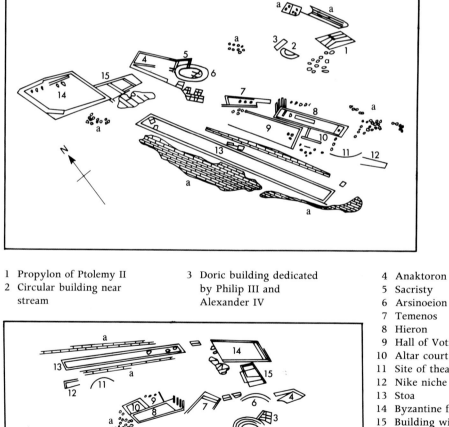

1 Propylon of Ptolemy II
2 Circular building near
  stream

3 Doric building dedicated
  by Philip III and
  Alexander IV

4 Anaktoron
5 Sacristy
6 Arsinoeion
7 Temenos
8 Hieron
9 Hall of Votive Gifts
10 Altar court
11 Site of theatre
12 Nike niche
13 Stoa
14 Byzantine fortification
15 Building with Milesian
   dedication
a Unassembled fragments

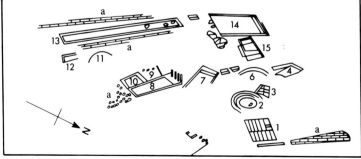

centre. An adjacent sacristy probably served for vesting and enrolling worshippers. The upper level of initiation, which involved witnessing sacred symbolic rites after the admission of sinfulness and purification, was undergone in the Hieron, a long Doric structure with wide deep porch at the north end with two rows of six columns each across it, an apse at the back and a double row of marble benches for spectators along the inside walls. Outside to the north, at an angle, was a rectangular temenos enclosure with an Ionic Propylon at its northeast corner, while to the west was a hall for votive gifts and an unroofed marble court enclosing an altar. Beyond them lay the theatre (now hard to trace) and a very long stoa on a higher level. South of the theatre in a rock-cut niche was a fountain-house where the Winged Victory, a sculptural masterpiece, stood on a prow over a pool. It is now in the Louvre.

On the hillside east of the stream bed was the elaborate Propylon entrance to the sanctuary; the columns of its outer porch were Ionic, those facing the sanctuary Corinthian. A circular building west of the stream, with rings of steps, was probably for witnessing some ritual.

Sfaktiria/**Sphacteria**

Near the southwest tip of the Peloponnesus, the great bay of Navarino is protected from the sea by the long island of Sphacteria enclosing its whole western side but leaving an entrance at the southern end. This superb natural break- water is nearly three miles long, running almost due north-south. In the oval bay within, the Turkish fleet of 82 warships was nearly totally destroyed by a much smaller force of British, French, and Russian ships on October 20, 1827,

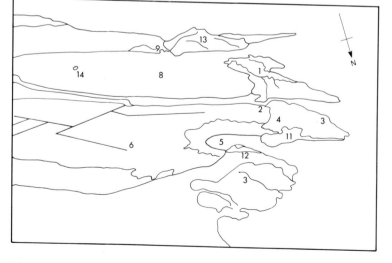

1 Sphacteria island
2 Sykia channel
3 Koryphasion hill
4 Classical Pylos
5 Bouphras/Voidokilia cove
6 Lagoon
7 Aigaleon range
8 Navarino Bay
9 Modern Pylos
10 Pylos islet
11 Neleus/Nestor cave
12 Mycenaean tholos
13 Mt San Nicolo
14 Chelonaki islet

completing the liberation of Greece from Turkish domination.

Sphacteria itself is famous for another battle, described at length by Thucydides. There, during the early stages of the Peloponnesian War, a picked band of Spartans held out for 72 days in the summer of 425 BC against an Athenian siege and blockade until the 292 survivors surrendered – thereby shattering the belief that Spartans always chose death before dishonour. Their camp was at the northern summit of the island amid the remains of a much earlier stone defence wall of Cyclopean style, now demolished. On the high hill just to the north across Sykia channel was a small fortified settlement, the Pylos of Classical times, which the Athenians held for many years. Some of its walls are incorporated into the medieval castle of AD 1278 later held by Venetians and Turks. At the southeast foot of the hill along the top of the bay can be seen some of the ancient Classical breakwater, and a cemetery nearby has yielded Hellenistic tombs. The shallow lagoon to the east did not exist in ancient times. The hill's name, Koryphasion, refers to its high crowning peak.

There is evidence of Neolithic and Mycenaean habitation on this hill and on its twin across the beautiful crescent cove Bouphras or Voidokilia,

and a Mycenaean tholos tomb has been discovered on the summit of the northern hill. This may well be the Tomb of Thrasymedes, son of Nestor, traditionally held to be in the area. The cove seems to have served as the harbour for Nestor's Pylos a few miles away to the north; it is ideally suited to the small ships of that period and its fine beach befits the 'sandy Pylos' which Homer assigns to Nestor, the talkative old man in the *Iliad* and *Odyssey*.

Off the southern edge of the cove is a large cave in the north cliff of Koryphasion below the Classical citadel. This is 60 ft long, 40 ft high and wide, with an arched entrance. Inside are massive stalactites, some looking like hanging animal skins. It was reputed to be a stable for the cows of Nestor and his father Neleus, and is also presumably the cave mentioned in the *Homeric Hymn to Hermes* where that god, still an infant, hid the cattle of the Sun which he had stolen in precocious exercise of his qualifications to be patron of thieves and merchants. Numerous fragments of Mycenaean pottery found in this cave indicate its extensive use.

Modern Pylos at the southeast edge of the great bay, with its fine sixteenth-century Turkish castle, is an entirely recent city, taking over the name of the Classical site and Nestor's before that.

Sikion/**Sicyon**

Sicyon, a very ancient city some ten miles west of Corinth along the gulf, was originally Ionian and known as Aigialeia, but c. 1100 BC was taken over by Dorians. Homer says its forces at Troy were led by Adrastus of Argos and he calls the 'spacious' city Sicyon. A brilliant and popular leader Orthagoras shook off the domination of Argos and established his own dynasty of autocrats in the seventh century BC, culminating in the city's most famous figure Cleisthenes – whose grandson later reformed the constitution of Athens. From this Archaic period Sicyon was a notable centre of art for generations with pioneer painters like Pamphilos and Pausias, the sculptors Boutades and Kanachos and many others including Polyclitus and Lysippus. Pliny says that all its youth were taught to draw, and Cicero

mentions Sicyonian shoes and dress as still widely admired in Roman times. Cleisthenes led the liberation of Delphi in the early sixth century BC and reorganized its Pythian Games. Later Sicyon allied mostly with Sparta and fought against Persia and Athens. It was under Theban power for a while in the fourth century BC, then in 303 the Macedonian ruler Demetrius Poliorcetes destroyed it, but soon built a new city away from the sea on the great high plateau two miles inland that has precipitous cliffs above the Helisson river. This new city, destroyed by an earthquake in AD 23, was partly excavated by American archaeologists in 1886–90 and by Orlandos in 1932–54. The view from its lofty acropolis is spectacular.

The most obvious ruin is the large theatre, dating from the early third century BC. It is

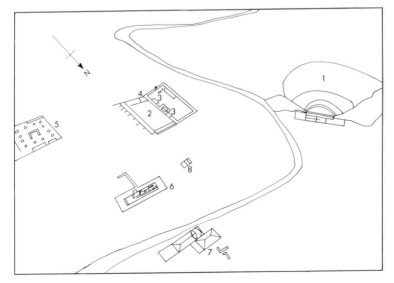

1 Theatre
2 Gymnasium
3 Fountains
4 Nymphaeum
5 Bouleuterion
6 Temple
7 Roman baths/museum
8 Steps to buried
    building

cut into the hillside with unusual lateral vaulted entrances and the largest number (16) of radial stairs of any theatre in Greece. There was an elaborate stage structure and in front a small temple to Dionysos, which Leake saw in the 1820s, but which is now gone. Officials of the Achaean League met in this theatre in 168 BC to plan their political strategy. A stadium can be traced in a ravine west of the theatre, with polygonal walls at its ends.

The gymnasium, a large double rectangle on two levels, is ascribed to Kleinias in the early third century BC but was repaired in Roman times. Each terrace has surrounding porticoes on three sides – the upper one Doric, the lower Ionic with a series of rooms outside. Stairs lead up at the middle from the lower to the upper level, with graceful fountain-houses at each side and in the south corner a Nymphaeum shrine. Another rectangular building can be traced just to the north, with stairs at the bottom. East of this is a long narrow temple of Hellenistic date but following an Archaic plan. It is perhaps the temple of Apollo by Proitos mentioned by Pausanias, who saw nearby a colossal statue of Attalus I of Pergamum over 15 ft high. The temple of Tyche Akraia, that of Peitho, an Asclepieion, a Heroön of Aratus, and a Hercules sanctuary with an ancient wooden statue (*xoanon*) which he also saw are still undiscovered.

A square Bouleuterion lies east of the gymnasium. It had four rows of four Ionic columns each to support its roof, open at the centre, with a raised speaker's platform and probably a porch on the agora side. East of it are foundations of a long stoa, probably not the Painted Stoa referred to in ancient sources, which has yet to be identified.

The Sicyonian Treasury at Delphi, and that at Olympia, were monuments to the city's pride in its achievements.

Sounion/**Sunium**

At the southeast tip of Attica, Cape Sunium projects abruptly, nearly 200 ft high, into the blue Aegean in a setting of famous charm. Homer speaks of the site as the 'holy promontory of Athens' and from early times there was a sanctuary of Zeus and Poseidon here to placate the sea from dangerously buffeting winds. Colossal statues of youths (*kouroi*) stood in the open and there was an altar nearby. Athena too was worshipped here from Archaic times. Numerous Egyptian objects are found in the area, testimony to Athens' vigorous foreign trade.

The town lay along the western harbour, with repair facilities for two ships – the berths cut into the cliffs for this in the late fourth century BC are still visible. Fortification walls, with a tower every 60 ft, protected both the harbour and the heights. They were built of a mixture of poros and marble (a sign of haste), as Thucydides records, in 413/412 BC to protect the town's and sanctuary's role for Athens' food-supply route. Houses in the enclosure date from the sixth century BC to Roman times. Every four years, in the Classical era, a nautical festival was held off Sunium, with mock sea-battles in Poseidon's honour.

On a hill-top some 1500 ft inland from the promontory's tip was a temple to Athena. The Archaic sixth-century shrine was built of limestone and sun-dried brick in Ionic style but shaped like an old Mycenaean megaron. It was destroyed by the Persians in 480 BC. Pericles had it rebuilt before 450 BC in marble, preserving the ancient plan and incorporating some of its ruins. Vitruvius cites it as an example of variation from the usual temple design, with 'what we find in the front in other temples here transferred to the sides'. Extant remains show a solid cella wall without frontal columns: a complete rectangle except for the opening for a door on the east side. Inside were four columns and a raised base at the back for the cult statue. A colonnade of Ionic pillars stood outside the cella – but only on the east and south sides, joined to the cella's northeast and southwest corners. Nearby, a little to the northeast, was a smaller Archaic shrine with walls of sun-dried brick, a cult-statue base inside, two free-standing columns, and an altar opposite the front.

More notable is the famous Poseidon temple on the cliff's edge, with its striking view over

1 Site of ancient town
2 Ancient shipsheds
3 Sanctuary defence wall
4 Site of temple of Athena
5 Propylon

6 Temple of Poseidon
7 North Stoa
8 West Stoa
9 Site of altar
10 Modern tourist pavilion

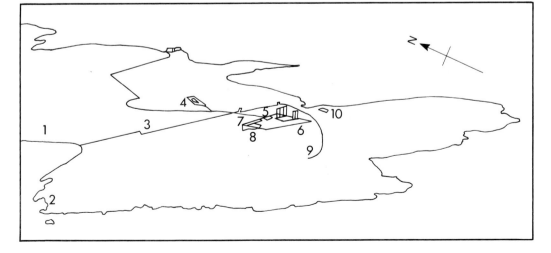

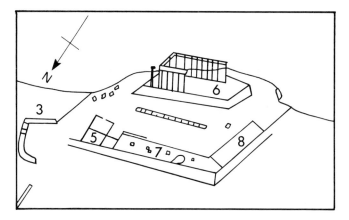

1 (*see p. 199*)
2 (*see p. 199*)
3 Sanctuary defence wall
4 (*see p. 199*)
5 Propylon
6 Temple of Poseidon
7 North Stoa
8 West Stoa

sea and islands. Built about 444–440 BC, apparently by the same architect later responsible for the Hephaisteion and Ares temples in Athens and of Nemesis at Rhamnous, it replaced an earlier structure which was unfinished when burned by the Persians in 480 BC. Its columns are unusually slim for Doric, and in flashing bright marble which made it a landmark guiding sailors towards Athens. An unusual feature is an Ionic room at the east end, formed by running an Ionic frieze around all four upper walls *inside* the east porch. There were sculptured pediments and floral acroteria. A formal Propylon gave access at the northeast corner of the terrace platform, with adjacent stoas along the northern and western edges.

Sparti/**Sparta**

Both feared and admired by other Greek cities, Sparta had a peculiar social and governmental system that made it the greatest military power in Greece but which also came to crush humane and cultural interests that until the end of the sixth century BC had fostered fine poetry, sculpture, and brilliant Laconian pottery. Thereafter monolithic militarism and totalitarian subordination of all to the benefit of the State turned Sparta into a heartless war machine and cut it off from economic and cultural progress. Only the Spartiates, a landed nobility, had full citizenship and leisure (supported by helot serfs who worked their farms), and spent their life in military and civic service under ruthless discipline. Crafts and commercial activity were left to associated neighbours (*Perioikoi*). There were two kings in command of the army, and political power lay in the hands of five Ephors elected annually and a Senate (*Gerousia*) of 30 elders, with concurrence of the Popular Assembly (*Apella*) of mature Spartiates over 30.

Sparta conquered the rich plains of Messenia in the eighth century BC and dominated the southern and central Peloponnesus. At constant war with Tegea, Argos, Corinth, Athens, Thebes, it helped oppose Xerxes' invasion of 480 BC and later destroyed Athens' pre-eminence in the Peloponnesian War, but was itself defeated by Thebes at Leuctra in 371 BC and was held in weakened isolation by the subsequent Arcadian and Achaean Leagues and by Macedonia. Sparta prospered under Roman rule but was sacked by Alaric in AD 396 and was later abandoned for Mistra. The modern city dates only from 1834. Homer's Sparta was some distance away, probably near where the Shrine of Menelaus and Helen has been found in the hills to the east of the Eurotas river. The Classical Sparta/Lacedemon was a Dorian foundation of the tenth century BC. The Byzantine city was confined to the ancient acropolis area.

Sparta was not interested in splendid public buildings and what little of it survives is mostly from the Archaic and Roman periods. British excavations in 1906–10 and again in 1925–29 have revealed meagre fragments and part of the six-mile circuit of late walls (third to eighth century AD) and G. Soteriou has uncovered some Byzantine churches above the theatre.

The acropolis is the highest of Sparta's six hills. Pausanias saw on it temples of Zeus, Aphrodite, Athena Ergane, the Muses, and Athena Chalkioikos – 'of the Bronze House' because the interior was lined with engraved metal plaques, the work of a local sixth-century artist, Gitiadas. Only a few fragments of this last temple have been identified above the theatre's retaining wall. East of this are medieval ruins, including a monastery with a pilgrimage tomb of St Nikon and his tenth-eleventh century Byzantine basilica. The large theatre cut into the hill seems to date to the second or first century BC and was reworked in Roman times. The wall east of the stage has an inscribed list of civic officials in the second century AD. At the southern edge of the acropolis was a Roman stoa.

The agora to the south is unexcavated. A small Hellenistic temple to the southwest is falsely called the 'Tomb of Leonidas' – which was in fact near the theatre. Northeast along the Eurotas is a large altar and a Heroön, and farther south at Limenaion is the sanctuary of Artemis Orthia, whose Archaic temple overlies a tenth-century BC cult site. The altar dates from the ninth century BC. The Romans built a circular theatral cavea in Sparta for witnesses of the temple rites, which had once included whipping contests to test the endurance of Spartan youths.

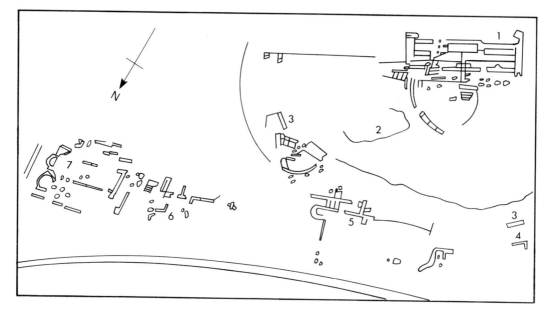

1　Theatre stage buildings
2　Theatre cavea
3　Retaining wall of theatre (fragments)
4　Site of temple of Athena Chalkioikos
5　Medieval foundations
6　Monastery and tomb of St Nikon
7　Basilica of St Nikon
8　Temple of Artemis Orthia
9　Altar
10　Temenos wall fragment
11　Roman theatral building

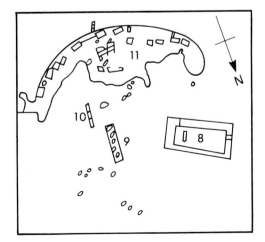

Stratos/**Stratos**

Now little known and rarely visited, Stratos in Classical and Hellenistic times was the largest and best fortified city in Acarnania and was for long its capital. There was a prehistoric settlement here on the low steep hill with four parallel ridges overlooking the right bank of the Acheloos river – with whose divine personification Hercules had wrestled for the hand of Deianeira. By the mid-fifth century BC, Stratos was an important centre of commerce and military strength in the area of west-central Greece. Allied with Athens, it fought off a Spartan and Ambracian attack in 429 BC during the Peloponnesian War and repulsed several later threats to its independence. The Macedonian king Cassander took control of it in 314 BC and greatly increased its size and importance by moving into it the populations of several small towns in the district, and he used it as a buffer against the Aetolian League. It later fell under Aetolian dominance in 263 BC, and after 188 depended on Roman protection against Macedonia. It declined notably, however, and around the middle of the first century BC was badly pillaged by invading Dolopes. French and Greek excavations in 1892, 1910–11,

1923–24, and more recently have only uncovered fragments of the large site, notably its temple and some of the walls.

It is argued whether the extant walls, unusually extensive and largely in good preservation, date to the fifth century BC and contributed to the repulse of the Spartan attack of 429, or (more likely, in view of the structural style) to the enlargement of Stratos by Cassander in 314 BC. The blocks are trapezoidal and pseudo-isodomic – a fourth-century fashion. The main gate is at the south, the fortified acropolis on the north opposite. An unusual feature of the site is a long transverse wall (*diateichisma*) running north-south from near the main gate to the acropolis, dividing the city into nearly equal halves. A theatre has been located just to the east of the centre of this transverse wall; only partly discernible now, it probably dates to the late fourth-century Macedonian period. The agora seems to have been to the west on the other side of the central wall where part of a stoa has been uncovered. Presumably most of the civic buildings were in this sector. An inscription indicates there was a gymnasium in the city. Much more remains to be found.

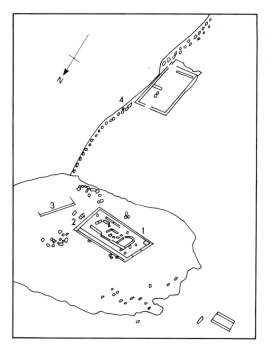

1 Temple of Zeus
2 Late bases
3 Altar ?
4 Fortification wall (southwestern sector)

Inside a sharp corner of the defence wall at its western extremity, and built into the ramparts (an unusual procedure), is the large temple of Zeus. It is on a raised terrace, and must have been prominent from afar. Built in a hard grey stone, it was never finished – fluting of the columns was begun but not completed and protective bosses on many drums and blocks were not removed. It probably dates from the late fourth and into the early third century BC.

The outer peristyle columns (11 × 6) were Doric, but within the cella (100 ft in length) the ten columns and two engaged columns near the door were Ionic, with an Ionic architrave and figured frieze. This central room may have been open to the sky; if roofed, it had to be with wood only. A large door 11 ft wide led into the cella from the pronaos over a raised lintel; there was a rear porch also. An inscription identifies Zeus as the divinity worshipped here.

Tegea/**Tegea**

A major city of ancient Arcadia, Tegea was said to have been organized out of nine rural demes by King Aleos. It was the birthplace of swift-footed Atalanta, heroine of the Calydonian Boar Hunt. Hercules here sired Telephus by the local nymph Auge.

Tegea long led the Arcadian resistance to Sparta until beaten into submission *c.* 560 BC. A contingent from Tegea fought at Thermopylae and at Plataea. After the decline of Sparta, Tegea was a reluctant member of the Arcadian League and later of the Achaean League. It was still flourishing in the second century AD when visited by Pausanias, but was later demolished by Alaric in the fifth century. It revived in Byzantine times, when its was known as Nikli. Little can be seen today of the ancient city; even its agora and temples to Apollo and Dionysos have been covered over again.

The major monument visible is the fine temple of Athena Alea, the solid foundations lying clean amid surrounding recent houses – and in the spring-time set off by a green carpet of grass. Off its northeast corner is an ancient fountain-house, traditionally associated with Auge and Hercules. Excavations by the French between 1889 and 1910 have especially clarified the temple's details.

An Archaic temple, the most famous sanctuary in Arcadia, where the Spartan king Pausanias had sought refuge like Orestes before him in legendary times, was burned down in 395 BC. When rebuilt some fifty years later, the sculptor Scopas was chosen as its architect. The new building was remarkable and imaginative in many ways. Above the foundations the structure was completely in marble – the first such instance in the Peloponnesus. Though

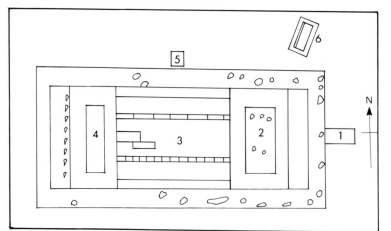

1 East ramp
2 Prodomos (east porch)
3 Cella (naos)
4 Opisthodomos (west porch)
5 North ramp
6 Fountain-house

essentially Doric it had an Ionic flavour: its exterior columns (6 × 14, an unusual configuration) were slimmer than traditional and its inner proportions long and uncrowded, with some Ionic elements in the decorative details. The columns inside the cella were embedded in the inner wall, giving much more room than was usual. They had Ionic fluting and notably refined Corinthian capitals. Square pilasters ingeniously fitted into the inside corners. There was an extra door at the middle of the north cella wall, with a ramp outside. The porches at the east and west ends each had two Doric columns between the projecting anta walls. All horizontal lines were slightly curved for aesthetic effect, and the peristyle columns leaned inwards a little as they rose. The carved molding was especially fine, as fragments in the local museum show. The east pediment sculpture represented the Calydonian Boar Hunt, with Atalanta, Meleager, and Theseus among the participants. On the west pediment were Achilles and Telephus battling beside the river Kaikos. Inside stood a famous Archaic statue of Athena in ivory, the work of Endoios; and Pausanias describes notable relics displayed within, including the hide of the Calydonian boar and a sacred couch of Athena. Scopas also decorated the altar in front with Zeus and Arcadian nymphs. His famous statues of Asclepius and Hygieia flanked the cult statue within the temple.

Thassos/**Thasos**

The northernmost of all Greek islands, facing the borders of Macedonia and Thrace, Thasos was prosperous from its widely-sought oil, wine, and marble, from its gold and silver mines and its proximity to those of Mt Pangaios to the north. It conducted an extensive sea trade with Phoenicia and Egypt, and was a northern outpost of Greek culture in a barbarian region. Ionians from Paros island colonized Thasos in the late eighth century BC. Archilochus, pioneer of personal poetry, was a mercenary soldier here and the great painter Polygnotus was born in Thasos. The island was seized by the Persians in 491 BC. It was later allied with Athens but often sided with Sparta. Philip of Macedon took control of it in the fourth century BC and later the Romans used it for military and trade advantage. French excavations since 1910 have uncovered the centre of the city and several outlying shrines and clarified its circuit of unique marble walls with their many sculptured gates.

From the air the relationship of port to agora is obvious, though obscured on the ground by intervening modern buildings. Part of the ancient harbour mole is visible under water. North of the port some of the housing district has been revealed and at the tip of the promontory ruins of an early Christian church overlie a sanctuary dating from the sixth century BC where inscriptions record the cults

1 North sanctuary
2 Theatre (under the trees)
3 Ancient houses
4 Poseideion
5 Dionysion
6 Artemision
7 Theoroi passage and shops
8 Northeast Stoa
9 Civic building with parascenia
10 Sanctuary of Zeus Agoraios
11 Northwest Stoa
12 Theogenes monument
13 Altar to Lucius and Gaius Caesar
14 Exedras
15 Southwest Stoa
16 Great Altar
17 Southeast Stoa
18 Glaukos monument
19 Prow monument
20 Ancient street
21 (see p. 210)
22 Odeion
23 Port
24 Ancient mole (under water)

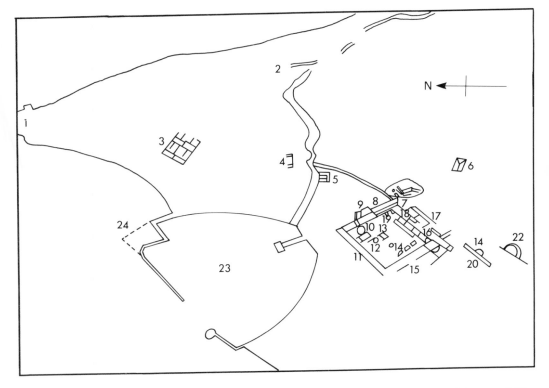

of Zeus, Athena, Artemis, Persephone, and the Nymphs. The theatre is cut into the hillside overlooking the port from the east. It is mentioned in the fifth century BC by Hippocrates and its comic actor Hegemon is credited by Aristotle with inventing the art of parody. A Hellenistic marble proscenium in front of the wooden stage had Doric columns and sculptured metopes above them. At the southern summit of the hill was a sanctuary of Apollo Pythius and on a terrace nearby a temple of Athena Poliouchos, both dating to the early years of the city's foundation. Lower down is a rock-cut grotto of Pan with a relief of the god playing his pipe amid attentive goats. Near the harbour and agora are the remains of a trapezoidal sanctuary of Poseidon, another to Dionysos with a choragic monument on a seven-stepped platform, and a temenos of Artemis Polo.

The agora is now fully uncovered. (A close-up view taken in 1950 is included to show the progress of the excavations.) It had a colonnaded stoa on each side, but the north corner is pre-empted by a rectangular building in poros and a civic structure, apparently an administrative centre, with projecting wings along the front like parascenia in a theatre. At the north angle of the square inside the stoas is a fourth-century sanctuary of Zeus Agoraios and a Hellenistic circular temenos enclosing an altar. To the south is the sanctuary of Theogenes, a local athletic hero, its stepped circular altar preserving an iron ring to which sacrificial victims were fastened. East of this is a Roman altar to Lucius and Gaius Caesar, Augustus' intended heirs. A monumental altar fills the southern corner of the agora, with a row of exedras to the west. At the northeast corner is a monument base with ship's prow and carved waves, and east of this an interesting memorial to Glaukos, a seventh-century friend of Archilochus mentioned in one of his extant poems. The Passage of the Theoroi (Ambassadors) lies outside the agora in this sector, with adjacent shops along a major street.

South of the agora is a rectangular building with a paved marble court, and east of this is the marble Odeion from the days of Hadrian. Farther southwest an Arch of Caracalla, a fourth-century BC monument to Thersilochos, and an elaborate Archaic Hercules sanctuary round off the site.

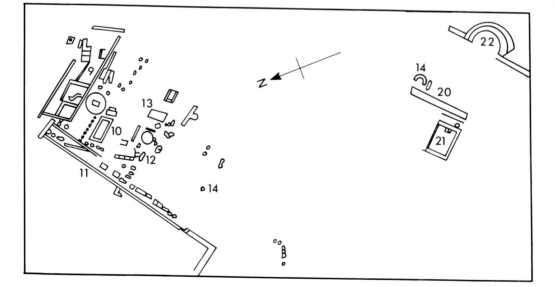

Thermon/**Thermon**

Lying south of the great Panaitolikon mountain range, on the slope of Mt Mega Lakkos to the east of the large and scenic Lake Trichonis, Thermon was the chief religious centre of Aetolia. Annual festivals and Games were held here in spring and autumn and for many years the Panaetolic Assembly met and chose its officials here. The sanctuary dates back to the end of the Mycenaean period and many remains have been found from the subsequent Geometric and Archaic periods. In the third century BC a strong wall with towers was built in a rectangle of some 660 × 1220 ft enclosing the sacred area. Nevertheless Philip V of

Macedon twice sacked the sanctuary, in 218 and 206 BC, reportedly destroying 2000 of its statues. There was no town here, only some houses adjacent to the temples and stoas. The site was long lost but was discovered and excavated by Soteriades and Rhomaios between 1897 and 1932 in several campaigns.

The finds are of special significance for the history of Greek architectural development. Several late Mycenaean or early Geometric houses survive in sufficient detail to make their ground-plan clear: a 'hair-pin' pattern with a long central room, a deep porch extending forwards and an elliptical apse at the rear. They

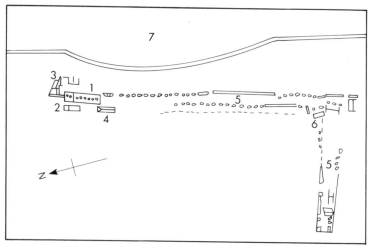

1 Temple of Apollo
  Thermios
2 Temple of Apollo
  Lyseios?
3 Geometric period houses,
  temple of Artemis?
4 Museum
5 Stoas
6 Fountain
7 Mt Mega Lakkos

presumably had pitched thatch roofs projecting over the walls. One of these houses, 'Megaron B', seems to have been adapted into a temple in the seventh century BC. Its back wall was only slightly curved, but a row of 36 stone slabs was arranged around it in an ellipse with apse. These carried wooden pillars, propped up by stone sockets at their base, and constituted the earliest known Greek peristyle – and the only curved one.

On top of this interesting structure's foundations was built a new stone and wood temple c. 630 BC. This pioneer Archaic temple's 100 ft long cella overlies Megaron B in a slightly different orientation. Down its centre ran a row of ten wooden columns on separate circular stone bases, with two more in the deep porch at the back. There is no fore-porch, but wooden doors at each side of the central column on the south front. The wooden roof was gabled. On the rectangular outer foundation wall (40 × 125 ft) was a peristyle of wooden columns, five across the front and back, 15 down the sides. The Doric frieze above them had wooden tri-glyphs framing painted terracotta metopes, some of which survive as key samples of Archaic painting style: Chelidon and Aedo plotting the death of Itys, Perseus with the Gorgon's head, animals, a hunter, etc. They show strong Corinthian influence or origin. There was a pediment only at the front, the back roof sloping down below the wall top. Terracotta antefixes from the roof also survive, with brightly coloured decoration. The temple was rebuilt more completely in stone in several stages in the sixth and fifth centuries BC and again after Philip's sacking in 206 BC. Its god was Apollo Thermios – referring to the hot springs nearby or to his function as warming sunlight. To the west another small temple may have existed to Apollo Lyseios; and to the northeast apparently one to Artemis amid other early ruins.

Two long parallel stoas stretched southward from the temple. The Aetolian Council Hall may have been between them. Another stoa runs westward inside the south temenos wall. A fountain nearby still flows copiously.

Thermopili/**Thermopylae**

The relentless advance of Xerxes' great army against Greece brought him in July of 480 BC to Trachis, south of Lamia, where he encamped along the Asopus river while his fleet lay off the coast of Magnesia east of Volos, blocked by the menace of the Greek ships at Cape Artemision. The general Greek strategy of defence had long before decided to hold the narrow defile of Thermopylae, just east of Trachis, the only feasible land route along the coast into Boeotia and Attica. Though the area is now broad and easy to traverse, due to silting from the Spercheios river, in the fifth century BC there was only a narrow road for four miles between the sea and the steep northern slope of Mt Kallidromon. The eastern entry into the narrows was near the small town of Alpenoi, the western below Anthela fortress; in the centre at the Middle Pass, it was somewhat broader, but still only a limited defile.

Here Leonidas, king of Sparta, took up position with 7300 men. Several times the vastly superior Persian forces were fought off with heavy losses. Xerxes was furious with frustration until Ephialtes, a local traitor, offered to lead the Persians around the defile by an upper mountain pass, the Anopaia, to attack the Greeks from the rear. Two thousand or more of the 'Immortals', the elite Royal Guard with their commander Hydarnes, set out in the evening, crossed the Asopus, and climbed the heights at night. Their route has been much argued, but it seems to have been settled by Pritchett's careful study of the topography and the ancient sources. This brings them up the slopes east of the Asopus Gorge (itself too steep, narrow, and slippery for a large force in heavy armour) to the plateau of the Kallidromon heights, eastward along that, routing in passage the thousand Phocians posted to guard the upper path, to the region near Alpenoi, then down to attack the Greek holding force in the rear from the east.

Meanwhile Xerxes had again mounted a massive assault from the west along the sea. Leonidas learned of the encircling manoeuvre

1 Kolonos (Leonidas' last stand)   4 Mt Kallidromon
2 Modern monument with Leonidas statue   5 Middle pass
3 Modern Athens–Lamia road

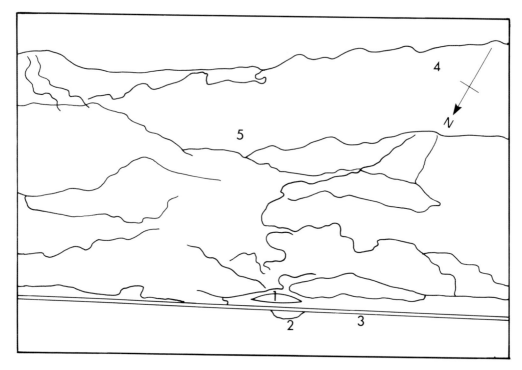

and sent away most of his troops except the 300 Spartans and the contingents from Thespiae and Thebes – the Thebans soon deserting to the foe. This gave the rest of the Greek forces time to withdraw to Athens and the Isthmus, while the Spartans could uphold their code of no surrender and win eternal glory (as they have) for their courage, however hopeless the odds. They fought fiercely but were overwhelmed by sheer numbers. Simonides' famous epitaphs still bring them honour. The story and its setting is graphically enshrined in Herodotus' dramatic account in Book Seven of his *History of the Persian Wars*. In 1955 a marble monument with a heroic bronze statue of Leonidas was erected here, being paid for by international contributions.

Excavations in 1939 established the low oval hill opposite the monument as the Kolonos, the site of Leonidas' last stand. Many arrowheads of different types (reflecting the varied national levies of the Persian host) were found, including the special Persian three-edged kind found also at Marathon, on the Acropolis, and at Persepolis. Nearby are the remains of an ancient wall, no doubt the one which Leonidas rebuilt before the historic battle. Thermopylae Pass was also fought over in many later invasions.

Thessaloniki/**Thessalonike**

Thessalonike, named after the half-sister of Alexander the Great by her husband Cassander, ruler of Macedonia, who founded it in 316 BC, replaced the small earlier town of Thermae nearby on the Thermaic Gulf. It took over from Pella as the chief port of Macedonia and further prospered commercially when the Roman Via Egnatia connected it with both the Adriatic opposite Italy, and Byzantium and the East. When the Romans conquered Macedonia in 146 BC they made Thessalonike its capital. Pompey found refuge here from Caesar in 49 BC, Cicero chose it for part of his exile, and St Paul for implanting Christianity in northern Greece. The Emperor Galerius made it his official abode when he took over the Eastern Empire from Diocletian. In the Byzantine era Thessalonike was second only to Constantinople, as today it is only to Athens in modern Greece. Several fine Byzantine churches are among its major reminders of a brilliant past.

Little can be seen now of the Hellenistic city except fragments in the agora area and some recently discovered graves. The Roman monuments are widely scattered, the most imposing being Galerius' Triumphal Arch southeast of the forum, erected to commemorate his victories over the Persians in Armenia and Mesopotamia at the end of the third century AD. Its badly weathered reliefs portray his military and religious activities. To the southeast can be traced Galerius' monumental hippodrome and to the west of the arch his huge palace is now being excavated, its great octagonal room 90 ft across presumably for the imperial throne and audience chamber. West of the palace are remains of a Nymphaeum fountain and much farther west a Serapis temple and a shrine for the Emperor-cult (*Caesareum*). A massive brick and mortar cylindrical rotunda northeast of the arch, adapted into a church of St George in the fourth century, was probably built to be Galerius' mausoleum but he in fact died and was buried in modern Bulgaria. In the upper town the acropolis heights are encircled by impressive Byzantine ramparts which incorporate parts of the older Greek wall.

From the air the most interesting sector of the ancient city is the forum area, only recently excavated in part. This overlies the earlier Hellenistic agora, of which little survives. Today's Via Egnatia passes nearby to the south and no doubt the forum extended that far or was connected to it by intervening structures. A long stoa portico at the southern end has part of its construction underground and may therefore be the Chalkeutike Stoa referred to in some Byzantine sources. The East Stoa, some 125 ft in length, had Corinthian columns and a series of steps into the forum. It dates from the first or second century AD, and may be the famous 'Enchanted' Stoa (*Goëtria*, *Encantada*) mentioned in medieval accounts which pretended that its caryatid pillars were women

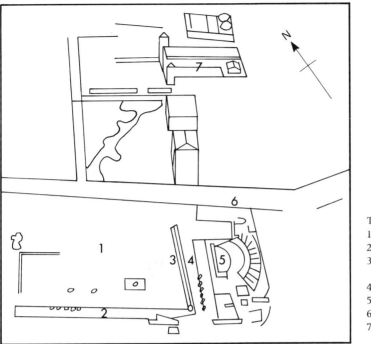

turned into stone by magical powers. To the east is a large Roman Odeion of the fourth century AD, its orchestra area paved with marble. There is evidence of stoas on the other sides of the forum also. The central open court, 230 ft north-south and 295 ft east-west, was paved and had a marble drain.

St Demetrius' church to the north, a fine old basilica with splendid mosaics (badly damaged by fire in 1917), is built over Roman baths.

Thira/**Thera**

According to ancient accounts Thera (probably = 'Wild Beast') was originally known as Kalliste ('Most Beautiful') or Stongyle ('Round'). The change of name probably reflects memory of the catastrophic explosion which destroyed life on the island and did enormous damage for hundreds of miles around – perhaps explaining the collapse of late Minoan civilization in the Aegean region, an increasingly popular theory though there remain serious chronological difficulties. A great central volcanic cone was pulverized in the eruption and the sea rushed into the six-mile-diameter gap, producing enormous seismic waves (*tsunamis*) that must have devastated the coastal areas of Greece, Crete, northern Egypt, and the Levant and may be behind the ancient story of Atlantis, the splendid city that disappeared beneath the sea. Recent excavations near Akrotiri are uncovering a Minoan site first discovered and partially explored a hundred years ago. Sensational finds of brilliant and imaginative wall frescoes, elegant decorated pottery, and a skilful architectural complex promise to make this 'Greek Pompeii' a most important revelation of Cretan art and life abroad. From the air however there is little of this to see other than the location, as all lies buried or under a protecting roof.

A little to the north, on the southeast slope of the island's highest remaining mountain, lie the considerable remains of a post-Mycenaean city, ancient Thera. Tradition reported prehistoric habitation of the island, perhaps by Carians from Asia Minor in the third millennium

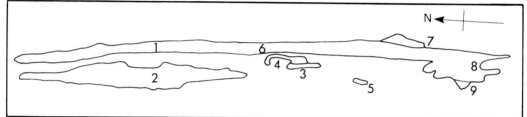

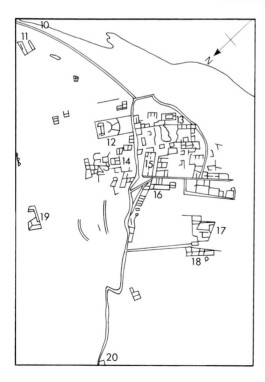

1 Thera island
2 Therasia
3 Old Kaimeni
4 New (Great) Kaimeni
5 Aspronisi
6 Phira town
7 Thera: Classical/Hellenistic city
8 Minoan site
9 Cape Akrotiri
10 Gymnasium of Ephebes
11 Temple of Apollo Karneios
12 Theatre
13 Peristyle court (Basilistai assembly?)
14 Agora/market
15 Royal stoa
16 Temple of Dionysos
17 Gymnasium?
18 Garrison headquarters
19 Broad terrace
20 Temenos of Artemidorus

BC. Early Greeks (Achaeans) absorbed them *c.* 1900 BC and Cadmus was said to have left colonists there on his way from Phoenicia to Thebes *c.* 1500. Dorians were dominant in Thera from around 1000 BC onwards and from there founded Cyrene, the only major Greek colony in Africa. The island continued under strong influence of Cretan and Cycladic traditions and its distinctive Geometric pottery, with a band of animals on the upper vase only and parallel rings below, is of great interest and charm. German excavations in 1835 and 1895–1903 have identified buildings from the Archaic period, the Classical period when Thera was subject to Athens, the Hellenistic era when the Ptolemies turned it into a military base for naval control of the central Aegean, and from Roman times.

The oldest extant sanctuary is that of Apollo Karneios at the eastern end of the ridge along which the city extended. Here the Archaic temple dated to the seventh century BC is much like an early house. It has a square court with a cistern, its cella at the side with a deep porch and two adjacent rooms, and a Propylon approach. Like many structures on Thera, this is on an artifical terrace supported by a massive Cyclopaean retaining wall.

The theatre shows four periods of construction, with a wooden stage in the third century BC, replaced in stone in the second century and a new cavea later, and reworking of the orchestra and proscenium in Roman times. A long royal stoa with central colonnade lies to the west of the agora, and a small temple of Dionysos is located nearby. A room at the northern end of the stoa was for the Imperial cult. South of the Ptolemaic military garrison is a large court that may have been a gymnasium, but there is no proof of its purpose. There are many rock-cut shrines. Large Hellenistic houses are numerous, with cisterns, courts, corridors and painted walls – one of the few extensive residential areas surviving from ancient Greece.

Thive/**Thebes**

Both in legend and in history Thebes was one of the most important cities of ancient Greece. The site was inhabited from Early Helladic times by a pre-Greek people who built on the hill-top a large stone structure with wide doors between rooms and a curved apse, very much like the contemporary great house at Lerna. Remains of this structure have been identified under the later Mycenaean palace, which was built *c.* 1500 BC – traditionally by Cadmus who had come from Phoenicia in search of his abducted sister Europa and settled at Thebes on the advice of Delphi. He was credited with introducing writing to Greece and many aspects of Eastern and Egyptian civilization. From the dragon's teeth he had sown in a field sprang warriors who founded the Theban nobility. Fertile in tragedy also, Thebes is the setting of the bitter stories of Oedipus, Antigone, Dirce, Polyneices, and the Seven against Thebes. It produced Pindar however, and the military genius Epaminondas who led it to supreme power in Greece for a short period in the fourth century BC. Constantly at war with Athens or Sparta, siding with the invading Persians, defeated by Philip at Chaeronea, Thebes was ruthlessly destroyed by Alexander in 336 BC and, after a partial revival, was divided by Sulla in 86 BC and faded away.

Its visible ruins are few and in miserable condition. The modern town covers the ancient city centre but does not fill the five-mile enclosure of the fourth-century walls. The low broad acropolis of the Kadmeion citadel is clearly visible from the air but hard to distinguish on the ground. Its famous seven gates are difficult to trace except the Electran on the old road to Athens, where the foundations of the round towers have survived both time and neglect. Keramopoullos uncovered a segment of the Mycenaean palace near the hill's centre between 1906 and 1921, and Platon in 1963–64 partially excavated some rooms to the south which yielded Babylonian cylinder-seals with cuneiform inscriptions, some fine ivories, and record-tablets in Linear B (Mycenaean Greek script). Earlier finds included parts of a wall fresco of nearly life-size women in procession, and treasures of gold, agate, and lapis lazuli jewellery. Cadmus' palace seems to have been

1 Ismenion hill
2 Temple of Apollo Ismenios

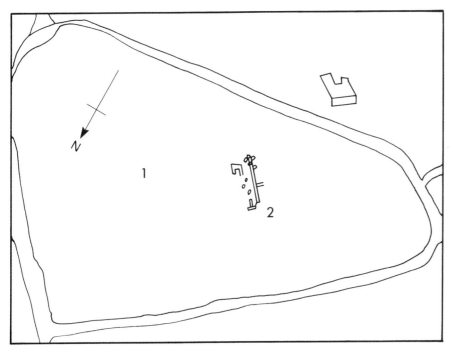

destroyed c. 1300 BC by fire (ascribed in tradition to Zeus' lightning) and its replacement was similarly destroyed some 30 years later. It was not rebuilt and Pausanias says a sanctuary of Demeter Thesmophoros was built on its site. A Mycenaean road has been found nearby, over 16 ft wide. In classical times the agora took over the old palace area. It boasted an altar by the sons of Praxiteles and an Archaic wooden statue of Dionysos. Pausanias mentions a theatre some distance to the north, two gymnasia, a stadium and a hippodrome. Mycenaean tholos tombs have been located in the environs and a major ancient cemetery.

Southeast of the citadel on a low hill are fragments of the temple of Apollo Ismenios, originally built of wood and brick in the Geometric period, perhaps without columns, replaced c. 700 BC by an Archaic Doric temple in poros stone, and praised by Pindar and Herodotus for its treasures. Rebuilt in 383 and again in 371 BC, with 6 × 12 columns, it had an Archaic wooden statue of Apollo by Kanachos, Scopas' Athena, and a Hermes by Phidias. To the west was a shrine of Hercules and to the north the tomb of Amphion who built Thebes' original walls. To the east was the spring where Oedipus washed off his slain father's blood.

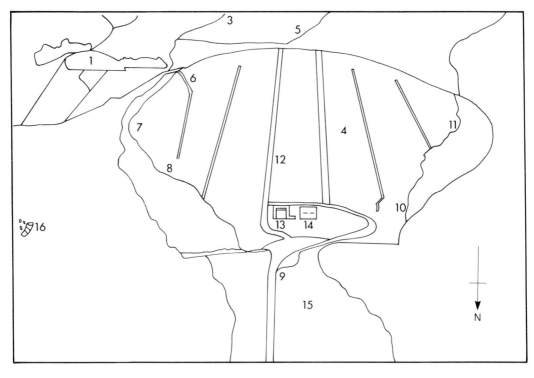

Thorikos/**Thorikos**

North of Sunium and the ancient silver mines of Laurium along the eastern coast of Attica, Thorikos was in an advantageous position for commerce as well as strategically located for the defence of the southern approach to Athens. A double conical hill lies inland from a promontory which has a harbour on each side. There was a Cretan trading post here, and pre-Greek houses have been traced on the hill's summit, dating back to perhaps 2000 BC. A Mycenaean fortification wall encircled the upper hill, and houses of that period overlie some of the earlier ones. Two tholos tombs have been discovered on the northeast side of the hill, while graves of the Geometric and Classical eras are known farther down the slope.

Demeter was said to have stopped at Thorikos on her way from Crete to Eleusis, and the early king of the city, Kephalos, was allied to Mycenaean Athens and according to ancient legend married Erechtheus' daughter Procris. Thorikos was one of the 12 independent towns of Attica, before Theseus unified the population of Athens, and later was an important deme in Athenian territory. Its fifth-century BC walls stretched along the lower slope (the 12 ft high square tower is of later date). These walls were supplemented by a fort on the promontory presumably built in 412 BC when Athens also fortified Sunium and Rhamnous to protect its food-supply routes during the Peloponnesian War. This maritime fortress had two walls across the Isthmus on the west and east sides, a tower and rear gate to the north, the main gate was on the south on the hill-top which was made into a small citadel. In Hellenistic times this fort was turned into an industrial centre for the port. Workshops for lead and silver products have been identified in the town area northwest of the theatre and

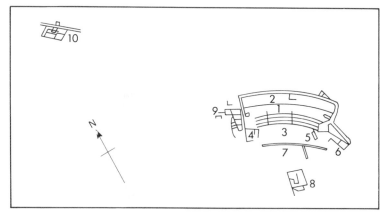

1 Theatre: earlier
cavea
2 Later extended cavea
section
3 Orchestra area
4 Temple
5 Altar
6 Old rooms (theatre
storage?)
7 Ancient terrace
8 Graves
9 Terraced rooms
10 Workshops,
industrial area of
town

houses and civic buildings in that region are currently under excavation. The double harbour to the north and south of the promontory served for commercial transport for Laurium's mines as well as for Athens' trade with Crete and the islands. The whole site was abandoned in Roman times. The American School at Athens excavated here in 1885–86, and the Belgians since 1963.

The most interesting remaining structure is the curious theatre cut into the lower slopes of the main hill. In its original form, perhaps dating from the late sixth century BC, it was probably only a rectangular assembly auditorium on the edge of the agora. About the mid-fifth century BC it was adapted for dramatic performances. The cavea of seats (31 rows are traceable) is a rough ellipse, with a distinct rectangular section in the middle between sharply curving side areas. The orchestra is also rectangular with curved inner corners. At its east edge pre-existing rooms (perhaps an early Council Hall) were possibly used for the storage of scenery and costumes. A small altar to Dionysos stands at the northeast edge of the orchestra, and a tiny temple to the god opposite on the west side is in Ionic style. There was no place for a stage building; probably a low wooden platform sufficed. Around the mid-fourth century BC the cavea was expanded with 12 more rows of seats at the top. Access was by ramps on each side. There is a vaulted space through the western support wall near three terraced rooms.

Farther west a Doric building with 7 × 14 columns, perhaps a temple to Demeter, lies buried.

Tilissos/**Tylissos**

In a valley among the foothills of Mt Ida some six miles west of Knossos, three Minoan country villas were excavated by Hazzidakis between 1909 and 1913, with further clearing and study by Platon in 1947–56. These are the best examples yet found of this type of structure, and therefore of particular interest. Among the ruins were recovered numerous works of art: three large bronze cauldrons, rhytons of obsidian, small bronze statuettes, painted pithoi and amphoras, and fragments of wall frescoes. The name, with its terminal -sos, reveals its Minoan origin. The site was inhabited from Early Minoan times, c. 2500 BC, until the general destruction of the mid-fifteenth century BC that engulfed Cretan settlements. Tylissos was re-occupied, however (as some of the greater sites were not) and some new building is identifiable from the Late Minoan III period after 1400 BC, and even in the Classical Greek era when it issued its own coinage. The three main villas date from the early Late Minoan or Neo-Palatial period, when the great palaces at Knossos, Phaistos, etc. were being rebuilt, c. 1600.

Each of the villas is a complex of rooms on two floors. Many of the staircases to the upper floor survive in their lower steps. They all had storerooms, in which a variety of objects were still *in situ*, indicating a sudden general destruction of the upper sections of the houses. Construction is careful and neat, in squared blocks of poros stone for the lower walls, the upper levels no doubt in brick and wood. There were courtyards open to the sky and windows and light-wells in adjacent rooms. Many of the rooms were paved with stone slabs.

Villa A preserved the huge bronze cauldrons on display in the Heraklion museum, some large pithoi storage urns, and several baked clay tablets inscribed in the Linear A script used in Minoan records. Fragments of frescoes from its upper storey reveal miniature figures in some form of contest, and decorative patterns.

Villa B is less well preserved and is the smallest of the three. Below its ruins can be discerned foundations of earlier structures from the Proto-Palatial period.

The best preserved plan is that of Villa C. Besides the usual storerooms, etc., it is possible to identify its vestibule off an atrium court, an entrance hall on the east with a porter's lodge or guardroom adjacent, a *polythyron* (room with several doors), bath, latrine, sanctuary for religious cult, stairs up to the second storey, and light-wells into inner rooms. Some of the walls retain their stucco covering and traces of red and white decoration. At the northeast

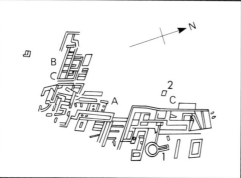

Tylissos

A Villa A
B Villa B
C Villa C
1 Cistern
2 Greek altar

corner a circular cistern was added in Late Minoan III, after 1400 BC. Its water channel has a filter basin at its northern end. Some Classical Greek walls overlie part of this villa, indicating use many centuries later. A Greek altar lies off the northwest corner.

A Minoan ritual sanctuary has been discovered on a hill-top in the vicinity.

Tinos/Tenos

Tenos, near the centre of the Cyclades north-west of Delos, was prosperous in ancient times and is today one of the most attractive of the islands, dotted with sparkling white towns and villages and fine views. It was colonized by Ionians in the tenth century BC and was known as Ophiusa from its many serpents – the later name may be based on the Phoenician word for snake: tenok. It prospered especially in the Geometric and Archaic periods but was also important through the Classical era. One of its ships deserted from forced service with the Persian fleet at Salamis and revealed the enemy's plan. Tenos contributed ten talents annually to the Athenian (Delian) Confederacy and joined Athens in the fateful attack on Syracuse in 415–414 BC. It was later allied with Rhodes. A notable local product was huge pithos storage jars with decoration in relief, represented by the amusing Trojan Horse

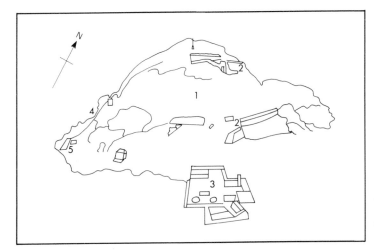

1 Xombourgo hill
2 Venetian fortress/castle
3 Monastery
4 Archaic wall of early city
5 Thesmophorion sanctuary

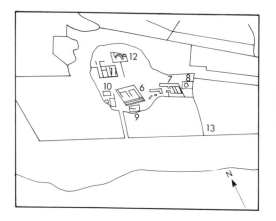

1–5 (*see p. 227*)
6 Temple of Poseidon and Amphitrite
7 Altar
8 Apsidal monument
9 Shrine for the Roman Emperor cult
10 Baths and pavement of Phileinos
11 Pilgrims' dining hall?
12 Stibadeion/fountain
13 Stoa site parallel to the sea

example which has recently been put on display in the Mykonos museum.

The early city lay some distance from the modern capital, on the west and southern slopes of conical Xombourgo hill, where Greek excavations have revealed parts of an Archaic polygonal wall dating back to the eighth century BC, some houses nearby, and a large public structure that may have had a religious purpose. Most significant is a long building from the eighth or seventh century BC with three major rooms, one of which encloses at its east end a small *naiskos* like a later temple with projecting anta walls, and an *eschara* sacred pit. This is probably a Thesmophorion of the Geometric/Archaic period dedicated to a female divinity. There is a small fountain nearby. Pithoi found in the temple-like room suggest that it was the sanctuary's *adyton*, the inner holy place. Doro Levi's investigations in Geometric tombs farther north at Kardiani have revealed much interesting pottery. There is evidence for a theatre and a Dionysos sanctuary in the Classical city, but neither of these has yet been adequately uncovered.

Along the coast northwest of the modern capital, some 500 ft inland from the sea, is the isolated sanctuary of Poseidon and Amphitrite partly revealed in Belgian excavations at the beginning of this century. Poseidon was honoured here for sending storks to rid the island of its serpents, and as the patron of commercial shipping. Amphitrite was also included in the cult from at least late Classical times. The sanctuary had its own mole out into the sea and a paved road leading to the beach. The temple, probably dating from the third century BC but replacing a much earlier one, is of peculiar design with an almost square cella and a 6 × 8 column peristyle with six steps to the supporting stylobate on the south and east sides. It is Doric and faces east. Some of its tiles bear dedications to Poseidon and fragments of marine beasts are among the decorative sculptural remains. The altar to the east had a square-U shape like the famous one at Pergamum, and a frieze of garlands and ox-heads. Two cult statues of Hellenistic style were found near it but probably belonged to the temple. An apsidal monument nearby seems to have been a family memorial. To the north of the temple was a pilgrims' ritual dining hall, mentioned by Strabo, and an exedra with a porticoed wing on each side with a Doric frieze above four columns – either a fountain or *stibadeion* for the Dionysos cult.

Tirins/**Tiryns**

Between Mycenae and the sea to Crete (Gulf of Argos), Tiryns stands on one of those geological phenomena so important to the development of independent city-states in ancient Greece: an oval limestone hill some 60 ft in height, accessible yet easily fortified and a prudent distance from the sea. A Bronze Age circular stone 'palace' some 90 ft in diameter has been traced, dated *c.* 2200 BC. In early Mycenaean times the hill was fortified, and again on a larger scale *c.* 1400, with a palace of considerable size near the centre. Walls and palace were rebuilt in the late Mycenaean period, 1250–1200 BC, but were soon after sacked and burned. Remains of an Archaic temple indicate renewed vitality in the seventh and sixth centuries BC, and Tiryns sent a contingent of 200 warriors against the Persians at Plataea in 479 but was conquered ten years later by Argos and the site faded into insignificance except for its imposing ruins – Pausanias compared its walls to the pyramids as a marvel (they were ascribed to the Cyclopes from Lycia, and are the most impressive of Mycenaean bastions, singled out by Homer and Pindar for admiration). In some accounts Hercules was born here, and all agree it was for Tiryns' king Eurystheus that he performed his mighty Twelve Labours.

Schliemann began excavations here in 1884, and work continued under Dörpfeld, Karo, and others. There was a town, as yet little explored, in the fertile plain around the citadel. Some fine fresco fragments and pottery from Tiryns are in the Athens and Nauplia museums.

The circuit of walls is nearly half a mile in length, and in some places they are as much as 25 ft thick. The main entrance through this encircling rampart was on the east, away from the sea, guarded by a massive tower. A long narrow corridor, easily defended, runs from there inside the eastern wall to an immense stone gateway much like the Lion Gate at Mycenae. A formal entrance, like later Classical Propylaea, leads to a large central court, to the north of which is another gate into the main megaron and royal quarters where the throne stood against the wall and four columns supported the roof, which was open over the central hearth. The floor was paved and painted, and stucco work decorated the walls: a boar

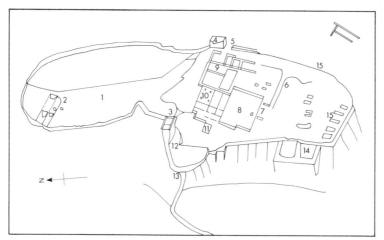

1 Lower enclosure
2 Entry to passages for water supply
3 West rampart bastion
4 East rampart tower
5 East (main) entry to citadel
6 Propylaea
7 Gate to palace area
8 Inner court, with altar
9 Royal family rooms (with 'Queen's Megaron')
10 King's Megaron
11 Bath
12 Stairs to west exit
13 West exit (Postern Gate)
14 Cisterns?
15 Trapezoidal galleries/ storerooms in south and east walls ('Grand Casemate')

hunt and a lady in formal pose partly survive. The complex of rooms to the east contains another smaller megaron, probably for the queen or for princes. To the west is a bath.

Inside the western wall a staircase winds down to a postern gate. Within the massive ramparts south and east are the trapezoidal galleries with fortified storerooms (the 'Grand Casemate').

The lower enclosure to the north was probably for livestock and for the protection of refugees from the houses outside the citadel in times of danger. Towards the northwest end are recently discovered passages tunnelled under the great wall for access to underground water springs outside.

Despite its splendid natural setting and colossal structures, Tiryns receives surprisingly little mention in ancient literature and history. Presumably it was eclipsed by its mighty neighbour Mycenae – or perhaps its people were too happy in its brightly elegant palace to be the theme of tragedy!

Trizin/**Troezen**

At the eastern edge of the Argolid, near the island of Poros, Troezen was an early colony of the Ionians and closely connected with Athens in legend, religious rites, and politics. It was here that Theseus was born, who later became king and organizer of Athens, and here also that his son Hippolytus by the Amazon Hippolyta met his death along the sea, when a monster sent by Poseidon frightened his horses as a result of his step-mother Phaedra's hatred – the theme of a famous extant tragedy by Euripides. Orestes came here to be purified after slaying his mother Clytemnestra. After the Persian break-through at Thermopylae, Troezen provided refuge for the citizens of Athens and Attica. An inscription found recently at Troezen

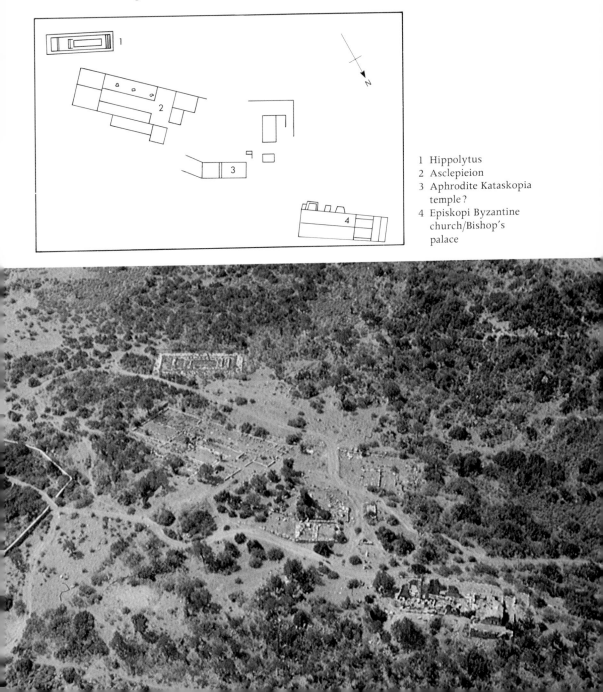

1 Hippolytus
2 Asclepieion
3 Aphrodite Kataskopia temple?
4 Episkopi Byzantine church/Bishop's palace

records Themistocles' plan for the evacuation of Athens and the mobilization of armed resistance at Salamis. (This decree may be a later glorified version of the strategy.) In resistance to the ambitions of Argos, Troezen fell under the influence and control of Sparta. It still flourished in Roman times.

Remains of the ancient city are widely scattered and not very substantial except for the Hippolytus sanctuary off to the northwest of the town centre and agora. The temple of Hippolytus here dates from the late fourth century BC, with 11 columns along the sides and six across the front and back. North of this is a large structure with adjacent buildings, apparently an Asclepieion (Asclepios was said to have brought Hippolytus back to life). Its main room on the south side had three Doric columns supporting a long ceiling, with a peristyle courtyard north of it, open to the sky at the centre. This was used either as a sacred dining room or as a ritual sleeping-hall for devotees. A small temple is included in the complex and a monumental fountain-house. The whole dates from the fourth or third century BC. A small temple north of the

Asclepieion may be that of Aphrodite Kataskopia, where Phaedra spied on Hippolytus in the ancient legend. Farther north, beyond the ruins of a Byzantine basilica and episcopal palace known as Episkopi, lay the stadium and gymnasium dedicated to Hippolytus.

The city centre was a good distance to the southeast. Pausanias describes at length its many temples and monuments, few of which are now visible or identified. The temple of Artemis Soteira ('Saviour') was near the agora, as was also one to Artemis Lykeia and a shrine to the Muses, plus a theatre, stoa, and a temple of Apollo Thearios. Half way up the hill to the south was a temple of Aphrodite Akraia, and higher up one to Pan. On the summit of the acropolis to the south was a temple of Athena Athenias. The sanctuary of Demeter and that of Poseidon were probably at the foot of the hill to the east. A long circuit of polygonal walls linked the acropolis to the city below. In the middle of the third century BC a transverse wall was constructed between the city area and the hill, at the expense of all citizens. A fine tower in this stretch is a fine example of Hellenistic fortification skill.

Vasse/Bassae

In austere isolation some 3700 ft up the side of Mt Kotilion amid deep ravines (bassai) from which it derives its modern name, the temple of Apollo Epikourios is the goal and reward for one of the most memorable excursions one can make in Greece. The air photographs bring out its striking setting far more adequately than any perspective on the ground.

Pausanias struggled up these elusive heights near Phigalia in Arcadia and admired the temple more than any other in southern Greece except Tegea's, praising its precise workmanship and the beauty of its stone. The hard local grey limestone needed no surface covering; the sculpture, interior capitals, and ceiling coffers and roofing were, however, of good marble.

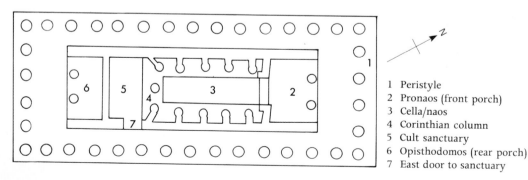

1 Peristyle
2 Pronaos (front porch)
3 Cella/naos
4 Corinthian column
5 Cult sanctuary
6 Opisthodomos (rear porch)
7 East door to sanctuary

The temple was built in thanksgiving to Apollo for aid in a local plague, probably the one of 420 BC known to have ravaged the area, and is therefore best dated to the end of the fifth century, somewhat later than the Parthenon, though some experts consider it to be earlier.

The architect is reported by Pausanias to have been Iktinos who also designed the Parthenon. Bassae's temple shows many marks of genius and bold innovation. It faces north, not the usual east, and is unusually long for its width (15 × 6 columns) – probably in imitation of the Archaic temple of Apollo at Delphi. Its porches are unusually deep, its cella unique – with five Ionic spur-columns projecting from the inner wall on each side, and with special handling of the capital scrolls; the back pair of columns is set at an angle and has between them a free-standing column with the first appearance of the Corinthian capital, modelled on clustered acanthus leaves. Furthermore, there is no back wall of the cella, but a new rectangular room with a door on the east, open towards the north into the cella proper. It is likely that this was a replacement of an earlier small shrine, traditionally oriented to the east, with the cult statue at its rear or centre, which the architect was obliged to preserve. He did so with brilliant ingenuity, boldly breaking from usual treatment of the cella and from the eastward facing of the whole. Morning light came through the little extra door, carefully positioned between the outer columns of the Doric peristyle, to illumine Apollo's statue and shrine with his own celestial radiance. Another colossal statue of Apollo in bronze stood outside the temple.

Above the inner Ionic and Corinthian columns, and across the opening of the main northern door, ran an Ionic continuous frieze with figures of Lapiths battling Centaurs and Greeks in combat with Amazons. Much of this strongly executed sculpture is now in the British Museum.

A ground plan is given here to help clarify the structural features described, no guide being necessary to identify the photograph's contents.

Vravron/**Brauron**

After Iphigeneia and her brother Orestes fled from Tauris (in the Crimea) with a primitive wooden statue of Artemis, they established the cult of the goddess at Brauron, 15 miles east of Athens where the little river Erasinos enters a great bay of the Aegean at the foot of a hill that had been inhabited since the Neolithic period. Another shrine to Artemis Tauropolos was set up nearby at Halae, four miles to the north. Euripides' great play *Iphigeneia in Tauris* 'prophesies' the establishment of Artemis' cult at both sites.

Though flourishing in the second millennium BC, the town at Brauron disappeared, according to archaeological evidence, in the late Mycenaean Age around 1300 BC – probably when its leading families were forced by Theseus to move to his newly-consolidated Athens. But the Artemis sanctuary continued. There is indication of cult there in the eighth century BC and thereafter until the early third century, when floods made the site unusable. An earlier, pre-Greek, mother-goddess of the region was absorbed into Artemis in the local traditions, which included the goddess' demand that young girls of Attica be dedicated to her service in reparation for the killing of one of her sacred bears. The ritual in Classical times involved ceremonies every four or five years in which girls from 5 to 10 years of age, dressed in saffron-hued robes, impersonated bears (*arktoi*). Charming little marble statues of these devotees have been found in the excavations carried out by Papadimitriou between 1946 and 1963, along with some fine relief panels, pottery, and gold jewellery.

The Artemis temple is on an elevation at the south edge of the site at the foot of the hill, near the late Byzantine chapel of St George put up to Christianize a pagan religious centre, as so frequently happened in Greece and Italy. Only parts on the south and east survive, but they reveal that the temple had a columned porch on the east front, an *adyton* (sacred area) at the back, and the central cella divided into three parts by a double row of columns. The building was Doric, 33 × 66 ft, probably of the fifth century BC, replacing an earlier structure of the seventh or sixth. An early retaining wall below to the north is, no doubt, the 'sacred stairway at Brauron' mentioned by Euripides. The altar was most likely situated outside on the east, within the temenos wall of the Archaic sanctuary. Below the temple's northwest corner is the Sacred Spring. Outside a small cave on the slope southeast of the temple is a ruined structure that was probably the traditional 'Tomb of Iphigeneia', with a priestess' house nearby. Her cult goes back at least to the eighth century BC.

Around 425 BC the sanctuary was greatly enlarged by the addition of an elaborate Doric peristyle court and stoa, 96 ft across. It has nine

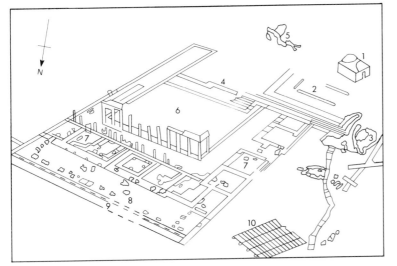

1 St George chapel
2 Temple of Artemis
3 Sacred Spring
4 Temenos wall
5 'Tomb of Iphigeneia'
6 Peristyle court
7 Rooms for 'Bears'
8 East Propylon
9 Stelae and dedicatory statues base
10 Bridge

columns down the west side, 15 along the east, and 11 across the north front; they are 12 ft high, with architrave and frieze above. Along the north and west sides are several rooms, with cuttings for beds and tables – presumably a sort of convent for the little girl 'Bears', referred to in Athenian inscriptions as the Parthenon (maidens' quarters). On the northern ledge outside the East Propylon are grooves to hold stelae records, and small statues of girl 'Bears' were recovered here.

Off the northwest corner of the complex is a stone bridge, its slabs resting on walls paralleling the stream's course. This is the only extant bridge that has survived from Classical times in Greece.

The Artemis Brauronia sanctuary on the Acropolis at Athens shows the cult's importance.

Xerxes' Canal

The easternmost of the three prongs of the Chalcidian peninsula that jut into the northern Aegean was called Akte in ancient times, and Holy Mountain today because of its many Orthodox monasteries that have dotted its shores for the past thousand years. The southern point is a fine pyramidal mountain, Athos, that towers 6670 ft above the sea. When attempting to round it in 492 BC on the way to punish Eretria and Athens, the Persian fleet of Darius under Mardonius was devastatingly shipwrecked in a fierce storm. When Xerxes planned a much more massive assault on Greece he resolved to take no chances of another such disaster here and ordered a canal to be dug across the peninsula's narrowest section near the town of Akanthos, broad enough for two triremes to sail through abreast.

Our only information on this great project is Herodotus' account and some confusing traces on the spot. Early nineteenth-century travellers like Leake, Bowen, Spratt reported seeing a series of wide shallow pools in a depression running westward from Hierissos village, which seems to be on the site of ancient Akanthos. Some of the low hills on the western shore appear to be artificial mounds, perhaps dumped earth from the canal construction. The soil here is marl and sand, making plausible both the original digging and the subsequent filling in of the channel by centuries of weathering and farming. Though a few ancient authors like Juvenal and some modern scholars are sceptical about the canal's existence, it seems to have been real. The distance is under a mile and a half, the terrain low and soft – unlike the Isthmus at Corinth which is solid rock 255 ft high.

Herodotus himself thinks the work superfluous and primarily an arrogant display of Persian might to terrorize the Greeks. But it was practical, rather than dragging the ships across on land – a very slow operation for so vast and impatient a fleet, and Xerxes had enormous resources at his command. He is said to have ordered the operation three years in advance of his setting out, and to have dispatched relays of workers from many nations, supplying them with ground grain in a market situated in a meadow next to the work site. Of special interest is a hoard of 300 Persian daric coins found in the area in the last century. Only the Phoenician workmen are said to have been foresighted enough to start their section much wider at the top and slope it down to waterlevel; the others' walls kept caving in. A giant Persian taskmaster named Artachaies supervised the labour which was done under the lash, as Herodotus reports with disgust. When Xerxes arrived at Akanthos, Artachaies died of an illness and was given a splendid burial. The mighty fleet then sailed through the canal and on to Artemision – and to unanticipated humiliation and disaster at Salamis. The psychological warfare aspect of the canal's flamboyant construction had failed; the Greeks were not petrified into surrender. Since its value to commercial shipping was not later considered commensurate to the endless labour of keeping it navigable, it has almost lapsed from view – but lives on in memory by the art of Herodotus, the father of history and of European prose.

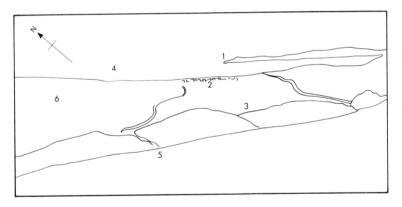

Zakros/**Zakros**

Until a few years ago the existence of a major Minoan palace on the extreme eastern edge of Crete was not known and hardly even suspected. There is no historical or literary tradition about it, and its discovery by Professor Platon has been one of the major windfalls of modern archaeology. The palace has a well-preserved ground plan and since it was not re-occupied after the disaster that destroyed it c. 1450 BC, along with the other great Minoan sites, its remains are of special importance in clarifying many aspects of Cretan architecture and life. Some splendid art objects were recovered from the ruins, precious documentation of Minoan civilization – which Zakros has illuminated in many new aspects. It has an added interest as a harbour town, prospering from extensive international trade.

The excavations are not yet complete, but the main area of the palace is now uncovered, along with an annex to the northeast and a block of houses along cobbled streets to the

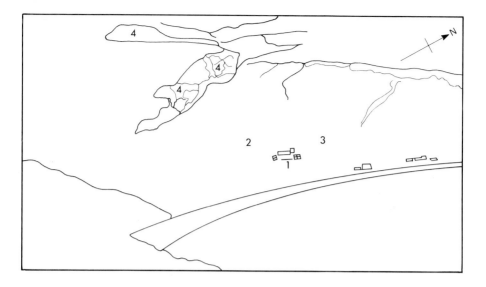

1 Palace
2 Site of southwest houses
3 Northeast slope (Hogarth)
4 Gorge of the Dead
5 Central Court of the palace
6 Queen's apartment?
7 King's apartment?
8 Hall of the cistern
9 Well in stepped enclosure
10 Storerooms
11 Reception lobby
12 Hall of Ceremonies
13 Banquet hall
14 Workshops
15 Stepped ramp
16 Inner paved court
17 Passage to the northeast
   annex
18 Kitchen and dining area
19 Northern sector: apartments
20 Northwestern sector: rooms
21 Archives room (Linear A)
22 Central shrine
23 Lustral basin
24 Treasury of the shrine
25 Southwest houses

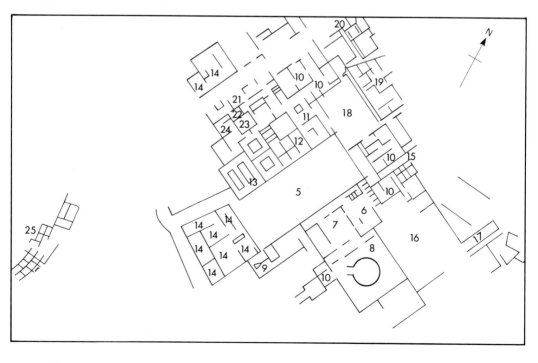

southwest – the sector which Platon first dug before finding the palace itself. The air view does not show the rooms north and northeast of the palace complex which have been excavated since 1967 but it is otherwise adequate since the main constructions were already then exposed, in their great setting near the majestic bay.

The ancient establishment was much more imposing than today's few houses, cafes, farms, and inn at Kato Zakro – which at least share their predecessor's fine beach and protectively enfolding mountains. The isolated grandeur and mystery of the site is augmented by the awesome Gorge of the Dead at the back, whose deep recesses guard Minoan and later tombs.

British excavations in 1901 under Hogarth discovered on the northeast slope several houses (interpreted as Mycenaean) and some artifacts, but it was 60 years before Platon, led by various clues and intuition, located the southwest houses and then in 1962 the great palace. Further structures to the north are still being uncovered, and there are almost certainly more on the east towards the sea. The excavator's account of the discovery and interpretation of this hitherto unknown royal Minoan town is most fascinating.

Some rooms to the north and northwest go back to the end of the Early Minoan era and the Proto-Palatial period, but the extant palace proper dates from after 1600 BC, with considerable rebuilding after the ruinous earthquake of the late sixteenth century BC. The large Central Court is oriented northeast-southwest, like all other Palatial examples in Crete. Rooms to the east of the court were probably royal apartments. The great hall beyond them, possibly an audience chamber, included a cistern for spring water. This, and a well enclosed in a stone casing with eight steps down to water-level, are an arrangement of internal supply unique in Cretan palaces. In a cup at the bottom of the well were found olives still preserved! A paved court to the east has a passage up to the north east annex rooms.

Near the lustral basin west of the court was the palace shrine, with benches for idols along its inner walls. In its adjacent treasury were found splendid stone and crystal vessels for ritual use. The archives room nearby had record tablets in Linear A script. A banquet hall and a ceremonial room adjoin the court on its west side. The large room northeast of the court is identified by its contents as the kitchen area, the only one yet found in a Minoan palace. There were clearly rooms above the main floor over most of the palace area; their contents fell to earth in the final disaster. Stairs and light-wells were provided. There were many store-rooms, and workshops for carving ivory, stone, and crystal and for pottery.

Rooms were brightly decorated. Many walls had stucco relief: often this was white spirals on a blue background with a rosette in the centre. Some floors had rectangular panels framed by stucco ridges and filled with some red material – a kind of raised carpeting.

Mediterranean Chronology

(Dates = BC. Based on Platon, Hammond, Mylonas, Michalowski; some dates controverted)

NEAR EAST, ETC.	CRETE	GREECE
	NEOLITHIC	
Çatal Huyük, Jericho: 7500 Predynastic Ur: 3400–2500 1st Writing (Sumer): *c.* 3300 Gilgamesh epic: *c.* 3000 Troy I: *c.* 3500– Troy II: *c.* 2800–	Late Stone Age: *c.* 6000–2600	Late Stone Age: *c.* 3900–2900 (to 2200 in N) 'Pelasgoi' *c.* 3200–
	EARLY BRONZE AGE	
Sumer: Dyn. 1: *c.* 2500 Sargon (Akkad): *c.* 2350– Troy III: *c.* 2300– Babylon and Assur founded: *c.* 2200 Gudea (Lagash): *c.* 2080–	*Pre-Palatial/Early Minoan* 1 (=EM 1): 2600–2400 2 (=EM 2): 2400–2250 3 {EM 3): 2250–1950 {MM 1a): 1950–1900 (pictographic script)	*Early Helladic* (Pre-Greek) 2600–1900 Lerna 'House of Tiles' *c.* 2200; destroyed *c.* 2100
	MIDDLE BRONZE AGE	
Hittite expansion: 1800– Hamurrabi (Babylon): *c.* 1792–1750 Troy VI: 1800– Alphabet invented in Syria: *c.* 1500	*Proto-Palatial/Mid. Minoan* (first palaces) 1 (=MM 1b): 1900–1850 2 (=MM 2a): 1850–1750 3 (=MM 2b): 1750–1700 (Kamares pottery) (palaces destroyed *c.* 1700) *Neo-Palatial/Mid.-Late Minoan* 1 {MM 3a): 1700–1650 {MM 3b): 1650–1550 (palaces rebuilt; Linear A script)	*Middle Helladic* (Primitive Greek) MH 1: 1900–1650 Achaeans arrive, *c.* 1900 (from Asia Minor?) Minyan Ware MH 2: 1650–1580 (first shaft graves: Circle B at Mycenae)
	LATE BRONZE AGE	
Thera quake? *c.* 1450 (Cretan palaces wrecked) Troy VII A: *c.* 1300– Urartu (Ararat, Armenia): 13th cent. – Ramses II checks Hittites: *c.* 1280 Sea Peoples invade Egypt: *c.* 1230 Gk. Thebes destr.: *c.* 1230 Trojan War: *c.* 1210–1200 Thera explosion: *c.* 1175? Tiglath-Pileser I takes Babylon: *c.* 1080 New Assyrian Empire: 885– Carthage founded: *c.* 800 Rome founded: *c.* 753 Cumae, 1st colony in Eur: 750 Medes' Empire: 715–550	2 (=LM 1a): 1550–1500 3 (=LM 1b): 1500–1450 (peak of Cretan power; palaces destroyed *c.* 1450) 4 (=LM 2): 1450–1350 (at Knossos only; rebuilt, under Greek control; 'Throne Room' built; Linear B script) *Post-Palatial/Late Minoan* 1 (=LM 3a): 1350–1300 2 (=LM 3b): 1300–1225 3 (=LM 3c): 1225–1120 (Greeks gone by 1190)	*Late Helladic* (=Mycenaean Age) LH 1: 1580–1500 (Grave Circle; tholoi) LH 2: 1500–1400 (Gk. colonies: Cyprus, Syria) LH 3a: 1400–1300 (Myc. palaces built) LH 3b: 1300–1190 (Atreus *c.* 1250) (Pylos destroyed *c.* 1190) LH 3c: 1190–1120 ('Dorian Invasion': Myc. etc. destroyed 1120)
	IRON AGE	
Troy VIII (Greek): *c.* 700– Sennacherib destroys Jerusalem 701, Babylon 689 Nebuchadnessar king of Babylon: *c.* 605–562 Cyrus: Persian Emp: 550– Hannibal: 247–182 Carthage destroyed: 146 Troy IX (Roman): 45–	*Sub-Minoan* (Dark Age): 1120–1000 *Proto-Geometric:* 1000–850 *Dorian Era:* 8–7th cent. *Classical Era:* 6–1st cent. *Roman Rule:* 67 BC– *Byzantine:* 5–9th cent. AD	*Sub-Mycenaean:* 1120–1000 *Proto-Geometric:* 10th cent. *Geometric:* *c.* 9th, 8th cent. *Archaic Age:* 750–480 *Classical Era:* 480–323 *Hellenistic Age:* 323–146 *Roman Domination:* 146– *Byzantine Era:* 395 AD–

Glossary

ABATON ('not to be trodden', 'sacred') a sanctuary building, as at Epidauros – a long hall where the sick lay awaiting a revelation or cure.

ACROTERION ('top-fixture', 'along the edge') decorative sculpture, often floral, at apex and two bottom edges of a pediment on a temple.

ADYTON ('not to be entered') innermost sacred room of temple or shrine.

ANAKTORON ('hall of lords') a rectangular sacred building, as at Samothrace.

ANTA ('opposite, facing') projecting front portion of a cella's side wall in a temple, often forming an enclosed porch.

ARCHEGESION ('place of the leader') a sacred structure for the cult of Apollo Archegetis on Delos, and of the legendary founder Anios.

ARCHITRAVE ('chief beam') horizontal supporting beam across columns of a temple, stoa, etc., supporting the pediment or roof-front.

ARTEMISION shrine or temple in honour of Artemis, as at Delos.

ASCLEPIEION temple or sanctuary in honour of Asclepius, the god of healing.

BOULEUTERION ('place of the Boule') Senate House.

CAVEA ('hollow area') concave auditorium of seats in a theatre, etc.

CELLA ('storeroom') enclosed inner 'house of the god', central room of a temple.

DIAZOMA ('girdle') horizontal passage in a theatre separating blocks of seat-rows.

DIATEICHISMA ('dividing wall') partition wall between zones of a city or sanctuary.

DIOLKOS ('drag-through') a slipway for pulling ships across strip of land between water areas.

DIPYLON ('double gate') an entrance with double gate.

DROMOS ('race, run-way') a narrow approach, as to a tholos tomb, walled on both sides.

ESCHARA ('fire-holder') a hearth or altar for burnt sacrifice, especially in Minoan palaces.

EXEDRA ('seat to side') a public bench, semicircular or U-shaped, along a street or processional way.

HELIAIA the rectangular hall for the chief Law Court of Athens, in the Agora.

HEROON ('hero's place') a shrine or monument to a Hero, glorified mortal.

HIPPODROME ('horse running area') a long stadium-like place for horse and chariot racing.

HYPOSTYLE HALL ('under-pillared') a large roofed room with many supporting interior columns.

ISCHEGAON ('earth-holder') a retaining wall supporting a temple terrace, as at Delphi.

KERATON ('of horns') structure housing the 'altar made from horns' on Delos.

KORE ('girl') archaic statue of standing clothed young woman.

KOUROS ('youth') archaic statue of standing nude young man.

MANTEION ('belonging to a prophet or oracle') seat of an oracle or prophetic centre.

MARMARIA ('marble quarter') lower sanctuary area at Delphi, where Tholos, temple of Athena Pronaia, etc. are.

MEGARON ('large room') the central main room of a Mycenaean palace, sometimes also applied to an old temple.

METOPE ('between beam-ends') rectangular space, usually carrying sculpture or other figured decoration, between the triglyphs in a Doric frieze of temples, stoas, etc.

NAISKOS ('little shrine') small shrine-like structure on a tomb, etc.; a façade with gabled roof and frontal pillars.

NAOS ('temple, shrine') the inner main room (=cella) of a temple; sometimes used of the whole temple.

NEORION ('ship-place') dockyard, protected anchorage for ships.

ODEION ('singing place') concert hall, in form of a small theatre, roofed over.

OPISTHODOMOS ('room at back') western back-porch room of a temple.

ORCHESTRA ('dancing area') flat area in front of stage of theatre, usually partially or fully circular, where chorus moved and sang – and in early times also the actors.

PALAESTRA ('wrestling place') rectangular open area surrounded by colonnade for sports and training practice.

PARADROMOS ('running along side') unroofed running course along gymnasium colonnade, etc.

PARASCENIUM ('next to the stage') a wing or side room flanking the stage structure, often projecting ahead of the stage into the Orchestra.

PARODOS ('way at side') a passage between Orchestra and stage for entry from side into theatre area.

PELOPION Shrine to Pelops, as at Olympia.

PERISTYLE ('pillar around') a row of columns surrounding a building (e.g. a temple) or open courtyard.

POLYANDREION ('for many men') a common burial monument for a group.

POMPEION ('procession-house') a storeroom for equipment used in solemn processions.

PROHEDRIA ('front seats') the front row of seats, in a theatre, etc., for honoured officials and guests, usually with backs.

PROPYLON ('front entrance') formal gateway into special area; plural = *Propylaea*.

PROSCENIUM ('in front of stage') a colonnaded platform between Orchestra and stage building of a theatre.

PROSTOON ('front shed') a colonnaded formal porch or portico.

PRYTANEION ('officials' building') the Magistrates' Court or town hall.

PYTHION temple or shrine of Pythian Apollo, as at Delphi.

SCENE OR SKENE ('tent, booth') back scene structure of a theatre behind the stage, replacing earlier players' booth.

SEBASTEION ('place of revered ones') shrine in honour of Emperors, *Augusti*.

SKENOTHEKE ('tent store') storeroom for stage equipment, scenery, costumes, etc.

SPHENDONE ('sling') the oblong area of a stadium with sloping sides and rounded end.

STOA ('shed') a roofed colonnade or portico, with one or more rows of columns parallel to back wall.

STYLOBATE ('pillar basis') the top step or platform on which temple or stoa columns rest. Loosely used of all three levels beneath the columns.

SYNEDRION ('place for sitting together') Council chamber, officials' hall.

TELESTERION ('perfecting place') sacred hall for initiation ceremonies of cult, as at Eleusis.

TEMENOS ('cut-off area') sacred enclosure fenced off from common use, for temples, etc.

THERSILION a large roofed (hypostyle) Council Hall at Megalopolis near the theatre.

THOLOS ('rotunda') a round building with conical roof –

either a 'beehive' tomb of Mycenaean period or a special civic structure with surrounding colonnade.

TRIGLYPH ('triple-carved') a decorative element of Doric frieze above architrave of temple or stoa, imitating primitive wooden beam-ends, with two vertical grooves between three raised vertical panels.

XENON ('of strangers') name for a hotel for transient visitors, as at Nemea.

XOANON ('carved') primitive carved wooden statue in log-like form.

XYSTOS ('trimmed') roofed colonnade in gymnasium, or in house, as walking area.

Bibliography

LIST OF ABBREVIATIONS

AAA	Athens Annals of Archaeology
AJA	American Journal of Archaeology
Ath. Mitt.	Athenische Mitteilungen des Deutschen Archäologischen Instituts
BA	Biblical Archaeologist
BCH	Bulletin de Correspondance Hellénique
BSA	Annual of the British School at Athens
EAA	Enciclopedia dell'Arte Antica
ILN	Illustrated London News
JDAI	Jahrbuch des Deutschen Archäologischen Instituts
JHS	Journal of Hellenistic Studies
PAE	Praktika tis Archaiologikes Etairias
SA	Scientific American

The following list of books and articles is highly selective. It makes no pretence of being complete – that would require a large volume by itself. Those items are listed which should be of special interest and usefulness as sources of fuller data on the sites covered in this book. Mostly only those in English are included, but where these do not provide the full picture, studies in French, German, Greek, or Italian are also cited. Excavation reports are not ordinarily in this list, except where more general synthesis and interpretation studies are not available. Special care is taken to indicate where ground plans of the sites may be found, to supplement with fuller detail (and often theoretical additions) the basic key given by the identification sketches in this book and the air photographs themselves.

Ancient sources are not normally included in the list, though they are often of interest for background

and explanation of the monuments. Those who desire this sort of information can readily find it in the standard editions of Herodotus, Pausanias, and Strabo – all of them translated in the Loeb Classical Library, with indexes, and Herodotus and Pausanias also in the Penguin Classics Paperbacks. Their use as companions to the study of the sites is warmly recommended.

Omitted from the Bibliography are the relevant pages in the following general guides, which it is assumed will be consulted for fuller data when desired. Because of their ready availability I thought it best to keep the commentaries in this book very succinct, there being no reason to repeat what is in these general guides:

The Princeton Dictionary of Classical Archaeology, edited by R. Stillwell (Princeton, projected for 1975): an alphabetical treatment of all Classical sites with basic historical and archaeological data and brief bibliographies.

Greece in World Guides series by Hachette (Paris, 1964), by R. Boulanger: very handy summary of data on all sites in Greece, often with ground plans.

Greece in Blue Guides series by Benn (London, 1973), by S. Rossiter: similar to the above title but more up-to-date, and fuller details on some sites.

Griechenlandkunde, 5th edition (Heidelberg, 1967), by Kirsten and Kraiker: like the two above but in German only; omits some sites, is especially good on others; basic bibliography on each site at end (but has numerous errors).

Oxford Classical Dictionary, 2nd edition (Oxford, 1970), edited by Hammond and Scullard: short historical account of major sites, but omits many others.

Real-Encyclopaedie der Classischen Altertumswissenschaft, edited by Pauly, Wissowa, Kroll, *et al.*

(Stuttgart, 1894–1971), many volumes and supplements: history and description of all sites, with citation of sources; occasional plans.

AEGINA
Berve, H. and G. Gruben, *Greek Temples, Theatres and Shrines*, London, 1963: 347–51 on Aphaia temple, with details and plan.

Furtwängler, A. *Aegina: Das Heiligtum der Aphaia*, Munich, 1906, 2 vols.

Webster, T. B. L. 'The Temple of Aphaia at Aegina'. *JHS* 51 (1931): 179–83 on sculptures only.

Welter, G. *Aigina*, Berlin, 1938: 64–90 on Aphaia temple, rest on other sites and art.

AEGOSTHENA/AIGOSTHENA
Benson, E. F. 'Aegosthena' *JHS* 15 (1895), 314–24: with plan.

Scranton, R. L. *Greek Walls*, Harvard, 1941: 81, 167, 176.

Winter, F. E. *Greek Fortifications*, Toronto, 1971: 142, 165, 189.

AGHIA TRIADHA/HAGHIA TRIADHA
Banti, L. 'Haghia Triadha'. *EAA* 3, 1087–93; with photos and plan.

Graham, J. W. *The Palaces of Crete*, Princeton 1962: 49–51, plan.

Halbherr, F. 'Scoperti ad Haghia Triadha presso Phaestos'. *Monumenti Antichi* 13 (1903), 6–74.

Marinatos, S. *Crete and Mycenae*, London, 1960: 58–62, 135–7, with photos, Banti's plan.

Mosso, A. *The Palaces of Crete and their Builders*, London, 1907: 69–91, with photos of early finds.

Nauert, J. P. 'The Haghia Triadha Sarcophagus: an iconographical study'. *Antike Kunst* 8 (1965), 91–8.

Pernier, L., and L. Banti, *Guida degli scavi Italiani in Creta*, Rome, 1947. 28–38.

AMFIARION/AMPHIAREION
Coulton, J. J. 'The Stoa of the Amphiareion at Oropos'. *BSA* 63 (1968), 147–83.

Petrakos, B. *O Oropos kai to Ieron tou Amphiaraou*, Athens, 1968: general study in Greek with plans.

Versace, F. 'Der Tempel und die Stoa im Amphiareion bei Oropos'. *Ath. Mitt.* 33 (1908), 247–72.

AMFIPOLIS/AMPHIPOLIS
Broneer, O. *The Lion Monument of Amphipolis*, Harvard, 1971.

Pelekides, C. and D. Lazarides. In *PAE* for 1920, 1956, 1957, 1959, 1961, 1962, 1965: excavation reports in Greek.

Pritchett, W. K. 'Amphipolis'. *Studies in Ancient Greek Topography*, vol. 1, University of California, 1965: 30–48, with photos and map of area.

ARGOS
Courbin, P. 'Discoveries at Ancient Argos'. *Archaeology* 9 (1956), 166–74: Mycenaean, Geometric tombs.

Roux, G. 'Le Sanctuaire d'Apollon sur l'Aspis'. *L'Architecture de l'Argolide aux IV et III Siècles*, Paris, 1961: 65–82.

Tomlinson, R. A. *Argos and the Argolid*, London, 1972: general history; photos and plans.

Vollgraff, W., *et al.* *Le Sanctuaire d'Apollon Pythéen à Argos*, Paris, 1956: with photos and plans.

Vollgraff, W. and J. Deshayes, P. Courbin, G. Roux, G. Daux. In *BCH* for 1904, 1906, 1907, 1920 and annually since 1954. Excavation reports with plans.

ATHINE/ATHENS
The Athenian Agora: Results of the Excavations conducted by the American School of Classical Studies in Athens, many volumes in progress, Princeton, 1953– : full data, photos and plans.

Berve, H. and G. Gruben. *Greek Temples, Theatres and Shrines*, London, 1963: 78–90, 371–97, plans.

Bowra, C. M. *Periclean Athens*, London, 1971: historical and cultural background.

Collignon, M. *Le Parthénon: Histoire, Archicture, Sculpture*, Paris, 1926: detailed account.

DeSolla Price, D. 'The Tower of the Winds'. *National Geographic Magazine*, April 1967, 587–96.

Dinsmoor, W. B. *Observations on the Hephaisteion*, Princeton, 1941: *Hesperia* Supplement 5.

Gouvoussis, J. and A. N. Oikonomides. *The Acropolis*, Athens, 1965: plan and three-dimensional reconstruction drawing, with description and sources.

Hill, I. T. *The Ancient City of Athens*, London, 1953: good synthesis of sources and studies.

Hopper, R. J. *The Acropolis*, London, 1970: description, many photographs.

Judeich, W. *Topographie von Athen*, 2nd edition. Munich, 1931: fullest data, some now out of date.

Karo, G. *An Attic Cemetery: Excavations in the Kerameikos at Athens*, Philadelphia, 1943.

Oikonomides, A. N. *The Two Agoras in Ancient Athens*, Chicago, 1964: data on early location theory.

Pickard-Cambridge, A. W., *The Theatre of Dionysos at Athens*, Oxford, 1946.

Plommer, W. H. 'The Archaic Acropolis: Some Problems'. *JHS* 80 (1960), 127–59.

Stevens, Gorham P., *Restorations of Classical Buildings*, Princeton, 1958: accurate drawings of many buildings in Athens.

— *The Setting of the Periclean Parthenon*, Princeton, 1940: *Hesperia* Supplement 3.

Stuart, J. and N. Revett, *The Antiquities of Athens*, 4 vols. London, 1762–1816: important drawings as monuments were in 18th century, with descriptions.

Thompson, H. A. (editor). *The Athenian Agora: A guide to the excavations and museum*, Athens, 1962.

Thompson, H. A. and R. E. Wycherley. *The Agora of Athens*, Princeton, 1972: summary of finds, data.

Travlos, J., *Pictorial Dictionary of Ancient Athens*, London, 1971: 721 photos, brief data on all main monuments, selective archaeological bibliography.

Wycherley, R. E. 'The Olympieion at Athens'. *Greek, Roman and Byzantine Studies* 5 (1964), 161–79. A model of the Acropolis, in 'Archaeological News'. *Archaeology* 13 (1960), 217: photo of fine scale model in Toronto.

AVDIRA/ABDERA
Graham, J. W. 'Notes on Houses and Housing

Districts at Abdera and Himera.' *AJA* 76 (1972), 295–301.

Lazarides, D. In *PAE* 1950, 1952, 1954, 1955, 1956, 1966: excavation reports in Greek.

Lazarides, D. and C. Doxiadis. *Abdera kai Dikaia*, Athens, 1971: general summary in Greek, with plans.

MacDonald, W. A. *The History of Abdera*, Baltimore, 1943.

AVLIS/AULIS

Daux, G. 'Chronique des Fouilles, 1961: Aulis'. *BCH* 86 (1962), 776–9, with plan of temple area.

Psarianos, O. 'Ho Archaios Limen tes Aulidos'. *Polemon* 3 (1948), 155–60: on the ancient harbour.

Threpsiades, I. In *PAE* for 1956 (94–104), 1958 (45–54), 1959 (26–33), 1961 (41–4): excavation reports in Greek.

DELFI/DELPHI

Berve, H. and G. Gruben, *Greek Temples, Theatres and Shrines*, London, 1963: 27–42, 326–42, with plan.

Coste-Messelière, P. de la and G. de Miré. *Delphes*, Paris, 1943: 248 fine photos of site and art.

Dinsmoor, W. B. 'Studies of the Delphian Treasuries'. *BCH* 36 (1912), 439–93 and 37 (1913), 5–83.

Ferri, S. 'Delfi'. *EAA* 3, 27–44, with plan, photos.

Flacelière, R. *Greek Oracles*, London, 1965: 33–59 on Delphi.

Haywood, R. 'The Delphic Oracle'. *Archaeology* 5 (1952), 110–18.

Holland, L. B. 'The Mantic Mechanism at Delphi'. *AJA* 37 (1933), 201–14.

Hoyle, P. *Delphi*, London, 1967: general account, with much on the oracle; with photos.

Parke, H. W. and E. W. Wormell. *The Delphic Oracle*, 2 vols. Oxford, 1956; history, extant responses.

Picard, C. and J. Replat. 'Sur la Tholos du 'Hiéron' d'Athéna Pronaia'. *BCH* 48 (1924), 209–63.

Poulsen, F. *Delphi*, London, 1920: good over-all survey.

Ridgway, B. S. 'The West Frieze of the Siphnian Treasury'. *BCH* 86 (1962), 24–35.

—— 'The East Pediment of the Siphnian Treasury'. *AJA* 69 (1965), 1–5.

Roux, G. *Delphes*, Paris, 1970; general study of oracle and monuments, in French; photos and plan.

Full data, plans, reconstructions in *Fouilles de Delphes*, Paris, 1902–: many volumes, in progress.

DILOS/DELOS

Berve, H. and G. Gruben. *Greek Temples, Theatres and Shrines*, London, 1963; 59–64, 363–6, with plan.

Bruneau, P. and J. Ducat. *Guide de Délos*, Paris, 1965: summary of data, with photos and plans.

Courby, F. 'Le Sanctuaire d'Apollon Délien'. *BCH* 44/45 (1921/22), 174–241.

Deonna, W. *La Vie privée des Déliens*, Paris, 1948.

Laidlaw, W. A. *A History of Delos*, Oxford, 1933.

Laurenzi, L. 'Delo'. *EAA* 3, 45–58: summary, with photos and plans.

Reinach, S. 'Le Colosse d'Apollon à Délos'. *BCH* 17 (1893), 129–44.

Vallois, R. *L'Architecture Hellénique et Hellénistique à Délos*, 2 vols. Paris, 1944, 1966.

—— 'Topographie Délienne'. *BCH* 48 (1924), 411–45 and 54 (1929), 185–315.

Full description and data, with plans and photos, in *Exploration Archéologique de Délos*, many volumes, in progress since 1909 (Paris).

DODONI/DODONA

Berve, H. and G. Gruben, *Greek Temples, Theatres and Shrines*, London, 1963: 52–3 on oracle, history.

Carapanos, C. *Dodone et ses Ruines*, 2 vols. Paris, 1878.

Dakaris, S. *Bodona*, Ioannina, 1971: summary guide, with plans, sketches, photos.

Gardner, P. *New Chapters in Greek History*, London, 1892: 402–12.

Nicol, D. M. 'The Oracle of Dodona'. *Greece and Rome* 5 (1958), 128–43.

Parke, H. W. *The Oracles of Zeus*, Harvard, 1967: 1–163, 259–86.

ELEFSIS/ELEUSIS

Berve, H. and G. Gruben. *Greek Temples, Theatres and Shrines*, London, 1963; 45–52, 399–404.

Kerenyi, C. *Eleusis: Archetypal Image of Mother and Daughter*, New York, 1967.

Kourouniotis, K. *Eleusis: A Guide to the Excavations and Museum*, Athens, 1936.

Mylonas, G. *Eleusis and the Eleusinian Mysteries*, Princeton, 1961; with photos and plans.

Mylonas, G. and K. Kourouniotis. *The Hymn to Demeter and her Sanctuary at Eleusis*, St Louis, 1942.

Noack, F. *Eleusis*, Berlin, 1927, 2 vols: full study, in German, with photos and plans.

Travlos, J. 'The Topography of Eleusis'. *Hesperia* 18 (1949), 138–47: with plans.

EPIDAVROS/EPIDAUROS

Berve, H. and G. Gruben. *Greek Temples, Theatres and Shrines*, London, 1963: 67–9, 358–63, plans.

Burford, A. *The Greek Temple Builders at Epidauros*, Liverpool, 1969: interesting data on planning, supervision, financing, artisans, records.

Gerkan, A. von, and W. Müller-Wiener. *Das Theater von Epidauros*, Stuttgart, 1961: full data, plans.

Kavvadias, P. *Fouilles d'Epidaure*, Athens, 1891: excavator's report, with photos and plans.

Lechat, H. and A. Defrasse. *Épidaure: Restaurations et description des principaux monuments du sanctuaire d'Asclépios*, Paris, 1895: plan, fine reconstructions, descriptive data.

Papadimitriou, J. 'Le Sanctuaire d'Apollo Maléatas à Epidaure'. *BCH* 73 (1949), 361–83.

Roux, G. *L'Architecture de l'Argolide aux IV et III Siècles*, Paris, 1961: 83–315 on Epidauros.

Schoder, R. V. 'The Theater at Epidauros as a Work of Art'. In *Greek Drama: Festival Papers*, edited by Grace L. Beede, University of South Dakota, 1967: 13–39, with photos, data.

ERETRIA

Auberson, P. and K. Schefold. *Führer durch Eretria*, Bern, 1972: general guide.

Eretria: Fouilles et Recherches, Bern, 1968–: vol. I on Apollo Temple, III on Heroön at W. Gate.

Fiechter, E. *Das Theater in Eretria*, Stuttgart, 1937.
Richardson, R. *et al.*: series of reports on history, topography, theatre, Dionysos temple, gymnasium, etc. in early excavations, in *Papers of the American School of Classical Studies at Athens*, vol. 6: 1890–97, Boston, 1897; reprinted from *AJA* 5–11.
Schefold, K. 'The Architecture of Eretria'. *Archaeology* 21 (1968), 272–81: survey, with photos.
Schefold, K. *et al.* excavation reports, with photos and plans, in *Antike Kunst* for 1964, 1966, 1968, 1969, 1971. Better plan in *Archailogikon Deltion* 17 (1961/62), 153.

FESTOS/PHAISTOS
Graham, J. W. 'Phaistos: Second Fiddle to Knossos?' *Archaeology* 10 (1957), 208–14: photos.
— *The Palaces of Crete*, Princeton, 1962: 34–41, photos and plan.
— 'Egyptian Features at Phaistos'. *AJA* 74 (1970), 231–9.
Hood, S. *The Minoans*, London, 1971: 72–5, with photos and plan.
Hutchinson, R. W. *Prehistoric Crete*, London, 1962: 190–5, with plan.
Levi, D. *Recent Excavations at Phaistos*, Lund, 1964: summary, with photos and new plan.
Marinatos, S. *Crete and Mycenae*, London, 1960: 131–5, with photos and plan.
Pernier, L. and L. Banti. *Il Palazzo Minoico di Festos*, 2 vols., Rome, 1935, 1951: full data, plans.

FILI/PHYLE
Chandler, L. 'The Northwest Frontier of Attica'. *JHS* 46 (1926): 3–6 Phyle.
Scranton, R. L. *Greek Walls*, Cambridge, 1941: 177.
Skias, A. In *PAE*, 1900, 38–50: excavation report in Greek.
Winter, F. E. *Greek Fortifications*, Toronto, 1971: 43, 139–40, 161–2, with plan, reconstruction.
Wrede, W. 'Phyle'. *Ath. Mitt.* 49 (1924), 153–224: fullest account, with photos, reconstruction sketch.
— *Attische Mauern*, Athens, 1933: 28, 55, 63, 66–7 on Phyle.

FILIPPI/PHILIPPI
Collart, P. 'Le Théâtre de Philippes'. *BCH* 52 (1928), 74–124.
— 'Le Sanctuaire des Dieux Egyptiens à Philippes'. *BCH* 53 (1929), 70–100.
— *Philippes: Ville de Macédoine,* 2 vols. Paris, 1937: full data, photos and plans.
Ducoux, H. and P. Lemerle. 'L'Acropole et l'Enceinte Haute de Philippes', *BCH* 62 (1938), 4–19.
Hoddinott, R. F. *Early Byzantine Churches in Macedonia and Southern Serbia*, London, 1962.
Krautheimer, R. *Early Christian and Byzantine Architecture*, London, 1965: 97–8, 182–3, plan.
Lemerle, P. 'Palestre Romaine à Philippes'. *BCH* 61 (1936), 86–102.
— *Philippes et la Macédoine Orientale à l'Epoque Chrétienne et Byzantine*, Paris, 1945.
O'Sullivan, F. *The Egnatian Way*, London, 1972.
Roger, J. *L'Enceinte Basse de Philippes'. BCH* 62 (1938), 21–41.

GLA
Gomme, A. W. 'The Ancient Name of Gla'. In *Essays and Studies Presented to William Ridgeway*, edited by E. C. Quiggin, Cambridge, 1914: 116–23.
Mylonas, G. 'The Citadel of Gla'. In *Mycenae and the Mycenaean Age*, Princeton, 1966: 43–4 and 84–5, with photos and plan.
Ridder, A. de, In *BCH* 18 (1894) 271–310: excavation reports with plans.
Threpsiades, J. In *PAE* 1955 to 1961: excavation reports in Greek.
Tsountas, C. and J. Manatt. 'The Fortress of Gla and other Minoan Works at Lake Copais'. In *The Mycenaean Age*, London, 1897: 374–82.

GORTIS/GORTYN
Colini, A. 'Ripresa dello Scavo del Pretorio a Gortina'. *Annuario di Scuola Italiana a Atene* 32 (1970), 439–50: new plan.
Levi, D. 'Country Life in Minoan Crete: II Gortyna'. *ILN*, Jan. 2, 1960, 16–18.
Pernier, L. 'L'Odeum nell'Agora di Gortina'. *Annuario di Scuola Italiana a Atene* 8 (1925), 1–69.
Pernier, L. and L. Banti. *Guida degli Scavi Italiani in Creta*, Rome, 1947: 15–27, photos and plan.
Savignoni, L. *et al.* 'Nuovi Studi e Scoperti in Gortyna'. *Monumenti Antichi* 18 (1907), 177–383.
Taramelli, A. 'Gortyna'. *AJA* 6 (1902), 101–65: survey, with plan.
Willetts, R. *The Law Code of Gortyn*, Berlin, 1967.

GOURNIA
Graham, J. W. *The Palaces of Crete*, Princeton, 1962: 47–9, with plan.
Hawes, H. B. *et al. Gournia, Vasiliki, and other Prehistoric Sites on the Isthmus of Hierapetra, Crete,* Philadelphia, 1908: full account, with photos and plan.
Hutchinson, R. W. 'Prehistoric Town Planning in Crete'. *Town Planning Review* 21 (1950), 199–220.
— *Prehistoric Crete*, London, 1962: 190, 287–9, with plan.
Matz, F. *Crete and Early Greece*, London, 1962: 106–9, with photos and plan.
Pendlebury, J. D. S. *The Archaeology of Crete*, London, 1939: 61, 191, 228.

HALIEIS
Bakhuizen, S. 'The Two Citadels of Chalkis on Euboea', *AAA* 5 (1972), 134–46.
Jacobsen, T. 'Halieis'. *Archailogikon Deltion* 23 (1968), 144-8.
— 'The Franchthi Cave near Porto Cheli, 1967–1968'. *Hesperia* 38 (1969), 343–81.
Jameson, M. 'Excavations at Porto Cheli: Halieis, 1962–1968'. *Hesperia* 38 (1969), 311–42: plans.
Young, J. H. 'A Migrant City in the Peloponnesus'. *Expedition* (Univ. Pennsylvania Museum) 5 (1963), 2–11, with photos from early excavation.

HALKIS/CHALCIS
Dondorff, H. *De Rebus Chalchidensium*, Halle, 1885: historical survey, appraisal in Latin.
Pappavasileiou, P. In *PAE* for 1900, 1901, 1906, 1910, 1911: excavation reports in Greek.

HERAION/ARGIVE HERAION

Berve, H. and G. Gruben. *Greek Temples, Theatres and Shrines*, London, 1963: 54–6, 346–7, with plan.

Blegen, C. W. 'Excavations at the Argive Heraeum, 1925'. *AJA* 29 (1925), 413–28.

— *Prosymna: The Argive Settlement Preceding The Argive Heraeum*, 2 vols. Cambridge, 1937.

Caskey, J. and P. Amandry. 'Investigations at the Heraion of Argos, 1949'. *Hesperia* 21 (1952), 165–274.

Waldstein, C. *et al. The Argive Heraeum*, 2 vols. Boston, 1902, 1905, with photos and plans.

HERONIA/CHAERONEA

Anti, C. and L. Polacco. *Nuovi Ricerche Sui Teatri Greci Arcaici*, Padua 1969: 17–44, with plan and photos of theatre.

Arias, P. *Il Teatro Greco Fuori di Atene*, Florence, 1934: 64–6.

Dilke, O. W. 'Details and Chronology of Greek Theatre Caveas'. *BSA* 45 (1950), 21–62: 35–7 on Chaeronea.

Hammond, N. G. L. 'Two Battles of Chaeronea'. *Klio* 31 (1938), 186–218.

Lethaby, W. R. 'Greek Lion Monuments'. *JHS* 38 (1918), 37–44.

Pritchett, W. K. 'Observations on Chaeronea'. *AJA* 62 (1958), 307–11.

ISTHMIA

Berve, H. and G. Gruben. *Greek Temples, Theatres and Shrines*, London, 1963: 344–5, with plan.

Broneer, O. *Hesperia* 1953, 1955, 1958, 1959, 1960, 1962: excavation reports, with photos and plans.

— 'The Isthmian Sanctuary of Poseidon'. *Archaeology* 8 (1955), 56–62, with photos and plan.

— 'An Archaeological Enigma'. *Archaeology* 9 (1956), 134–7 and 268–72: stadium starting line markings.

— 'Isthmiaca'. *Klio* 39 (1961), 249–70, with plan, photos: good general survey.

— 'The Apostle Paul and the Isthmian Games'. *BA* 25 (1962), 2–31.

— *The Temple of Poseidon (Isthmia Excavations I)*, Princeton, 1971: photos and plans.

Gebhard, E. *The Theatre at Isthmia*, Chicago, 1972: full study, with photos and plans.

Pearson, L. 'Pausanias on the Temple of Poseidon at Isthmia'. *Hermes* 88 (1960), 498–502.

Wiseman, J. R. 'A Trans-Isthmian Fortification Wall'. *Hesperia* 32 (1963), 248–75.

ITHAKI/ITHACA

Bérard, V. *Ithaque et la Grèce des Achéens*, Paris, 1947.

Brewster, F. 'Ithaca: A Study of the Homeric Evidence'. *Harvard Studies in Classical Philology* 31 31 (1920), 125–66.

Burrage, C. *The Ithaca of the Odyssey*, Oxford, 1928: with map.

Dörpfeld, W. *Alt-Ithaka: Beitrag zur Homer Frage*, 2 vols. Munich, 1927.

Fraser, A. D. 'Homer's Ithaca and Adjacent Islands'. *Classical Philology* 23 (1928), 213–38.

Gell, W. *The Geography and Antiquities of Ithaca*, London, 1807.

Heurtley, W. A., *et al. BSA* for 1930, 1932/33, 1934, 1938, 1948, 1952, 1953: excavation reports; summary of results, *BSA* 1939/40, 1–13.

Rodd, R. *Homer's Ithaca: A Vindication of Tradition*, London, 1927.

— 'The Ithaca of the Odyssey'. *BSA* 33 (1932), 1–21.

KABIRION/KABEIRION

Bruns, G. 'Das Kabirenheiligtum bei Theben'. *Archäologische Anzeiger* in *JDAI* 1939, 581–96; *JDAI* 1964, 231–65: photos and plan; *JDAI* 1967, 228–73; 'Kabeirion'.

Cook, R. M. *Greek Painted Pottery*, London, 1960: 102–3 on Kabiric vases.

Dörpfeld, W. and W. Judeich. 'Das Kabirenheiligtum bei Theben'. *Ath. Mitt.* 13 (1888), 81–99.

Winnefeld, H. 'Das Kabirenheiligtum bei Theben, III: die Vaserfunde'. *Ath. Mitt.* 13 (1888), 412–28.

Wolters, P. and G. Bruns. *Das Kabirenheiligtum bei Theben*, I, Berlin, 1940: photos and plans.

Wolters, P. and E. Szanto. *Ath. Mitt.* 15 (1890): 355–419 on architectural finds and inscriptions.

KALIDON/CALYDON

Dyggve, E. 'A Second Heroön at Calydon'. *Studies Presented to David M. Robinson*, vol. 1, St Louis, 1954, 360–4.

Dyggve, E. and F. Poulsen. *Das Laphrion: Der Tempelbezirk von Kalydon*, Copenhagen, 1948: with photos and plans.

Dyggve, E. and F. Poulsen and K. Rhomaios. *Das Heroön von Kalydon*, Copenhagen, 1934: with photos and plans.

Lawrence, A. *Greek Architecture*, London, 1957: plan and reconstruction of Heroön, 220.

KEA

Caskey, J. L. 'Excavations in Keos, 1960–1961'. *Hesperia* 31 (1962), 263–83.

— 'Excavations in Keos, 1963'. *Hesperia* 33 (1964), 314–35.

— 'Excavations in Keos, 1964–1965'. *Hesperia* 35 (1966), 363–76.

— 'Excavations in Keos, 1966–1967'. *Hesperia* 40 (1971), 358–96: with plans.

— 'The Early Bronze Age at Ayia Irini in Keos'. *Archaeology* 23 (1970), 339–42.

Lewis, D. 'The Federal Constitution of Keos'. *BSA* 57 (1962), 1–4.

KENCHREE/KENCHREAI

Hawthorne, J. G. 'Cenchreae: Port of Corinth'. *Archaeology* 18 (1965), 191–200.

Scranton, R. S. 'Glass Pictures from the Sea'. *Archaeology* 20 (1967), 163–73.

Scranton, R. S. and E. S. Ramage. 'Investigations at Kenchreai, 1963'. *Hesperia* 33 (1964), 134–45, 'Investigations at Kenchreai, 1964–1966'. 36 (1967), 124–86: with plans.

Shaw, J. W. 'Shallow-Water Excavation at Kenchreai'. *AJA* 71 (1967), 223–31.

KERKIRA/CORFU

Bérard, V. *Les Phéniciens et l'Odyssée*, 2 vols. Paris,

1902–3: I. 481–591, especially 523–41 on Alcinous' palace site, with map of area; restated in his *Les Navigations d'Ulysse*, Paris, 1927–9, vol. 4, 9–92: 'Chez Alkinoos', especially 45–6, with map opp. 41.

Borrelli, L. V. 'Corfu'. *EAA* 2, 832–6: survey of archaeological sites, art finds, with general plan of ancient city, photos.

Dondas, G. 'Le grand sanctuaire de Mon Repos à Corfou', *AAA* 1 (1968), 66–9.

Johnson, F. and W. Dinsmoor. 'The Kardaki Temple'. *AJA* 40 (1936), 46–56.

Rhomaios, C. 'Les Premières Fouilles de Corfu'. *BCH* 1925, 190–218.

Rodenwaldt, G. *et al. Korkyra: Archäische Bauten und Bildwerke*, 2 vols. Berlin, 1939–40.

Reports in Greek on later excavations in Palaeopolis and in Mon Repos area, in *PAE* 1939, 1955 to 1961, and in *Archaiologikon Deltion* 1962, 1963.

KNOSSOS

Evans, A. *The Palace of Minos At Knossos*, London, 1921–36, 7 vols.: full data, illustrations.

Graham, J. W. *The Palaces of Crete*, Princeton, 1962: 23–33, 51–8, plans.

Hood, M. F. 'The Last Palace and the Reoccupation at Knossos'. *Kadmos* 4 (1965), 16–44.

Hood, S. *The Minoans*, London, 1971: 67–72, plan.

Hutchinson, R. W. *Prehistoric Crete*, London, 1962: 164–6, 170–81, 270–9, plan.

Marinatos, S. *Crete and Mycenae*, London, 1960: 121–30, photos and plan.

Palmer, L. R. *A New Guide to the Palace of Knossos*, London, 1969, photos and plan.

— *The Penultimate Palace at Knossos*, Rome, 1969: data for his chronology.

Pendlebury, J. *A Handbook to the Palace of Minos*, London, 1954: photos and plan.

KORINTHOS/CORINTH

Carpenter, R. and O. Broneer. *Ancient Corinth: A Guide to the Excavations*, 6th edition Athens, 1954: brief history, description of monuments, with plans, photos, reconstructions.

Corinth: Results of Excavations conducted by the American School of Classical Studies at Athens, Princeton, 1929–: full publication by various authors, in progress, many volumes.

Dewaele, J. J., *Corinthe*, Paris, 1961: useful survey in French, with plan, reconstructions, photos.

O'Neil, J. G. *Ancient Corinth, with a topographical sketch of the Corinthia, to 404 BC*, Baltimore, 1930: good general history, but before the major excavations.

Robinson, H. S. *Corinth: A brief history of the city and a guide to the excavations*, Princeton, 1964: shorter guide but more up to date; 2nd edition 1969.

— *The Urban Development of Ancient Corinth*, Athens, 1965: with photos and phase-plans.

Reports by J. Wiseman on new excavations in the Gynasium area, and R. Stroud and N. Bookides on the Demeter Sanctuary in *Hesperia* 1965 (1–24); 1967 (13–41, 402–28); 1968 (299–330); 1969 (64–106, 297–310); 1972 (1–42, 283–331), with photos and plans; also Wiseman, J. 'Ancient Corinth: The Gymnasium Area'. *Archaeology* 22 (1969), 216–25.

KOS/COS

Bean, G. and J. M. Cook, 'Cos', *BSA* 52 (1957), 119–27: historical data.

Herzog, R. and P. Schazmann, *Kos: Ergebnisse der deutschen Ausgrabungen und Forschungen: Band I: Das Asklepieion*, Berlin, 1932: full details, photos, plans, reconstruction.

Laurenzi, L. 'Coos'. *EAA* 2, 794–800: with photos and plans.

— 'Nuovi Contributi alla Topografia storico-archeologica di Coo'. *Historia* 5 (1931), 592–626 (on Odeum, other finds).

Modono, A. N. *L'Isola di Coo nell'Antichità Classica*, Rhodes, 1933.

Morricone, L. 'Scavi e Recherche a Coo, 1935–1943'. *Bolletino d'Arte* 35 (1950), 54–75, 219–46, 316–31: with photos, plans of Agora and Roman area excavations.

LERNI/LERNA

Caskey, J. L. 'An Early Settlement at the Spring of Lerna'. *Archaeology* 6 (1953), 99–102.

— 'The House of Tiles at Lerna: An Early Bronze Age Palace'. *Archaeology* 8 (1955), 116–20.

— 'Excavations at Lerna'. *Hesperia* for 1954, 1955, 1956, 1957, 1958, with latest plan 1958 p. 128.

— 'Where Hercules Slew the Hydra'. *ILN* Jan. 12, 1957, 68–71.

— 'Lerna in the Early Bronze Age'. *AJA* 72 (1968), 313–16.

LINDOS

Blinkenberg, C. *Lindos: Fouilles de l'Acropole, 1: Les Petits Objets*, 2 vols. Berlin 1931.

Blinkenberg, C. and K. F. Kinch. *Lindos: Fouilles de l'Acropole, II: Inscriptions*, 2 vols. Berlin, 1931–41.

DeVita, A. 'Lindos'. In *EAA* 4, 638–44: with plan.

Dyggve, E. and V. Poulson. *Lindos: Fouilles de l'Acropole, III: Le Sanctuaire d'Athena Lindia et l'Architecture lindienne, avec Catalogue des Sculptures trouvées*, 2 vols. Berlin 1960.

Kähler, H. *Lindos*, Zurich, 1971: general summary, with photos and plans.

MALIA/MALLIA

Banti, L. 'Mallia'. In *EAA* 4, 796–802: with plan.

Gallet de Santerre, H. 'Mallia: Aperçu Historique'. *Kretika Chronika* 3 (1949), 363–91.

Graham, J. W. *The Palaces of Crete*, Princeton, 1962: 41–6, 62–8, with plans, reconstructions.

Tiré, C. and H. van Effenterre, *Guide des Fouilles françaises en Crète*, Paris, 1966: 3–80, photos and plan.

Full publication, with photos and plans, in French School at Athens' *Etudes Crétoises*, vols. 1, 2, 4, 5, 6, 7, 9, 11, 12, 13, 16, 17, 18: Paris, 1928–70.

MANTINEA/MANTINEIA

Arias, P. *Il Teatro Greco Fuori di Atene*, Florence, 1934: 95–7.

Dilke, O. A. W. 'Details and Chronology of Greek Theatre Caveas'. *BSA* 45 (1950), 45–7.

Fougères, G. *Mantinée et l'Arcadie Orientale*, Athens, 1898: full data, maps, photos and plan.

Pritchett, W. K. 'The Battles of Mantineia'. In *Studies in Ancient Greek Topography*, II, University of California, 1969, 37–72.

Winter, F. *Greek Fortifications*, Toronto, 1971: 216–7, 227, 240, 272–3.

Woodhouse, W. J. 'The Campaigns and Battle of Mantineia in 418 BC'. *BSA* 22 (1916–18), 51–84.

MARATHON

Burn, A. R. *Persia and the Greeks*, London, 1962: 239–56 on the battle.

Marinatos, S. 'Further News and Discoveries at Marathon'. *Athens Annals of Archaeology* 3 (1970), 63–8, 153–66, 349–66: on Plataean tumulus and other tombs in the area.

Pritchett, W. K. 'Marathon'. *University of California Publications in Classical Archaeology* 4 (1960), 137–90.

— 'Marathon Revisited'. In *Studies in Ancient Greek Topography*, I, University of California, 1965, 83–93; also 'The Deme of Marathon'. *Ibid*. II, 1969, 1–11: with plan.

Vanderpool, E. 'A Monument to the Battle of Marathon'. *Hesperia* 35 (1966), 93–106: with plan of area.

MEGALOPOLIS

Arias, P. *Il Teatro Greco Fuori di Atene*, Florence, 1934: 100–12 on Megalopolis theatre.

Bather, A. G. 'The Development of the Plan of the Thersilion'. *JHS* 13 (1892/93), 328–37.

Benson, E. F. 'The Thersilion at Megapolis'. *JHS* 13 (1892–3), 319–27.

Bury, J. B. 'The Double City of Megalopolis' *JHS* 18 (1898), 15–22.

Dinsmoor, W. G. *The Architecture of Ancient Greece*, London, 1950: 242–3, 249–50 on Thersilion and theatre.

Gardner, E. A. *et al*. 'The Theatre at Megalopolis' *JHS* 11 (1890), 294–8.

— *Excavations at Megalopolis, 1890–1891*, London, 1892: with plans.

MESSINI/MESSENE

Borrelli, L. V. 'Messene'. In *EAA* 4, 1082–4.

Leake, W. *Travels in the Morea*, 4 vols. London 1830: I, 366–83, is an account before excavations.

Scranton, R. *Greek Walls*, Cambridge, 1941: 80–1, 112–13, 128–9.

Winter, F. *Greek Fortifications*, Toronto, 1971: 31–2, 111–14, 164–5, 173–5.

Excavation reports (in Greek) in *To Ergon tis Archaiologikis Etairias* 1958, 1959, 1960, 1961, 1962, 1963, 1964, and especially 1969 (97–132), 1970 (100–31), 1971 (144–73): with plans.

Summary of new excavations, with plan, in *AJA* 75 (1971), 309–10.

MIKINE/MYCENAE

Graham, J. W. 'Mycenaean Architecture'. *Archaeology* 13 (1960), 46–54.

Marinatos, S. *Crete and Mycenae*, London, 1960: 154–61, plans, photos.

Mylonas, G. *Mycenae and the Mycenaean Age*, Princeton, 1966: 5–8, 15–35, (on citadel), 58–83 (palaces and houses), 89–110 (Grave Circles), 120–5 (tholoi), with photos and plans.

—— *Mycenae: a Guide to its Ruins and its History*, 4th edition, Athens, 1973: with photos, plans.

Mylonas, G. and J. Papadimitriou. 'The New Grave Circle at Mycenae'. *Archaeology* 8 (1955), 43–50.

Samuel, A. *The Mycenaeans in History*, New Jersey, 1966.

Schliemann, H. *Mycenae*, London, 1878: report of excavation, finds.

Taylour, W. *The Mycenaeans*, London, 1964.

Verdelis, N. 'A Private House at Mycenae', *Archaeology* 14 (1961), 12–17.

Wace, A. 'Mycenae'. *Antiquity* 10 (1936), 405–16.

— *Mycenae: An Archaeological History and Guide*, Princeton, 1949: photos and plan.

Wace, H. *Mycenae Guide*, 6th edition, Athens, 1971: photos, plan and brief data.

NAXOS

Bent, J. T. *Aegean Islands*, London, 1885: Chapter XIV (329–71), a general account.

Casson, S. 'An unfinished Colossal Statue at Naxos'. *BSA* 37 (1936), 21–5.

Curtius, E. *Naxos*, Berlin, 1846.

Gruben, G. and W. Koenigs. 'Der "Hekatompedos" von Naxos'. *Archäologischer Anzeiger* 83 (1968), 693–717, and 85 (1970), 135–53: with plan.

Kontoleon, N. Excavation reports (in Greek) in *PAE* since 1937, still in progress; plan of Mycenaean area and of Agora/Stoa area in 1970, 146–55, report.

Welter, G. 'Altionische Tempel'. *Ath. Mitt*. 49 (1924), 17–22: with plan of temple on islet.

NEMEA

Berve, H. and G. Gruben. *Greek Temples, Theatres and Shrines*, London, 1963: 357–8, with plan.

Blegen, C. Excavation reports in *Art and Archaeology* 19 (1925), 175–84 and 23 (1927), 189.

— 'Excavations at Nemea 1926'. *AJA* 31 (1927), 421–40.

Daux, G. 'Chronique des fouilles et découvertes archéologiques en Grèce en 1964'. *BCH* 89 (1965), 703–6: summary of 1964 excavations, with revised plan.

Clemmensen, N. and R. Vallois. 'Le Temple de Zeus à Nemée'. *BCH* 49 (1925), 1–20.

Hill, B. H. *The Temple of Zeus at Nemea*, edited by Charles Williams, Princeton, 1966: full description and many large plans of whole site and of temple details.

NIKOPOLIS/NICOPOLIS

Hammond, N. G. L. *Epirus*, Oxford, 1967: 62, description.

Kahrstedt, U. 'Die Territorien von Patrai und Nikopolis in der Kaiserzeit'. *Historia* 1 (1950), 549–61: historical survey.

Kitzinger, E. 'Mosaics at Nikopolis'. *Dumbarton Oaks Papers* 6 (1951), 83–122.

Leake, W. M. *Travels in Northern Greece*, I, London, 1935: 186–99, description, plan.

Philadelpheus, A. *Nicopolis: Les Fouilles 1913–1926*, Athens, 1933: 28 p. summary, with photos.

Philadelpheus, O., *et al.* in *PAE* for 1913–30, 1937, 1938, 1940, 1956, 1959, 1961: excavation reports in Greek.

OLIMBIA/OLYMPIA

Ashmole, B. and N. Yalouris. *Olympia: The Sculptures of the Temple of Zeus*, London, 1967.

Berve, H. and G. Gruben. *Greek Temples, Theatres and Shrines*, London, 1963: 14–27, 316–26, with plan.

Curtius, E. *Olympia*, Leipzig, 1935: survey, in German, by the excavator.

Dinsmoor, W. B. 'An Archaeological Earthquake at Olympia'. *AJA* 45 (1941), 399–427: on dating of sculptures, etc.

Drees, L. *Olympia: Gods, Artists, Athletes*, London, 1968: excellent illustrations, plan.

Gardiner, E. N. *Olympia: Its History and Remains*, Oxford, 1925: general summary.

Kunze, E. and H. Weber. 'The Olympian Stadium, the Echo Colonnade, and an Archaeological Earthquake'. *AJA* 52 (1948), 490–6.

Morgan, C. H. 'Pheidias and Olympia'. *Hesperia* 21 (1952), 295–339 and 24 (1955), 164–8.

Richter, G. M. A. 'The Pheidian Zeus at Olympia'. *Hesperia* 35 (1966), 166–70.

Saflund, M.-L. *The East Pediment of the Temple of Zeus at Olympia*, Gothenburg, 1971.

Trendelenburg, A. *Pausanias in Olympia*, Berlin, 1914: his account applied to the remains.

OLIMBOS/OLYMPUS

Baud-Bovy, D. *La Grèce Immortelle*, Geneva, 1919: chapter on Olympus.

Heuzey, L. *Le Mont Olympe et l'Acarnanie*, Paris, 1860.

Kern, O. *Nord-Griechische Skizzen*, Berlin, 1912: 47–77 'Olymp und Helikon'.

Kurz, M. *Le Mont Olympe*, Paris, 1923: description, history, exploration; maps, photos.

Phoutrides, A. and F. Farquhar, 'With the Gods on Mt. Olympus'. *Scribner's Magazine* Nov. 1915, 558–77: with photos.

OLINTHOS/OLYNTHOS

Boethius, A. 'Ancient Town-Architecture and the New Material from Olynthos'. *American Journal of Philology* 69 (1948), 396–407.

Gude, M. *A History of Olynthos*, Baltimore, 1933.

Mylonas, G. 'The Olynthian House of the Classical Period'. *Classical Journal* 35 (1940), 389–402.

Robinson, D. M. 'Olynthus: The Greek Pompeii'. *Archaeology* 5 (1952), 228–36: summary, photos.

Robinson, D. M., *et al.* *Excavations at Olynthos*, 14 vols., Baltimore, 1929–52: full data, photos and plans.

Scichilone, G. 'Olinto'. *EAA* 5, 661–7, summary, with photos and plans.

PELLA

Petsas, P. 'New Discoveries at Pella, Birthplace and Capital of Alexander'. *Archaeology* 11 (1958), 246–54; with photos.

— 'Pella: Literary Tradition and Archaeological Research'. *Balkan Studies* 1 (1960), 113–28.

— 'Ten Years at Pella'. *Archaeology* 17 (1964), 74–84: with photos, house plan.

Summaries of annual finds, with photos, in *BCH* 1958 (761–5); 1959 (702–5); 1960 (783–8); 1961 (802–12); 1962 (805–13); 1966 (871–5); 1968 (898–901).

PERAHORA/PERACHORA

Coulton, J. J. 'The Stoa by the Harbour at Perachora'. *BSA* 59 (1964), 100–31.

— 'The West Court at Perachora'. *BSA* 62 (1967), 353–71.

Dunbabin, T. J. 'The Oracle of Hera Akraia at Perachora'. *BSA* 46 (1951), 61–71.

Hammond, N. G. L. 'The Heraeum at Perachora and Corinthian Encroachment'. *BSA* 49 (1954), 93–102.

Payne, H., *et al.* *Perachora: The Sanctuaries of Hera Akraia and Limenaia*, 2 vols. Oxford, 1940, 1962: full report, with photos and plans (at end of vol. I).

PILOS/PYLOS

Alsop, J. 'Pylos'. *New Yorker Magazine* Nov. 24, 1962: long account of Blegen and his finds.

Blegen, C. 'The Palace of King Nestor' *Archaeology* 5 (1952), 130–5, and 6 (1953), 203–7.

— 'King Nestor's Palace'. *SA* May 1958, 110–18: with photos.

Blegen, C. and M. Rawson. *Guide to the Palace of Nestor*, Cincinnati, 1962: with plan, photos, data.

Blegen, C., M. Rawson and M. Lang. *The Palace of Nestor at Pylos in Western Messenia*, 2 vols., Princeton. 1960, 1969): with photos, reconstructions, full data; Palace plan in II, plate 142.

McDonald, A. W. 'Where Did Nestor Live?' *AJA* 46 (1942), 538–45.

Mylonas, G. *Mycenae and the Mycenaean Age*, Princeton, 1966: 52–8 on Pylos palace, with plan.

PIREEFS/PIRAEUS

Amit, M. 'Le Pirée dans l'histoire d'Athènes à l'époque classique'. *Bulletin de l'Association Guillaume Budé: Lettres d'Humanité* 20 (1961), 464–74.

Fiechter, E. *Das Theater im Peiraieus*, Stuttgart, 1950: with plan.

Lorenzen, E. *The Arsenal at Piraeus*, Copenhagen, 1964.

Scranton, R. *Greek Walls*, Cambridge, 1941: 14, 42, 114–20.

Ulrichs, H. *Topography of the Harbours and position of the Long Walls of Athens*, London, 1847.

Excavation reports (in Greek) in *PAE* for 1885 (63–71); 1933–35 (159–95); 1951 (93–127); 1953 (61–71): with plans.

PLATEE/PLATAEA

Burn, A. R. *Persia and the Greeks*, London, 1962: 519–46 on battle.

Grundy, G. B. *Topography of the Battle of Plataea and the City of Plataea*, London, 1894.

Pritchett, W. K. 'New Light on Plataea'. *AJA* 61 (1957), 9–28; map.

Washington, H. S. 'Description of the Site and Walls of Plataia'. *AJA* 6 (1890), 452–62: with map and plan, (account of excavations, *ibid.* 445–52).

— 'Discovery of a Temple of Archaic Type at Plataia'. *AJA* 7 (1891), 390–407.

RAMNOUS/RHAMNOUS

Dilke, O. W. 'Details and Chronology of Greek Theatre Caveas'. *BSA* 45 (1950), 21–62: 28–30 on Rhamnous theatre.

Dinsmoor, W. B. *The Architecture of Ancient Greece*, London, 1950: 89, 181–3, 363.

— 'Rhamnountine Fantasies'. *Hesperia* 30 (1961), 179–204: on peristyle entablature.

Orlandos, A. 'Le Sanctuaire de Nemesis'. *BCH* 48 (1924), 305–20, with photos and plan.

Plommer, H. 'Three Attic Temples'. *BSA* 45 (1950), 66–112 (94–109 on Rhamnous Nemesis temple).

Pouilloux, J. *La Forteresse de Rhamnonte*, Paris, 1954.

Trevor Hodge, A. and R. Tomlinson. 'Some Notes on the Temple of Nemesis at Rhamnous', *AJA* 73 (1969), 185–92.

RODHOS/RHODES CITY

Bradford, J. 'Fieldwork on Aerial Discoveries in Attica and Rhodes'. *Antiquaries Journal* 36 (1956), 57–69: with high air photo of acropolis and plan.

Kondis, J. 'Zur Antiken Stadtbauplan von Rhodos'. *Ath. Mitt.* 73 (1958), 146–58: with air photos of harbour area and acropolis.

Laurenzi, L. *I Monumenti dell'Antica Rodi: Memorie dell'Istituto Fert di Rodi*, I, 1938.

Maiuri, A. 'Note sulla Topografia Antica di Rodi'. *Annuario della Scuola Italiana* 3 (1921), 259–62.

— 'La Topografia Monumentale di Rodi'. In *Clara Rhodos* I (1928), 44–55.

Maryon, H. 'The Colossus of Rhodes'. *JHS* 76 (1956), 68–86: with sketches.

Matton, R. *Rhodes*, Athens, 1959: general description (in French) of city and island sites.

Morriconi, L. 'Rodi' in *EAA* 6, 743–54: with plan, bibliography.

Rostovzeff, M. 'Rhodes'. *Cambridge Ancient History* 8 (1930), 619–42: general history survey.

SALAMIS

Burn, A. R. *Persia and the Greeks*, London, 1962: 540–75, with map.

Green, Peter *The Year of Salamis*, London, 1970: historical context of battle.

Hignett, C. *Xerxes' Invasion of Greece*, Oxford, 1963: 193–239, 397–417, with map.

McLeod, W. 'Boudoron, An Athenian Fort on Salamis'. *Hesperia* 29 (1960), 316–23.

Pritchett, W. K. 'Toward a Re-Study of the Battle of Salamis'. *Transactions of American Philological Association* 63 (1959), 251–62.

— 'Salamis Revisited'. In *Studies in Ancient Greek Topography*, I, Berkeley and Los Angeles, 1965: 94–102.

Wallace, P. 'Psyttaleia and the Trophies of Salamis'. *AJA* 73 (1969), 293–303.

SAMOS

Berve, H. and G. Gruben. *Greek Temples, Theatres and Shrines*, London 1963: 56–9, 447–56, with plans.

Borrelli, L. V. 'Samo' in *EAA* 6, 1091–1101: with photos and plans.

Brent, J. T. 'An Archaeological Visit to Samos'. *JHS* 7 (1886), 143–6.

Goodfield, J. 'The Tunnel of Eupalinus'. *SA* June 1964, 104–12: with photos and plan.

Reuther, O. *Der Heratempel von Samos*, Berlin, 1957: summary in *AJA* 64 (1960), 89–95.

Tölle, R. *Die Antike Stadt Samos*, Mainz, 1969: brief guide with map, photos (omits Heraion).

Walter, H. *Das Griechische Heiligtum: Heraion von Samos*, Munich, 1965: with photos and plans.

SAMOTHRAKI/SAMOTHRACE

Hemberg, H. *Die Kabiren*, Uppsala, 1950: on the cult.

Lazarides, D. *Samothrace and its Peraia* (Ancient Cities 7), Athens, 1971: with maps and plans.

Lehmann, K. *Samothrace: A Guide to the Excavations and the Museum*, 3rd edition. Locust Valley, NY, 1966: with plans, reconstructions, photos, brief data and history.

Lehmann, K. *et al. Samothrace: Excavations Conducted by the Institute of Fine Arts of New York University*, New York, 1958– : four volumes so far of full report, with plans, photos.

McCredie, J. R. 'Samothrace: Preliminary Report on the Campaigns of 1962–1964, and 1965–1967'. *Hesperia* 34 (1965), 100–25 and 37 (1968), 200–34, with updated plan, photos.

SFAKTIRIA/SPHACTERIA

Burrows, R. M. 'Pylos and Sphacteria'. *JHS* 16 (1896), 55–76; 18 (1898), 147–55; 28 (1908), 148–50.

Compton, W. C. and H. Awdry, 'Notes on Pylos and Sphacteria'. *JHS* 27 (1907), 274–83.

Gomme, A. W. 'Thucydides and Sphacteria'. *Classical Quarterly* 17 (1923), 36–40.

Grundy, G. B. 'Investigation of the Topography of the Region of Pylos and Sphacteria'. *JHS* 16 (1896), 1–54; 18 (1898), 232–5.

Marinatos, S. on Mycenaean tholos, in *Crete and Mycenae*, London, 1960: 161 and plates xxxii-iii.

Pritchett, W. K. 'Pylos and Sphacteria'. *Studies in Ancient Greek Topography*, I, Berkeley and Los Angeles, 1965: 6–29, with map.

SIKION/SICYON

Fossum, A. 'The Theatre at Sicyon'. *AJA* 9 (1905), 263–76.

Guerrini, L. 'Sicione'. *EAA* 7, 276–9: with plan, data.

McMurtry, W., W. Earle, C. Brownson, C. Young: excavation reports on theatre, in *AJA* 5 (1889), 267–92; 7 (1891) 281–2; 8 (1893), 388–409.

Philadelpheus, A. 'Note sur le Bouleutérion de Sicyone'. *BCH* 50 (1926), 174–82.

Roux, G. *Pausanias en Corinthie*, Paris, 1958: 133–61 on Sicyon remains, with photos and plan.

Skalet, C. H. *Ancient Sicyon*, Baltimore, 1928: history, monuments, art; with photos and plan.

SOUNION/SUNIUM

Berve, H. and G. Gruben. *Greek Temples, Theatres and Shrines*, London, 1963: 397–9.

Kenney, E. J. 'Ancient Docks at Sunium'. *BSA* 42 (1947), 194–200.

Oikonomides, A. 'The Makeshift Temples of Poseidon and Athena at Sounium'. *Athene* 24 (1963), 3–8.

Plommer, W. H. 'The Temple of Poseidon at Sunium'. *BSA* 45 (1950), 73–94; 55 (1960), 218–30.

Thompson, H. A. and W. B. Dinsmoor Jr. *The Sanctuary of Athena at Sounium*, Princeton, 1974.

SPARTI/SPARTA

Chrimes, K. M. T. *Ancient Sparta*, Manchester, 1949.

Dawkins, R. N. *The Sanctuary of Artemis Orthia at Sparta*, London, 1929.

Jones, A. H. M. *Sparta*, Oxford, 1967.

Oliva, P. *Sparta and her Social Problems*, Amsterdam, 1969.

Soteriou, G. in *PAE* 1939, 107–18: on Christian buildings above theatre (in Greek).

Excavation reports in *BSA*, especially 12 (1905), 277–479; 13 (1906), 1–218; 14 (1907), 1–158; 15 (1908), 1–157; 16 (1909), 1–61; 26 (1923), 116–310; 27 (1925), 173–254; 28 (1926), 1–106; 29 (1927), 1–107; 30 (1928), 152–254.

STRATOS

Bonacasa, N. 'Stratos'. *EAA* 7, 516–7: with good plan.

Courby, F., C. Picard, *et al. Recherches Archéologiques à Stratos d'Acarnanie*, Paris, 1924: full data, analysis, with plans, reconstructions.

Martin, R. *L'Urbanisme dans la Grèce Antique*, Paris, 1955: 194–5.

Orlandos, A. 'Ho en Strato Naos Dios'. *Archaiologike Ephemeris* 8 (1923), 1–51: full study (in Greek), with ground-plans, reconstructions, photos.

Winter, F. E. *Greek Fortifications*, Toronto, 1971: 34, 112–3, 224.

TEGEA

Berve, H. and G. Gruben, *Greek Temples, Theatres and Shrines*, London, 1963: 354–7, with plan.

Dugas, C. 'Le Sanctuaire d'Aléa Athéna à Tegée avant le IVe Siècle'. *BCH* 45 (1921), 335–435.

Dugas, C., J. Berchmans, M. Clemmensen, *Le Sanctuaire d'Aléa Athéna à Tegée au IVe Siècle*, Paris, 1914: full report, with plans, photos, reconstructions.

THASSOS/THASOS

Bernard, P. *et al. Guide de Thasos*, Athens, École Française, 1968: brief data, photos and plans.

Launey, M. *et al. Études Thasiennes*, Athens, École Française, 1944–   : eight volumes so far, with full data on history and monuments, plans, reconstructions, photos; 6 (1959) on Agora.

Lazarides, D. *Thasos and its Peraia* (Ancient Cities 5), Athens, 1971: with plans, maps.

Pouilloux, J. 'Thasos: Cultural Crossroads'. *Archaeology* 8 (1955), 198–204: with plans of city.

THERMON

Berve, H. and G. Gruben, *Greek Temples, Theatres and Shrines*, London 1963: 309–11, with temple plan.

Borelli, L. V. 'Thermos' in *EAA* 7, 825–7.

Croon, J. H. 'Artemis Thermia and Apollo Thermios'. *Mnemosyne* 9 (1956), 193–220; on name-basis.

Payne, H. 'On the Thermon Metopes'. *BSA* 27 (1925/26), 124–32.

Poulsen, F. *Thermos*, Copenhagen, 1934: general survey with plans.

Robertson, D. S. *Handbook of Greek and Roman Architecture*, Cambridge, 1929: 51–3, 66–7, with plan of Megaron B and Apollo Thermios temple, 52.

Soteriadis, G. 'Greek Excavations at Thermos'. *Records of the Past* I (1902), 172–81.

THERMOPILI/THERMOPYLAE

Burn, A. R. 'Thermopylae and Callidromos'. In *Studies presented to David M. Robinson*, I, St Louis, 1951, 480–9: with map of area.

— *Persia and the Greeks*, London, 1962: 362–422, with good map, 408.

Daskalakis, A. *Problèmes historiques autour de la Bataille de Thermopyles*, Paris, 1962.

Evans, J. A. S. 'The "Final Problem" at Thermopylae'. *Greek, Roman, and Byzantine Studies* 5 (1964), 231–7: on why Leonidas stayed to fight.

— 'Notes on Thermopylae and Artemision'. *Historia* 18 (1969), 389–406.

Grant, J. N. 'Leonidas' Last Stand'. *Phoenix* 15 (1961), 14–27.

Marinatos, S. *Thermopylae: An Historical and Archaeological Guide*, Athens, 1951: summary of Herodotus' account of area and battle, description of excavations; with maps, photos.

Pritchett, W. K. 'New Light on Thermopylae'. *AJA* 62 (1958), 202–13 and plates 54–5: best analysis of Ephialtes' route and local topography.

THESSALONIKI/THESSALONIKE

Kinch, K. F. *L'Arc de Triomphe de Salonique*, Paris, 1890.

Makaronas, C. In *PAE* 1950, 303–21, and *Archaiologikon Deltion* 20B (1965), 407–9; 21B (1966), 331–4; 22B (1967), 387–91: with plan; 24B (1969), 294–7: excavation reports in Greek of Galerian Palace and Octagon.

Papadopoulou, P. In *Archaiologikon Deltion* 18B (1963), 196–9; 19B (1964), 329–31; 22B (1967); 379–84: plans; 23B (1968), 328–30; 24B (1969), 294–5: excavation reports in Greek of Agora/Forum area and Odeion.

Petsas, Ph. 'The Agora of Thessaloniki', *AAA* 1 (1968), 156–61.

Tafrali, O. *Topographie de Thessalonique*, Paris, 1913.

Vacalopoulos, A. E. *A History of Thessalonike*, Thessalonike, 1963.

THIRA/THERA

Borelli, L. V. 'Thera' in *EAA* 7, 821–3: brief data, city plan.

Dörpfeld, W. 'Das Theater von Thera'. *Ath. Mitt.* 29 (1904), 57–72: with plan.

Hiller von Gaertringen, F. *et al. Thera: Untersuchungen und Ausgrabungen*, 4 vols. Berlin, 1899–1909: full data, with photos and plans.

Knidlberger, L. *Santorin*, Munich, 1965: general account of island, people, with fine photos.

Luce, J. V. *The End of Atlantis*, London, 1969: account of new excavations and theories; fine photos.

Marinatos, S. *Excavations at Thera*, I–V, Athens, 1968–1974: with photos.

— *Treasures of Thera*, Athens, 1972: short description, colour photos of frescoes, vases.

Vermeule, E. 'The Promise of Thera'. *Atlantic Monthly*, Dec. 1967: significance of new excavations.

THIVE/THEBES

Cloché, P. *Thèbes de Béotie: des Origines à la Conquête romaine*, Louvain/Namur, 1952.

Gomme, A. W. 'Literary Evidence for the Topography of Thebes'. *BSA* 17 (1910–11), 29–53.

Keramopoullos, A. Full account (in Greek) of his excavations, with photos, city plan, in *Archaiologikon Deltion* 3 (1917), 1–503.

Mylonas, G. *Mycenae and the Mycenaean Age*, Princeton, 1966: 9–10, 82, 201–4, 226–8.

Platon, N. On new palace excavations and finds, *ILN* Nov. 11 and Dec. 5, 1964.

Spyropoulos, T. 'The Discovery of the Palace Archives of Boeotian Thebes'. *Kadmos* 9 (1970), 170–2.

Vian, F. *Les Origines de Thèbes: Cadmos et les Spartes*, Paris, 1963.

THORIKOS

Arias, P. E. *Il Teatro Greco Fuori di Atene*, Florence, 1934: 24–32, with plan.

Bieber, M. *History of the Greek and Roman Theatre*, 2nd ed. Princeton, 1961: 57, with plan.

Dilke, O. A. W. 'Details and Chronology of Greek Theatre Caveas'. *BSA* 45 (1950), 21–62: 25–8 on Thorikos, with plan.

Miller, W. and L. Cushing. 'The Theater of Thorikos'. *Papers of the American School of Classical Studies at Athens* 4 (1885–6), 1–34: original excavation report, with theatre plan.

Mussche, H. F. 'La Forteresse maritime de Thorikos'. *BCH* 85 (1961), 176–205: with plan of promontory and fort.

— 'Recent Excavations at Thorikos'. *Acta Classica* 13 (1970), 125–36: with general plan.

Mussche, H. F., J. Bingen, J. Servais, *et al. Thorikos: Rapport Préliminaire*, Brussels 1968–71, 5 vols. so far on campaigns of 1963–8, 1968–71, with detailed account, photos.

TILISSOS/TYLISSOS

Graham, J. W. *The Palaces of Crete*, Princeton, 1962: 59–62, with plan.

Hazzidakis, J. *Tylissos à l'Epoque Minoenne*, Paris, 1921.

— *Les Villas Minoennes de Tylissos*, Paris, 1934: with photos and plans.

Hutchinson, R. W. *Prehistoric Crete*, London, 1962: 239, 243.

Platon, N. 'Tylissos'. In *EAA* 7, 1042–3.

TINOS/TENOS

Cristofani, M. 'Tino' *EAA* 7, 869–70.

Demoulin, H. 'Fouilles de Tenos'. *BCH* 26 (1902), 399–439: with plan.

Demoulin, H. and P. Graindor. In *Musée Belge* (1904), 64–100; (1905), 286–91; (1906), 309–61; (1907), 5–51; (1908), 213; (1910), 5–53: excavation reports of Poseidon-Amphitrite Sanctuary, with plans.

Kontoleon, N. In *PAE* (1949), 122–34; (1950) 264–8; (1952), 531–46; (1953), 258–67; (1955), 258–62; excavation reports in Greek of Xombourgo site, with plans.

Levi, D. *Annuario della Scuola Italiana di Atene* 8–9 (1926), 202–34: on Geometric graves at Kardiani.

Orlandos, A. In *Archaiologike Ephemeris* 1937 B, 608–20; on north exedra as fountain.

Picard, C. In *Comptes Rendues de l'Académie des Inscriptions et Belles Lettres* 1944, 147–52: on north exedra as *Stibadeion*.

TIRINS/TIRYNS

Daux, G. 'Chronique des fouilles et découvertes archéologiques en Grèce en 1962'. *BCH* 87 (1963), 751–5: on newly found water-supply system.

Frickenhaus, A., G. Rodenwaldt, K. Müller, G. Karo, *Tiryns: Ausgrabungen des Deutschen Instituts* 4 vols. Berlin/Athens, 1912–38.

Karo, G. 'Der Schatz von Tiryns'. *Ath. Mitt.* 55 (1930), 119–40.

Marinatos, S. *Crete and Mycenae*, London, 1960: 84–92, 172–6, plates 152–5.

Mylonas, G. 'The Citadel of Tiryns'. *Ibid.* 46–52.

Schliemann, H. *Tiryns: The Prehistoric Palace of the Kings of Tiryns*, New York, 1885.

Voigtländer, W. *Tiryns*, Athens, 1972: illustrated booklet guide.

In *Mycenae and the Mycenaean Age*, Princeton, 1966: 11–15 with plan: 'The Palace of Tiryns'. *Ibid.* 46–52.

TRIZIN/TROEZEN

Cristofani, M. 'Trezene' *EAA* 7, 981–2: with plan.

Dodwell, E. *A Classical and Topographical Tour Through Greece During 1801, 1805, 1806*, London, 1819, vol. 2: 265–71.

Frickenhaus, A. and W. Müller, 'Troezenia'. *Ath. Mitt.* 36 (1911), 31–5.

Jameson, M. 'A Decree of Themistocles from Troezen'. *Hesperia* 29 (1960), 198–223; 'A Revised Text of the Themistocles Decree'. *Hesperia* 31 (1962), 310–15.

— 'Waiting for the Barbarian: New Light on the Persian Wars'. *Greece and Rome* 8 (1961), 5–18.

— 'The Provisions for Mobilization in the Decree of Themistocles'. *Historia* 12 (1963), 385–403.

Legrand, P. 'Fouilles à Troèzene'. *BCH* 21 (1897), 543–51; 29 (1905), 269–318.

Welter, G. *Troezen, und Kalaureia*, Berlin, 1941: with photos, plans, reconstructions.

VASSE/BASSAE

Berve, H. and G. Gruben, *Greek Temples, Theatres and Shrines*, London 1963: 351–4.

Cooper, F. A. 'The Temple of Apollo at Bassae: New Observations on its Plan and Orientation'. *AJA* 72 (1968), 103–11.

Dinsmoor, W. B. 'The Temple of Apollo at Bassae'. *Metropolitan Museum of Art Studies* IV/2 (1933), 204–7.

— 'Sculptured Friezes from Bassae'. *AJA* 60 (1956), 401–52.

Roux, G. *L'Architecture de l'Argolide*, Paris, 1962: 21–56.

Scully, V. *The Earth, Temple, and Gods*, Yale, 1962: 122–9.

VRAVRON/BRAURON

Papadimitriou, J. In *PAE* for 1945, 1949, 1950, 1955, 1956, 1957, 1959: excavation reports in Greek.

— 'The Sanctuary of Brauron'. *SA* June 1963, 110–20: with photos and plans.

XERXES' CANAL

Burn, A. R. *Persia and the Greeks*, London, 1962: 295, 318, 338.

Bowen, G. *Mt. Athos, Thessaly and Epirus*, London, 1852: 56–7: description of its traces.

Green, P. *The Year of Salamis*, London, 1970: 53, 75, 89.

Herodotus, *Histories*: 7, 22–24, 37, 122.

How, W. and J. Wells. *A Commentary on Herodotus*, 2 vols. Oxford, 1928: 2. 135–6.

Leake, W. *Travels in North Greece*, 3, London, 1835: 143–7, account of its traces.

Macan, R. W. *Herodotus: Seventh, Eighth, and Ninth Books*, I, part 1, London, 1908: 34–7.

Spratt, Colonel, in *Journal of the Geographic Society* 17 (1847), especially 145–8: a detailed description, with measurements.

ZAKROS

Huxley, G. 'The Ancient Name of Zakro'. *Greek, Roman, and Byzantine Studies* 8 (1967), 85–7.

Platon, N. *Zakros: The Discovery of a Lost Palace of Ancient Crete*, New York, 1971: excellent account of discovery, finds, interpretation: with photos and plans.

— Chapter on Zakros in *Ancient Crete*, edited by S. Alexiou, London, 1967: with photos and plan.

— Summary account, with photos, in *Archaeology* 16 (1963), 269–75, and *Horizon* 1965, 76–80.

Spanakis, S. *Crete: A Guide*, Iraklion, 1968: 368–78, with plan.

Fullest plan in *To Ergon tis Archaiologikis Etairias* 1971, 232.

Index